Aviation & Foreign Policy

Aviation & Foreign Policy

CONVERGENCE

SANAT KAUL

KNOWLEDGE WORLD
KW Publishers Pvt Ltd
New Delhi

IFFAAD
International Foundation for Aviation, Aerospace And Drones

ISBN 978-93-91490-60-7 Hardback
ISBN 978-93-91490-61-4 ebook

Published in India by Kalpana Shukla

KNOWLEDGE WORLD
KW Publishers Pvt Ltd
4676/21, First Floor, Ansari Road
Daryaganj, New Delhi 110002
Phone: +91 11 43528107
Marketing: kw@kwpub.in
Editorial: production@kwpub.in
Website: www.kwpub.in

Printed and Bound in India

Contents

Table, Boxes and Maps

Acknowledgements

Aviation as a subject always fascinated me. My stints in the Indian Ministry of Civil Aviation and thereafter, with the International Civil Aviation Organisation, made me determined to look into the subject. A group of us enthusiasts floated a non-profit society called International Foundation for Aviation and Development. Thereafter, on return to India I, along with some friends, floated another similar but independent non-profit Society, initially called "International Foundation for Aviation and Development". With this background I also wrote extensively in newspapers on current issues of drones.

In a chance meeting with Ambassador Nalin Surie, the former Director General of Indian Council of World Affair, the idea of writing something which connects aviation with foreign policy emerged. This was a new subject where the challenge was to synthesise the two policies. Foreign policy has a lot to do with connectivity. In today's times, it's connectivity by air that's becoming important. So, I took up the challenge, and finally here is the book.

In government, turfs and silos play an important role. Often the right hand does not know what the left hand is doing. I have tried to bring this aspect out in the book and offered a solution.

I am also grateful to Professor Ram Jakhu, of the Institute of Air and Space Law, McGill University, Montreal for going through the draft. I am grateful to Mr. Vivek Pattanayak, formerly India's Representative and Director at the International Civil Aviation Organisation, for going through the manuscript. Finally, I am also grateful to Prof. D. B. Gupta of the National Council of Applied Economic Research for helping me with his comments on the book. All shortcomings and lapses are, of course, mine.

New Delhi

Sanat Kaul

Preface

This is an unusual topic for a book. Use of Aviation for economic growth of a country has been attempted earlier. The two prime examples of this are Singapore and Dubai who have managed to use aviation as a catalyst to growth successfully. But these are small city states. To use aviation for enhancement of foreign relations and strengthening of foreign policy is a new concept. To the best of my knowledge, a book on this subject has not been attempted earlier. As a matter of fact, even think tanks do not consider this a doable thing. On this issue they are unable to think "out of the box".

What is hard and soft power? Hard power is directly related to military power while soft power is the acceptability of a powerful country as a role model—something other countries look up to. India was a great soft power in spite of its weak military at the time of independence in 1947. Over time this got eroded and now it is aspiring to be a hard power, especially a regional power, but its soft power has declined over time.

As India embarks on foreign policy with the aspiration to be called at least a regional power, if not a much bigger power, there are missing links without which it cannot be considered sufficiently matured. One factor is the missing people-to-people contact. This is done by modern communications—through telephone, internet or direct air connectivity. The Romans, the Spanish and the Portuguese all used their sea power and connectivity to reach out. Currently, instead of the sea it is the air connectivity which is important. The US became the main power in the twentieth century with air power—both military and civil. Its airlines connected them to the world. Of late, China is emerging as one and its civil air power is growing, connecting the world, which is described in this book. For India, connectivity by air based on its foreign policy emphasis is yet to achieve the same status. This book will try to delve into our foreign and aviation policies simultaneously to see the lack of coordination in the two and how they can be synergised.

India has declared an intent of creating a $5 trillion economy by 2024 and considers it challenging but reachable.[1] How does it plan to reach such an objective? Globalisation has helped China achieve its present status of the second biggest economy in the world. Realising that the same globalisation has not worked well for India, India has declared in 2020 a policy of Atmanirbhar, or self-reliant and not isolation. However, even to achieve Atmanirbhar status, we need a much better world connectivity especially in areas in India's neighbourhood.

This book delves into the need for such connectivity, its growing outbound traffic and its direction. It looks into the need to divert it in the right direction to help our foreign image and policy.

Note

1. *The Economic Times*, June 20, 2019 as reported by Mihir Sharma from Bloomberg.

Abbreviations

AAI	Airports Authority of India
ACI	Airports Council International
ACP	Act East Policy
ADS	Approved Destination Status
ANI	Andaman and Nicobar Islands
ASA	Air Service Agreement
ASAM	ASEAN Single Aviation Market
ASEAN	Association of Southeast Asian Nations
BIMSTEC	Bay of Bengal Initiative for Multi-Sectoral Technical and Economic Cooperation
CLMV	Cambodia, Laos, Myanmar, Vietnam
CPEC	China-Pakistan Economic Corridor
DGCA	Director General of Civil Aviation
EEZ	Exclusive Economic Zone
GNI	Great Nicobar Island
IAC	International Air Connectivity
ICAO	International Civil Aviation Organisation
ICCR	Indian Council for Cultural Relations
ICS	International Connectivity Scheme
ICS	International Connectivity Scheme
IMO	International Maritime Organisation
INSTC	International North-South Transport Corridor
IORA	Indian Ocean Rim Association
ITDC	India Tourism Development Corporation
LEP	Look East Policy
MEA	Ministry of External Affairs

MHA	Ministry of Home Affairs
MOCA	Ministry of Civil Aviation
NCAP	National Civil Aviation Policy
NEFA	North-East Frontier Agency
ONGC	Oil and Natural Gas Commission
OTOAI	Outbound Tour Operators Association of India
RCS	Regional Connectivity Scheme
RDG	Route Dispersal Guidelines
SAARC	South Asian Association for Regional Cooperation
UDAN	Ude Desh ka Aam Naagrik (same as Regional Connectivity Scheme)
UNDP	United Nations Development Programme
VFR	Visiting Friends and Relatives
VGF	Viability Gap Funding
WTO	World Trade Organisation

1
Foreign Affairs and Aviation: Politics of Soft Power

Introduction: The Context

Can a country achieve the status of a Superpower, or even a regional power, without proper connectivity with its neighbours? Historically, empires were built up with good connectivity. The Roman Empire built an excellent road network. The Mughals in India also had a good network of roads. The British built up their empire through sea connectivity. The Chinese are building up a global network of roads and ports through their Project called 'One Belt-One Road' or 'OBOR'. Its international air connectivity is already taking on our countries. India has announced its ambition to become a $5 trillion economy by 2024 (a target unlikely to be achieved). At the same time India is also building its own answer to OBOR, which is described in the chapter on Foreign Policy. However, while road and sea-based connectivity is important, air connectivity has become crucial in the present context. This is the current challenge to Indian Foreign Policy. Is the current air connectivity from India to countries where we want our influence to grow sufficient or is it missing? Do such desired countries have a favourable impression of India? While it may not be possible to quantify an answer, informal perceptions are possible to access. We feel that to improve this perception and to enhance economic trade India needs to establish direct connectivity to start with. Direct air connectivity is urgently needed in cases where there are none to bring about the dividends of mutual contacts. India is generally regarded in its neighbourhood as a reluctant emerging power. It has to shed this image. Air connectivity has also proven to be a catalyst of growth and trust. The preamble to the Convention on International Civil Aviation, better known as the "Chicago Convention of 1944" states:

> Whereas the future development of international civil aviation can greatly help to create and preserve friendship and understanding amongst the nations and the peoples of the world, yet its abuse can become a threat to the general security.

Soft Power

While we find mention of Soft Power these days, there is no clear definition of it. Prof. Joseph Nye of Harvard University, the proponent of this concept, has defined it as follows:

> Soft power is the ability to affect others to obtain the outcomes one wants through attraction rather than coercion or payment. A country's soft power rests on its resources of culture, values, and policies. A smart power strategy combines hard and soft power resources. Public diplomacy has a long history as a means of promoting a country's soft power and was essential in winning the cold war. The current struggle against transnational terrorism is a struggle to win hearts and minds, and the current over-reliance on hard power alone is not the path to success. Public diplomacy is an important tool in the arsenal of smart power, but smart public diplomacy requires an understanding of the roles of credibility, self-criticism, and civil society in generating soft power.[1]

India is now a $ 2.68 trillion economy, the fifth largest and the fastest growing economy in the world. The latest IMF report[2] released at Davos on January 22, 2018 projects India's growth at 7.4 per cent in 2018 and 7.8 per cent in 2019. There was a contraction of 26 per cent in the Gross Domestic Product of India during the second quarter of 2020-2021due to Covid Pandemic, but the latest IMF projections give hope. For the year 2020-2021 IMF has pegged the contraction at 8 per cent but has projected a growth of 11.5 per cent for the year 2021-2222.[3] In order to grow faster and for India to have a major role in world affairs, there is a need to think in terms of a wider role that civil aviation can play in its future activities. We have seen the rise of two states, Singapore and the United Arab Emirates, in our region as centres of tourism, trade and developing into financial centres mainly on account of having a very aggressive aviation policy. They have both become strong financial and tourism centres mainly due to becoming international aviation hubs. Their beginnings were largely on account of India-based traffic 'hubbing' in these two places. People from India used both Singapore and Dubai as their hubs to connect to the rest of the world only because India never had a good airport or an aggressive aviation policy. Both these tiny countries are now important political forces, well regarded and accepted in the comity of nations.

COVID-19 has created its own international disequilibrium. China has been accused of releasing the pandemic to the rest of the world. Whether the virus started from Wuhan laboratory or the wholesale food market in Wuhan, remains a matter of dispute. The vaccine development is yet another international event. While the developed countries have overbooked the vaccines for their people, India has led the world in donating the vaccine to poorer countries along with giving it to its own people. All vaccines have been transported to various countries by civil carriers.

The power and status of a country also depends upon how well the country is connected. Britain used their maritime power to conquer the colonies and become an empire. In today's times, civil aviation determines the reach of a country. While India has a thriving domestic aviation industry, it is limited in its spread of international connections. Lee Kuan Yew, the renowned former Prime Minister of Singapore, has stated in his autobiography, *From Third World to First World* how after breaking with Malaya in 1965 he decided to use international aviation for economic and foreign policy purposes. He followed this by strengthening Singapore Airlines to make what Singapore is today. Dubai has also followed a similar policy.

This study endeavours to analyse some issues of the weakness in our foreign policy along with contradictions in aviation policy, and attempts to bring about a synergy between the two to make a greater impact on our neighbouring countries.

Ambassador Rajiv Sikri, a former Indian diplomat, in his book, *India's Foreign Policy: Rethinking Challenge and Strategy*,[4] has explained,

> Diplomacy can no longer be conducted in a rarefied atmosphere. Nor is it the exclusive preserve of diplomats and officialdom. The Government will always remain the central player in India's foreign policy but it is not the only one.

He further elaborates that,

> Foreign Policy issues require understanding and support among India's political class, corporate leaders, journalists, academics and all other sections of intelligentsia. (page 294)

At another place he goes on to explain that,

> ...till recently, India's attention was primarily on domestic issues; foreign policy was not seen as a matter to which the country needed to give special attention or an area where India needed to work out a careful strategy. ... Half a century later, the situation is quite different. India is stronger, more confident, more ambitious and increasingly globalised. It remains subject to outside pressures, but it is no longer a mere pawn on the world stage; it is also a player (pages 14-15) ... India can emerge as an influential regional and global player—an independent "pole" in the world ... regrettably, an impression has gained ground among India's neighbours that India is a soft State whose nose can be tweaked with immunity (pages 285-86). ... India's "Look East" Policy has been one of the most significant foreign policy moves with long term ramifications. In a psychological, political and strategic sense, India's membership of East Asia Summit (EAS) has bridged the gap between India and East Asia. Despite China's

> obstructionist approach, India will have to make sure that it continues to work with other Asian countries, in particular Japan, to develop a regional architecture for Asia. (page 286)

He then goes on to talk about the concept of Connectivity and 'public diplomacy'—of building bridges between peoples and gives the example of India-ASEAN Car Rally which took place in 2004 from Guwahati in Assam and ended in Batam in Indonesia, after passing through Myanmar, Thailand, Laos, Vietnam, Cambodia, Malaysia and Singapore. It brought India into small villages throughout the region.

Rajiv Sikri considers that implementation of foreign policy needs a much greater people-to-people connectivity. A good connectivity is, therefore, an important and critical input into the success of a foreign policy. One may go further and add that people-to-people contact through tourism and business brings the goodwill and the soft power as propounded by Prof. Joseph Nye. This could be further refined as the soft portion of our foreign policy.

This book has taken inspiration from Ambassador Rajiv Sikri's book described above. It has analysed how the importance of air connectivity in international affairs was given by the Indian Foreign Ministry earlier by use of Air India when it was a government-owned monopoly for outbound flights from India. However, this practice stopped once Air Corporation Act of 1953 was abrogated in 1994 and Air India lost its monopoly over outbound flights. Thereafter, in 2003 Prime Minister Atal Bihari Vajpayee realised the importance of the matter and attempted to rectify this important vacuum by unilaterally offering to SAARC and ASEAN countries connectivity to India. This well-intentioned strategy, however, failed as it was not well conceived. Again, Minister Jayant Sinha took up the cause of inter-connectivity between our neighbours under the proposed extended UDAN scheme but again there were no takers. MEA did not consider this worthy of their consideration. Finally, India's Foreign Minister late Sushma Swaraj during her visit to Uzbekistan in 2018 talked of a dialogue for an Air Corridor between India and CIS countries.

Unfortunately, although our outbound civil aviation traffic (mainly Indians going abroad for tourism purposes) is growing strong, its direction is not in sync with our foreign policy requirements. The question that comes up is whether India's National Civil Aviation Policy 2016 is in sync with our Foreign Policy. If not, then there is need for a course correction for both. It is surmised that when the National Civil Aviation Policy 2016 was approved by the Cabinet, the foreign ministry had obviously not made any contribution to it. This study attempts to look into these aspects and suggest measures that may contribute to better understanding.

We also need to look into our freight policy. About 30 years back India declared unilaterally an 'Open Sky Policy' for cargo, about the only country to do so. However, the benefits of this policy never materialised. In this book an attempt will be made to analyse these issues.

India never had a formalised Aviation Policy until 2016.[5] For over a decade it remained a draft. It was never given its importance. The present National Civil Aviation Policy 2016 (NCAP 2016) document is a welcome sign of a realisation that Aviation as a sector has a major role to play in economic development as well as in employment generation. It States:

> The Government has proposed to promote the growth of Indian aviation in a significant manner as this sector has a multiplier effect on the economy. As per an International Civil Aviation Organisation (ICAO) study, the output multiplier and employment multiplier are 3.25 and 6.10 respectively.

Unfortunately, NCAP 2016 has no synergy with our foreign policy. While it provides for protecting our airlines within 5,000 km radius from Delhi from stronger airlines and talks of open sky beyond 5,000 km, it does not talk of building a strong international airline network in the region to help our 'Act East' and 'Look West' Foreign Policy (explained in later chapters). It talks of a Regional Connectivity Scheme (RCS), but does not talk of an International Connectivity Scheme (ICS). This book hopes to fulfil this lacuna.

Air Connectivity is not simply an issue for Ministry of Civil Aviation alone as it involves the entire gamut of issues of economic, commerce, and tourism (including medical tourism), foreign policy as well as disaster relief. It involves Make in India, Digital India and other policies. International Air Transport Association (IATA)[6] has predicted India to be the third largest aviation market by 2026 and 478 million passengers by 2036.[7] Since only about 2-5 per cent of the 1.33 billion population travels by air, there is tremendous scope for its growth and also growth outbound. Further, the air connectivity pattern is much skewed. More than 80 per cent of the flights take place between the top six metro cities. While this is understandable as metro cities are engines of growth, the potential of the rest of the areas, including remote areas, is also tremendous, and their latent opportunities are yet to be exploited. Ministry of Civil Aviation has schemes for promotion of regional and remote air connectivity but not international.

World Bank's Air Connectivity Index

The World Bank, in their "Air Connectivity Index"[8] of 2007, has stated, "to capture various dimensions of performance in a single numerical indicator—Air Connectivity Index (unfortunately the World Bank has not published this index since then). A country's connectivity score is higher if the cost of moving to other countries in the network is relatively low." While the USA scores 22.7 per cent, India is 3.82 per cent. Clearly, India has a lot of catching up to do. Aviation has played a major role in economic growth in the world in the last half century. Although the road and railways have their advantage, the catalytic power of aviation is immense.

India's Regional Connectivity Scheme (RCS) or UDAN and our proposed International Connectivity Scheme (ICS) will go a long way to improve India's Air Connectivity Index. RCS/UDAN scheme is described in chapter 2 and the proposed ICS is described in chapter 6.

Box 1: World Bank Air Connectivity Index

This index considers country wise connectivity in the global air transport network, covering 211 countries and territories for the year 2007. It is grounded in network analysis methods, and is based on a gravity-like model that is familiar from the international trade and regional science literatures. It is a global measure of connectivity, in the sense that it captures the full range of interactions among all network nodes, even when there is no direct flight connection between them. The best connected countries are the United States, Canada, and Germany; the United States' score is more than two-thirds higher than the next placed countries, and connectivity overall follows a power law distribution that is fully consistent with the hub-and-spoke nature of the global air transport network. The measure of connectivity is closely correlated with important economic variables, such as the degree of liberalisation of air transport markets, and the extent of participation in international production networks. It provides a strong basis for future research in areas such as air and maritime transport, as well as international trade. Air cargo transport is getting increasingly important to the global economy. Be it for exports of perishable goods like vegetables or cut flowers, medical products like blood, expensive but light products like diamonds or the movement of highly specialised component parts within transnational production networks, the ability to move goods quickly, reliably, and at a reasonable price is a crucial ingredient in the trade performance of a wide range of countries.

To capture the various dimensions of performance in a single numerical indicator—the Air Connectivity Index (ACI)—air connectivity was defined as an important item for a country within the global air transport system. A country is considered to be better connected the stronger is the overall "pull" it exerts on the rest of the network. A country's connectivity score is higher if the cost of moving to other countries in the network is relatively low. It is considered to be less well connected if the dispersion of those costs is high. These two factors are both important in the context of a network industry. Combining them means that, for example, a spoke country with a strong connection to only one other country cannot have a high connectivity score: although the cost of moving from one country to the other is low, the dispersion of costs across all markets is very high. A regional hub with strong connections to a moderate number of destinations receives an intermediate

(*continued ...*)

Box 1 (*continued ...*)

connectivity score, since costs are relatively dispersed across the remainder of the network, although to a lesser extent than for a pure spoke country. Finally, a global hub with strong connections to many others countries in the network receives a relatively high connectivity score.

Ease of Doing Business

The "Ease of Doing Business" index is another index created by the World Bank Group. Higher rankings (a low numerical value) indicate better, usually simpler, regulations for businesses and stronger protections of property rights, etc. Economies are ranked on their ease of doing business, from 1 to 190. A high ease of doing business ranking means the regulatory environment is more conducive to the starting an operation of a local firm. The rankings are determined by sorting the aggregate distance to frontier scores on 10 topics, each consisting of several indicators, giving equal weight to each topic. The rankings for all economies are benchmarked to June 2017. India jumped up 30 notches in 2017 into the top 100th rank on the World Bank's "Ease of Doing Business" index, thanks to major improvements in indicators such as resolving insolvency, paying taxes, protecting minority investors and getting credit.

"The significant jump this year is a result of the Indian government's consistent efforts over the past few years and India's endeavour to strengthen its position as a preferred place to do business," said Annette Dixon, Vice President, South Asia region, World Bank at the release of *Doing Business 2018: Reforming to Create Jobs.*[9]

However, in order to reach the top 50 in the "Ease of Doing Business" a lot of work will be required to be done by Government. Aviation industry too will contribute in an overall manner to the Air Connectivity Index. It is an important first step in Ease of Doing Business. While these two schemes reach into India's interior, the next step should be to provide a much greater direct air connectivity into India's international neighbourhood by connecting direct schedule flights to destinations not connected so far and thereby not only increasing India's links with its neighbours culturally and economically but also making India an international transit hub just as Singapore and Dubai are today. Here our foreign policy objectives can be merged with creation of an international hub in India.

In 1992, Airports Council International (ACI),[10] an Association of Airports worldwide, published a report titled "Airports—Partners in Vital Economics", based mainly on European airports and considered direct, indirect, induced and catalytic employment. It also considered the wide economic impact known as the 'catalytic effect'. It concluded that airports are the primary factor for locating industries. A survey of Hamburg found that 80 per cent of manufacturing industries reported air services connection as important as getting customers to come and look at their products. Some airports with land available nearby have also developed business parks to capitalise on the Air Service Connectivity. Airports play a vital role in modern-day tourism. Spanish and Greek islands have grown in popularity because of their air connectivity. There is no doubt that as India develops and connects the country to new airports, as is happening under the Regional Connectivity Scheme, the catalyst effect will reach smaller cities and regions.

Since international civil aviation is dependent upon bilateral air service negotiations and do not come under World Trade Organisation (WTO), each country has the right to decide its international aviation services based on its bilateral air service negotiations with each country. International Civil Aviation Organisation (ICAO) recognises this and has accepted this aspect. While a large air power like the USA wanted more access and insisted on some form of 'open skies', many countries like India went in for a restricted bilateral civil aviation policy, more to protect its own aviation industry than look at the larger national goal of economic growth. Consequently, the Indian position relative to other countries in international connectivity declined. It may be mentioned in passing that Air India was a leading airline in the 1950s to the 1980s, and was in fact the first all-jet airline in the world. What role has aviation played in India's economic development, especially in international trade and commerce? It is difficult to assess but there is little doubt that because India followed a very restrictive bilateral air service policy some potential growth was presumably lost. It is, however, never too late to recover lost ground. Good policies and good implementation are essential.

A good airport is essential for creating a financial or trading centre. New York, London, Hong Kong, Dubai and Singapore are examples of it. Besides many essential requirements for a financial centre such as good broadband connectivity, an essential ingredient is to have a well-connected airport. The city of Mumbai, which is India's financial centre, has a serious problem with its airport. Mumbai airport has reached its peak capacity and cannot be expanded as it does not have space for more than one parallel airstrip. Further, its land has been encroached by 100,000 squatters and the State Government is unable to remove them in spite of having taken money from the Airports Authority of India for this purpose a couple of decades back. New Airport proposals like Navi Mumbai International Airport are still in the planning stage. Mumbai financial centre will not be able to grow unless the issue of the new airport at Mumbai is sorted out. A good airport in Mumbai is, therefore, not just an essential but a critical requirement for it to develop into an international financial centre. An early solution could have been to build an airport on the sea like Hong Kong and many other airports around the world. In the meantime, Delhi airport has already overtaken Mumbai airport as the busiest airport in terms of number of passengers. Kolkata (formerly known as Calcutta), which was India's leading airport till the 1960s, gave way to Mumbai and now it's Delhi. The reason is simple: decline of one city and rise of another due to poor city governance.

With Boeing[11] raising forecast in November 2019 for demand for civil aircraft in India to 2,380 new planes by 2038, valued at $ 330 billion, based on an elaborate method of calculation, there is no doubt that the airline sector in India is also poised for a big growth. The post COVID forecast is yet to take place and remains an unknown. Like the telecom sector, this sector can provide answers to many other economic sectors which are stuck in a quagmire. It has been adequately proved by economists that aviation is a catalyst to growth. Further, tourism (both domestic and international) can be a major provider of economic prosperity as well as employment. International inbound tourism is entirely dependent upon aviation and domestic tourism is increasingly also aviation dependent. However, unless the Tourism Ministry plans its tourism circuits and arranges to have air connectivity at competitive rates, the results will be poor. Most Indians themselves find it cheaper to holiday abroad in Thailand than in India in spite of the fact that the Thai Baht has gone up in value over the years. One major reason for this is high price of domestic air tickets due to high taxes and fees and the high price of domestic air turbine fuel.

Similarly, globalised industry requires good air connectivity (both domestic and international) and Indian industry tends to concentrate in a few urban areas largely because only a few cities are well connected by air. Eighty per cent of our civil air traffic is between 6 metro cities. That is why the five industrial corridors currently being planned and executed have provision for airports at its major clusters to attract business people.

International Civil Aviation and Chicago Convention of 1944[12]

Principles of Air Service Agreements and Ownership and Control Restrictions were all worked out under the overall umbrella of the Chicago Convention of 1944.[13] This Convention declared that all Air Space above a country is its sovereign air space. Since then, international air services between countries have operated under a system of bilateral Air Service Agreements (ASAs) negotiated between two countries. Typically, these ASAs specify which airlines could operate between the two countries, the routes carriers could operate (e.g., which airports they could fly to), whether carriers could offer beyond services (fifth freedom rights), limits on the frequency and capacity (seats) that the carriers could operate. As a result, the development of international air service has been as much a function of government policy as it has been a function of commercial considerations. Air Service negotiations take place between countries as and when they mutually agree to do so. Normally, a representative of the Foreign Ministry/Indian Embassy is also present. The Chicago Convention has been ratified by nearly all the countries of the world and is universally accepted.

Freedoms of the Air

The Air Transit Agreement and the Air Transport Agreement, both forming a part of the Chicago Convention of 1944, laid out the rules of the game for international commercial traffic and are known as the "Freedoms of Air".

The agreements propose that for scheduled international air services each nation grants to all others, with the possible exception of former enemy countries, these five "Freedoms of Air":

1. To fly across its territory without landing.
2. To land for non-traffic purposes.
3. To put down passengers, mail, and cargo taken on in the territory of the country whose nationality the aircraft possesses.
4. To take on passengers, mail, and cargo destined for the territory of the country whose nationality the aircraft possesses.
5. To take on passengers, mail, and cargo destined for the territory of another agreeing nation and to put down passengers, mail, and cargo coming from any such territory.

What Do They Mean?

Freedoms 3, 4, and 5 are essentially commercial privileges that encourage economic enterprise in the air. Freedoms 1 and 2 keep the skies open as an obligation by the contracting states who have ratified the Chicago Convention and the two Agreements.

The ready reception which the delegates to the conference gave to the first privilege indicated that the military fear is subsiding. With the first freedom in force, any plane on a regularly scheduled run can cross any nation's territory on designated routes without other preliminary agreement.

The second freedom means that, with certain limitations, the bases controlled by one country are open to the planes of any other agreeing country. Thus, the United States can no longer close the Pacific by denying foreign lines the use of Hawaii if the other nation involved has accepted the second freedom with respect to American planes desiring to land in its territories. And Britain can no longer deny the use of

Newfoundland or Bermuda to the lines of other nations accepting the second freedom.

The third, fourth, and fifth freedoms, insofar as they are now in force, make it economically useful to send planes from one country to another since they can thus pick up, carry, and discharge passengers and cargo en route both ways.

Without the fifth freedom a plane going, say, from New York to Calcutta would be unable to pick up new passengers on the way even if it has landing rights in a third country. Under pre-war conditions this was not always possible—with the result that it was not profitable to operate long international routes without the help of heavy governmental subsidies.[14]

Then there is the sixth Freedom of Air: the right or privilege, in respect of scheduled international air services, of transporting, via the home State of the carrier, traffic moving between two other States.

There is also a seventh Freedom of Air: Seventh freedom of the air refers to the right of a country's aircraft to fly between two foreign countries while not offering flights to one's own country. This freedom is hardly ever used, or agreed to.

Issues of Ownership of an Airline

In addition to the bilateral Air Service Agreements (ASAs), most countries have also placed foreign ownership and control restrictions on the airlines. In part, this was to ensure that the airline complied with the national ownership requirements in the ASA. In order for an airline to be designated by a country in the ASA, it typically needed to be "substantially owned and effectively controlled" by nationals of that country. However, these ownership restrictions were also justified for various strategic, safety and defence reasons, for example, governments wanted the ability to control the airlines in times of national emergency. Typically, the ownership restrictions specify the maximum percentage of airline shares (stocks) that can be owned by foreign nationals. For example, the United States requires that foreign ownership of domestic and international US airlines be restricted to no more than 25 per cent of voting shares (stocks) while for Japanese airlines the limit is 33 per cent; and the European Union limits non-EU ownership of the airlines of its member states to 49 per cent.[15] India has also increased foreign ownership limit by a foreign airline to 49 per cent. This ensures that there are no "fly-by-night" operators in the airline business as there are in the commercial shipping sector.

In the last two decades there has been a trend towards liberalisation of the international air market as governments recognised the benefits of allowing market forces to operate. Most countries, however, still insist that an airline being designated by a country in its ASA must be "substantially owned and effectively controlled" by the citizens of that country.

Bilateral Air Service Agreements (ASA) in India

Most of the Bilateral Air Service Agreements to which India is a signatory remain restrictive in nature, with most having limits on capacity, designated airports and approved airlines of the nation. Of the 109 ASAs by March 2019,[16] only the ASA with the US is an open skies agreement without restriction on capacity, routing or pricing. Although not quite open skies, the ASA with the UK was also significantly liberalised in 2004. It should be noted that Governments typically require reciprocity when negotiating the terms of an ASA. Therefore, it is possible that restrictions within an ASA are not due to the policies of the Indian government but due to the policies of the opposite country. India restricts foreign ownership of Indian carriers to 49 per cent of voting equity (increased from 40 per cent in 2004).

Liberalisation would also provide considerable benefits for passengers. Average fares have declined in real terms by 31 per cent with market access liberalisation, by 19 per cent with ownership and control liberalisation and by 50 per cent when both forms of liberalisation are undertaken. These fare reductions provide increases in consumer surplus of between INR 20.8 billion and INR 62.3 billion. The increase in air service and passenger traffic is forecast to generate employment in a number of ways.[17]

Bilateral Air Service Agreements provide the basic relationship on aviation issues between two countries. These agreements consist of a basic agreement which discusses many issues like security, safety, and three basic material issues: the capacity which each country can operate with the other country, the level of freedoms and the number of points (or cities) where each country's airlines can operate. These three guiding principles are dynamic in nature and either of the two countries request for another round of bilateral negotiations whenever they feel that the existing capacity has been exhausted or about to get exhausted. In the Indian context India had weak airlines and it was rare that India sought a revision of Bilateral Agreement. The request always came from the other countries. This was so because India has been an excellent market for India outbound, with weak airlines. While Air India was a great and a preferred airline, it lost its brand equity slowly over the last four decades or so. In the meantime, airlines from the east, specially Singapore's Singapore Airlines, and from the Gulf in the west, especially Dubai's Emirates, came into India in a big way. These countries realised that India was a pot of gold for them to pick up passengers and transport them to their country and beyond. However, unlike India, they had built up a very good aviation infrastructure, including friendly terminals and excellent air navigation facilities. They became hubs for Indians going abroad as Indian airports were in a bad shape till 2010 when the first modern Indian Airport opened in Delhi.

While India had a conservative bilateral air agreement policy, perhaps to the detriment of the Indian economy, an artificial shortage was created due to it. In the 1980s and 1990s availability of international air seats during the winter season was always difficult. During Bilateral Air Service discussions with other countries India was always receiving requests for more seats, and Indian airlines, mainly Air India, but also Indian private airlines going abroad, were resisting Indian Government giving away more seats. This practice still continues.

One of the problems which India has created for itself is in giving away too many points in India to some of these airlines. As a result, airlines of India are finding it difficult to compete even in India's Tier

II and III cities as these airlines offer better connectivity at their end by taking passengers from interior points of India to their hub airport, and then to destinations beyond.

Box 2: International Airlines Operations to/from India

Bilateral Air Service Agreements are based on mutual advantage. Ideally, it should be a win-win situation for both parties. However, this is not always the case. Often a country with strong airlines wants to deploy greater capacity in a country like India which has had 'good outbound' passenger traffic. This causes friction and political leveraging comes into play. The United States has been a great advocate of 'Open Sky' policy. While open sky could mean many things to many people, the United States always wanted an unlimited capacity exchange between two countries, which become properly known as "Bermuda type". While India did go in for a Burmuda type Bilateral Agreement with the US, it did not lead to any great boon as US Airlines did not fly into India in any big way and the same goes for airlines of India. The traffic between India and the US was serviced by European Airlines and later the Gulf Airlines joined in creating 5th Freedom traffic across the Atlantic.

Singapore, after separating from Malaysia, started creating an aviation hub. It was successful in transporting a large number of Indian passengers from Indian airports to Singapore for onward flights to the east.

Subsequently, on the west of India, Dubai followed the Singapore model using Indian passengers to start with. In such a case, bilateral were sought, not for 3rd and 4th freedoms, but mainly for 5th freedom traffic.

In India the state-owned monopoly airline, Air India, and later Jet as well as Kingfisher, which were permitted to go abroad, were not sufficiently strong to take on the competition, while countries from the Gulf and Singapore continued to put pressure for more capacity. As both inbound and outbound traffic of India grew, Indian Airlines were not able to meet the demand. While the India portion of the bilateral capacity between India and the regional hubs was never fully utilised due to incapacity of Indian airlines, Foreign carriers East and West of India were able to exhaust their portion. At the same time Indian airlines would resist allotment

(*continued ...*)

Box 2 (*continued ...*)

of more capacity to these countries as they considered it 3 and 4 freedom traffic but they were themselves not able to utilise their approved capacity.

In such bilateral negotiations, other considerations also came up. Besides some corrupt practices in allotment of seats, some countries started demanding greater seat capacity as a barter against other items of trade like oil and gas.

Hundred Years of Aviation in India

India celebrated 100 years of Civil Aviation in 2014. India has had a tradition of private airlines. India was one of the 52 signatory countries which attended the Chicago Convention in 1944 (surprisingly, before India became an independent country). At the time of independence in 1947 India had 11 private airlines which were nationalised in 1953 by passing of Air Corporation Act of 1953 and consolidated into two public sector airlines: Air India for International routes and Indian Airlines for domestic. During the Kashmir operations of 1947 all private airlines were mobilised by the government to airlift troops to Srinagar. It was the biggest troop movement in world history then. During World War II a large number of airstrips were built in support of the war. The land and airstrips remain in possession largely of Airports Authority of India even now. The number of airports in various conditions with AAI and State Governments is 449.[18] These come in handy in the Regional Connectivity Scheme (RCS)/UDAN scheme which is discussed in later chapters.

Vayudoot—First Attempt at Regional Connectivity in 1981

Building a countrywide Aviation Infrastructure to connect a large number of small towns was initiated for the first time in 1981 with Vayudoot Airlines,[19] an airline jointly promoted by Air India and Indian Airlines, then the monopoly airlines, on January 20, 1981. Vayudoot services lasted for about ten years and in 1991 it eventually closed down due to continuous losses which its parent companies could not sustain. At its peak the operations of Vayudoot connected over

100 cities of India with small aircraft, a feat which is restarted through the Regional Connectivity Scheme (RCS). This was done as Vayudoot could operate with small aircraft on unviable routes and Air India and Indian Airlines would meet its losses. This also helped them getting more passengers from smaller towns. However, in 1994, after repeal of Air Corporation Act of 1953, when the monopoly of erstwhile public sector airlines was abolished, this Vavudoot's losses could not be sustained by its parents, that is, Air India and Indian Airlines, and was shut down.

Route Dispersal Guidelines (RDG) 1994—Second Attempt at Regional Connectivity

After the collapse of Vayudoot, air connectivity in India shrank in its coverage. As a result, DGCA issued a (notice) CAR on Route Dispersal Guidelines (RDG) to all commercial airlines to cross-subsidise internally and connect to remote airports of the North-East, Jammu and Kashmir (J&K) and Island territories of India. This has been a tremendous success and many of these unviable routes have since then become viable. This is a form of internal cross-subsidy by commercial airlines and has no budgetary implications. While it is not considered the best way of granting subsidy, it is the most practical way as it does not involve government/finance ministry. While the Naresh Chandra Committee Report[20] on "Civil Aviation in India: The Way Ahead" had recommended to change it to a budgetary system, realising the practical difficulties, it was decided not to implement this part of the recommendation.

National Civil Aviation Policy (NCAP) 2016

In 2016 the Government announced a National Civil Aviation Policy for the first time. The National Civil Aviation Policy of 2016 is a fairly comprehensive document. While one can pick many holes in it, the fact that it has come out after remaining in a draft form for over ten years is to be complimented. This also shows the indifference of government to Civil Aviation as a sector. The policy has stated up front that India has the potential to be among the top three in terms of domestic and international passenger traffic. While this is certainly possible, it is necessary to have the right policy with the flexibility to tweak it when necessary.

The National Civil Aviation Policy categorises civil aviation services into four categories. These are as follows:

> The first deals with international connectivity. It proposes adopting a liberal bilateral aviation policy and encourages development of an international hub in our airports, be it Delhi, Bengaluru or Hyderabad. This can be achieved if we strategise our bilateral Air Service negotiations in future and work towards creation of a hub.

The second category is our existing domestic policy where all airlines are welcome to fly anywhere in the country as long as they follow RDG based on DGCA orders, mentioned earlier. At present the most lucrative routes are in connecting Metro cities. However, Tier I and even Tier II cities are catching up.

The third category is that of the existing Route Dispersal Guidelines (RDG[21]) where remote and inaccessible areas of our country are made accessible. These are remote areas like Jammu and Kashmir and Ladakh, Andaman and Nicobar Islands and Lakshadweep Islands, Himachal Pradesh, Uttarakhand and North-East India which are cut off especially during bad weather, and are included in this scheme. This remote area connectivity scheme has been on since 1994 by a DGCA notification. This Policy was reiterated with some minor changes in the National Civil Aviation Policy of 2016.

The fourth category is a newly introduced category of Regional Air Connectivity Scheme (RCS/UDAN).[22] This will help mainly second and third tier towns, which is so essential for regional economic growth. In India, we are privileged to have 449 airports and airstrips, generally unused or underused, except for the top 126 airports, including defence airports, where flights operate. The rest of the airports barely exist or are under-utilised/unutilised as they are not viable.[23] Here with revival of abandoned airstrips and starting of commercial flights through RCS/UDAN the role of Aviation as a catalyst to economic growth comes in. This scheme is discussed in the following paragraphs.

Regional Connectivity Scheme (RCS)/UDAN: Third Attempt at Regional Connectivity

An innovative scheme introduced in the NCAP 2016 is the Regional Connectivity Scheme (RCS), also known as UDAN. The main features of this scheme are:

> Under the new Policy NCAP of 2016 another subsidised scheme called Regional Connectivity Scheme (RCS) has been introduced. This scheme will connect many "under-served" and "unserved airports existing in India by improving them and offering airlines many incentives to start operations. This scheme is based again on funding largely from airlines, contribution by state governments and by the Airports Authority of India. RCS/UDAN policy is based on the fact that while India has on its books 449 airports, only 126 are operational. The rest of the airports are on books, with land generally available with AAI and, in some cases, with state Governments. NCAP 2016 has defined these airports as "unutilused" or "under-utilised". Routes connecting these airports have been thrown open to airlines operators with certain concessions and conditions. A Fund called Regional Connectivity Fund (RCF) has been created in order to subsidise airlines which are selected under this scheme for three years. This subsidy is also called Viability Gap Funding (VGF). All civil flights connecting major cities (as defined in the order) will be required to pay into RCF. This scheme is an excellent scheme as it will deepen the penetration of civil aviation. Private airlines would be allotted routes based on reverse auction for subsidy out of RCF which will give them exclusive rights on a route for three years. SpiceJet has announced that while they will participate in the bidding, they will not seek any subsidy. The airline so selected will have to give a commitment to maintain a fixed schedule throughout the year of three

flights minimum a week. A default penalty has also been provided. A conceptually good scheme, it will have many long-term benefits to the economy. It is also expected that with a three-year exclusive right will enable the operator to make the route viable. It is a great scheme for connecting another 100 plus regional locations in India from exiting non-functional/non-viable airports. The Government has sanctioned Rs. 4,500 crores to improve these airports.

What NCAP 2016 Did Not Take into Account was our Foreign Policy Need

Yes, it should certainly have, at our present stage of growth. India's "Look East Policy" developed during the Prime Ministership of Mr. Narasimha Rao in 1991,[24] was further reinforced by Prime Minister Vajpayee (1998-2004) and refined by Prime Minister Narendra Modi in 2014 as "Act East Policy", and, along with the Look West Policy, should have been important components of the NCAP 2016 had there been better coordination between the two wings of the government. How do you best implement such a policy? The question also arises as how to maximise the impact of this policy. The answer will be in our hypothesis that good connectivity will leverage the maximum impact both politically and economically. It will also improve India's World Bank Air Connectivity Index and thereby help improve our position in "Ease of Doing Business"[25] index further, help our trade as well as our foreign investment, both incoming and outgoing. Further, while road and ship connectivity have their place, air connectivity in modern times is the catalyst. Taking the example of the ten ASEAN member States, we have good connectivity with only three, namely, Singapore, Thailand and Malaysia. Our connectivity with the Philippines, Vietnam, Cambodia, Laos, Indonesia, Brunei and Myanmar is either very poor or non-existent. Just as Singapore and Malaysia had requested us to open our doors to them, we should do the same with the rest of these countries (we already have bilateral rights with all these countries). In a similar way, we have Indian Ocean rim countries like Mauritius and Seychelles where we should foster better air links. The same applies to Iran in West Asia and other central Asian countries. This is bound to lead to better economic results. India spends substantial amount of funds on extending cultural activities in foreign countries for political purposes through Indian Council for Cultural Relations (ICCR) (with about 34 offices abroad). We also maintain tourism offices in some countries abroad to encourage inbound tourism. Why can we not maintain direct flights to some of these countries in a similar manner as has been proposed for regional connectivity under RCS? This will, perhaps, have a better impact than these offices can have when there is no direct connectivity.

This book will, therefore, examine issues of international air connectivity to countries where it is felt direct air services will be useful politically, which could open opportunities for future economic cooperation between the peoples of the two countries and promote tourism, but may not be viable for the present. This may involve concessions in some form or the other. Details of this aspect will be discussed in chapter 4.

Third Stage of Our Aviation Story

It is worth mentioning that in 2011[26] we celebrated a hundred years of aviation in India. India started with private airlines and moved on to two public sector monopolies in 1953, and then back to a private airline system in the 1990s. This is the third stage of our aviation story. During the monopoly period of Air India and Indian Airlines, they together started a domestic regional airline Vayudoot in 1981 which connected 100 cities at its peak but collapsed due to unsustainable losses. Similarly, Air India subsidised some foreign routes on foreign policy considerations as long as it had a monopoly of foreign routes. With competition from our private airlines for foreign routes and decline of profits, Air India closed these loss-making routes. After liberalisation and the collapse of Vayudoot, Government introduced Route Dispersal Guidelines in 1994 and in 2016 Regional Connectivity Scheme (RCS). A major feature of the National Civil Aviation Policy (NCAP 2016) is of providing backward integration in air connectivity through RCS thereby setting the foundation of a proper and deep penetrating aviation infrastructure for the country—work that was abandoned after Vayudoot Airline closed down in 1993. This is bound to lead to greater business, industry and tourism in regions which lacked air connectivity. However, what the NCAP 2016 did not do was to provide forward linkage of International Connectivity, which is the main theme of this book.

This policy has interesting dimensions. It is for the first time that two subsidy schemes are running in parallel, that is, the Route Dispersal Guidelines (RDG) scheme for remote area connectivity and Regional Connectivity Scheme (RCS) for unserved and under-served airports. The first scheme is outside the budget with no government funds, while the second scheme is also largely outside the budget but may have implications in terms of subsidies by State Governments, Airlines and Airports Authority of India. With this background, a new scheme for forward linkage is proposed in this book, called International Connectivity Scheme (ICS). Like the RCS which induces the backward integration in the aviation infrastructure, ICS will provide the forward integration, connecting foreign countries in the region, and complete India's foreign policy aspirations of a regional/global power. In course of time, it will bring economic benefits to the economy.

Why an International Connectivity Scheme?

As already mentioned, India has reached a level of growth that needs to synergise its Civil Aviation Policy with Foreign Policy. This will enhance India's strategic depth in world affairs. The Act East Policy of 2014, the Look West Policy as well our policy towards Indian Ocean Rim countries will get the required gravitas with International Connectivity Scheme and will give a major thrust to our foreign policy through projection of our soft policy. A policy with regard to Andaman and Nicobar islands for enhancing India's image in the Bay of Bengal, with direct connectivity to ASEAN countries and beyond, to leverage our soft potential has also been recommended.

South-East Asia/West Asia, Central Asia and Indian Ocean Region also need good air connectivity with India keeping in mind India's future plans and the huge thrust that China is giving by pushing its airlines with subsidies on new routes, even from its smaller towns, all over the world and in particular in countries coming under our Act East Policy (see Chapter 4 for China Outbound as a Tool of Foreign Policy). China's 122 million outbound tourists in 2016[27] spent an estimated $ 109.8 billion. They provide vast incomes to certain countries by pushing their tourists to those countries. At the same time, they deny some countries their tourists for political reasons. India outbound is also large and growing fast and was expected to reach 50 million by 2020.[28] It was voted as the no. 3 place to go by *New York Times* in January 2017. However, it was in eighth position in Kuoni's top ten in 2019[29] and thirteenth in 2020.[30] The proposed International Connectivity Scheme will incentivise our outbound tourist into desired countries and will be the forward linkage to the aviation infrastructure like RCS and RDG providing the backward linkage. This will be discussed in Chapter 8.

On the subject of potential role of civil aviation in supporting its country's foreign policy there is hardly any literature available. Civil Aviation as a commercial entity was started by Governments in the developed western world, including Australia and Japan. All airlines were generally government-owned except for the United States of America, which always had private airlines. India also started with private airlines but all airlines were nationalised in 1954 when two state entities were created, called Air India and Indian Airlines. Governments tend to protect their own airlines. Use of Government-owned airline for foreign policy purposes was possible as long as it had monopoly rights. For India, as a developing country, use of Air India for political/diplomatic purposes did take place when Air India was nudged to fly in a limited way to certain countries even when it was not a commercially viable route. It did so from its own profits without any subsidy. The case of Singapore and Gulf Airlines also comes up. Singapore Airline was a state-owned airline which became famous as a quality airline. Gulf Airlines, especially Emirates, but also the other airlines, provided excellent service and connections. Their financial relations remain little known. US Airlines have accused the Emirates of receiving government subsidy, which they deny. On the other hand, the airlines of the Gulf accuse airlines of US receiving government subsidies, and they have been in court on this issue. The year 2020 was a washout due to COVID-19 pandemic, especially for travel and tourism. While domestic travel has picked up in most countries in 2021, international tourism was badly down due to travel restrictions by countries and a serious lack of traveller confidence. Holiday travel remained in the dumps. Business travel was substituted by digital video conferences, including seminars and conferences, for which the technology became available.

Finally, the case of China using its huge outbound tourist traffic as an instrument of its foreign policy has been discussed in Chapter 4. This is, perhaps, the most obvious case of Chinese Government's use of subsidy to help China outbound. China has also directed its huge outbound travellers to countries they want them to visit and not visit countries they want to discipline. Since they visit in groups under state supervision, the government is able to use it as a lever to influence its foreign policy requirements.

Notes

1. Joseph Nye Jr., "Public Diplomacy and Soft Power", at jestor.org.
2. Livemint, January 22, 2018, at live.mint.com.
3. *Business Standard*, January 27, 2021, p. 1.
4. Rajiv Sikri, India's Foreign Policy: Rethinking "*Challenge and Strategy*" (Sage Publications, 2009).
5. Press Information Bureau, Government of India, Ministry of Civil Aviation, June 15, 2016, at pib.nic.in.
6. International Air Transport Association (IATA) is an association of Airlines around the world consisting of over 190 airlines from 120 countries formed in 1945. See www.iata.org
7. media india.EU/aviation/IATA-predicts-india-to-become-the-third-largest-aviation-market-by-2025/
8. "Air Connectivity Index: Measuring Integration in the Global Air Transport Network", available at documents.worldbank.org. The last one was done in 2007. There would be many changes since then and, therefore, it should be taken as indicative only.
9. Ease of doing business as an index has since been given up by the World Bank due to internal problems.
10. Airports Council International is a non-profit organisation of 641 members operating 1953 airports in 176 countries. See www.aci.aero

11. Boeing.co.in; "Boeing Forecast demand for New Planes in India 2019", in *Outlook*, November 6, 2019, at https://www.outlook india.com/news roll/Boeing-forecast-demand-for-2380-new-aircraft-in-india-by-2038/1656378
12. Convention on International Civil Aviation, signed at Chicago on December 7, 1944 (Chicago Convention).
13. Two more Agreements were signed along with the Chicago Convention in 1944. They are: International Air Transit Agreement and International Air Transport Agreement. See Dr. Sanat Kaul, *1944 Chicago Convention Revisited*, at http://www.mcgill.ca>IASL>files>iasl
14. See American Historical Association, "What are Freedoms of Air", at historians.org
15. Ownership and Control Rules, at http://centreforaviation.com/reports
16. CAG Report no. 40 of 2016, p. 59.
17. Please see, "Impact of Air Service Liberalisation on India", prepared by Inter VISTAS-EU Consulting Inc., July 2009, for IATA, available at www.iata.org
18. "How many airports and airstrips in India"?, at www.quora.com
19. See www.en.m.wikipedia.org
20. Naresh Chandra, former Cabinet Secretary and India's Ambassador to the USA, chaired a government committee on aviation, better known as Naresh Chandra Committee, which gave its report in 2003.
21. See, www.mdoner.gov.in>node and civilaviation.gov.in on "Amendments of Route Dispersal Guidelines".
22. See, www.aai.aero>rcs-udan
23. "Airports of India", knowindia.net>aviation3
24. See the objectives of Look East Policy at http://www.quora.com>What-Are_the
25. See, The World Bank, www.doingbusiness.org
26. See, Murari N. Krishnaswamy, "One Hundred Years of Flying", at www.theHindu.com>article2584818
27. See "Chinese Outbound Tourism Statistics", February 3, 2017, at Travel168.net
28. Based on www.iby.org projection. See on "Kuoni Travel Report India 2007".
29. Kuoni, "The Worldwide Travel Report 2019", www.kuoni.uk
30. Kuoni, "The Worldwide Travel Report 2020", www.kuoni.uk

2
Current Status of Civil Aviation Industry in India[1]

Introduction

In May 2019 it was reported that from the fastest growing domestic civil aviation market earlier the civil aviation industry in India had dropped to 4th position[2]. India was then the 9th largest civil aviation market set to become 3rd largest civil aviation market in the world by 2037 after displacing the UK, behind the United States and China. "notwithstanding the ongoing turbulence due to rise in fuel prices, domestic airline industry has been able to grow at a steady pace. India's domestic aviation market topped the growth chart for the 12th time in 13 months in July, posting 47th consecutive month of double digit growth at 18.3 per cent."[3] Yet about 5 per cent of the population travel by air presently. The Civil Aviation industry has ushered in a new era of expansion, driven by factors such as low-cost carriers (LCCs), modern airports, Foreign Direct Investment (FDI) in domestic airlines and airports, advanced information technology (IT) interventions and growing emphasis on regional connectivity. It became the fastest growing sector of the economy, averaging a double-digit growth. As incomes grow in India the affordability of air travel goes up. Since, as already stated, only about less than 5 per cent of Indians travel by air, the future potential market is huge in view of India's growing economy. IATA predicted that India will serve 572 million passengers in 2037. With the coming of Low Cost Carriers (LCC) since 2003, the price sensitive market is seeing a boom with fierce competition amongst various airlines. Even the character of travellers is changing. Since 2003 passenger preference has made it the preferred mode of transportation over long distances, subject to pricing. Indian government which had treated air travel as a rich man's transport is slowly revising its views with the introduction of UDAN Scheme. Covid spoilt the party for aviation sector. However, hopes are back with post-Covid revival of the economy and relaxation of all restrictions imposed on Airlines due to Covid. This chapter analyses and suggests policy prescriptions.

The Domestic Scene

The Impact of Low Cost Carriers (LCCs) by 2003

The impact of coming of LCC in 2003 was disruptive. It shook the airline industry's full service airlines like Air India and Jet Airways who in turn also started their Low Cost subsidiaries. There was a full shift in the airline model in India with full service declining and LCCs dominating the industry. The full service carriers had to adjust to the new trend in passenger behaviour. Over a few years after 2003 the entire industry had turned upside down with LCCs having 70 per cent of the market. The tremendous growth in the aviation sector can be attributed largely to the emergence of LCCs.

An analysis of the Domestic Scene

The switchover of passengers from railways II-tier to air travel by first time travel was a major development caused by the introduction of Low Cost Carriers (LCC)s. In fact, in a newspaper article[4], it has been analysed that 'Over the last few years, the expense of travelling by train has increased to a great extent, while air travel expense has significantly reduced. In fact, there are certain routes that would cost you less when travelled by flight rather than train. In fact, Comptroller and Auditor General (CAG) reports suggest that air travel is the cheapest mode of transportation in 17 directions for advanced reservation period for 120 days. The report also suggests for 60 days advance reservation period, travel by air was found to be cheapest in 19 directions. Then again, for 30 days advance reservation period, air travel was cheaper in 17 directions.'

According to a report by travel portal Make My Tripp 'Air travel is no longer just faster than top-end overnight train rides; it is also cheaper. The study compared air ticket prices with the fares of air conditioned (AC) first class seats in trains during September and October.'[5]

The report further stated that on an average, train travellers spent Rs. 4,100 per ticket for a Mumbai-Delhi trip as compared the Rs. 3,400 that fliers spent on each ticket, stated the report. The trend was observed in seven out of the 12 routes that were compared in the above-1,000 km category.

The report also claimed that for distances between 500 km and 1,000 km, air fares were 5 per cent higher than that of the long distance trains. But for shorter trips (within 500 kms) train rides were 30 per cent cheaper.

"The air travel market in India has grown rapidly over the last year due to lower airfares, increased seat capacity and the expansion of the Indian economy resulting in higher disposable incomes," said Rajesh Magow, chief executive officer of Make My Trip.

The report also showed that domestic air travel in India was considerably cheaper than domestic air fare charges in Europe and the US.

For instance, the average one-way economy class fare for Mumbai-Kolkata (1,967 km) was Rs. 6,501. But a shorter distance flight from Amsterdam to Rome (1,647 km) was priced at Rs. 7,128. The difference in fares was for flights booked up to six days ahead of the journey. On an average, long distance flights (above 1,000 km) in India were 58 per cent cheaper than those in Europe, the study added. When compared with the US, Indian domestic fares for mid-haul routes (500 km to 1000 km) were 62 per cent cheaper and short haul routes (within 500 km) were 90 per cent cheaper, the report added.

Rajdhani and similar trains are no longer going full between metro cities like Delhi and Mumbai as LCC have taken over their passengers. There were about 100 daily flights between Delhi and Mumbai (before

COVID-19 spoilt the party), all going with high seat occupancy. As the market size expands and deepens, air travel becomes the preferred option for long-distance flights. Besides the time saved in air travel, it is the safest mode of transport worldwide, and the more so in India where road and train accidents are very high. Further, unlike the Railways, the government has taken many more steps for passenger facilities on issues like delayed flights or cancellation charges. Domestic air traffic continued its double-digit growth till COVID-19 lockdown came into force. The passenger traffic on the Indian Railways, however, grew by only 0.7 per cent in 2017-2018. This shows both the growing popularity of aviation as well as the rising willingness to pay a little more than rail fare to save time. This is in spite of the fact that taxation on air travel is much higher than on railways or roadways.

There were, pre-pandemic, over 650 commercial aircrafts in India , and another over 900 are under order awaiting delivery over the next few years. India's SpiceJet was the sixth fastest growing airline in 2017 based on a study done by "Routesonline." At the same time, Indira Gandhi International Airport has become South Asia's busiest airport, handling 60 million passengers in 2017.

According to data released by the Department of Industrial Policy and Promotion (DIPP), FDI inflows in air transport (including airfreight) between April 2000 and March 2017 stood at US$ 1.01 billion. India is estimated to see an investment of US$ 25 billion in the next decade in the airports sector, a demand for 935 more planes and traffic growth of 13 per cent, according to Morgan Stanley. According to them, the share of air travel in air and rail travel combined in India will grow to 15.2 per cent by 2027 from 7.9 per cent now.

Capital Expenditure plans (pre- pandemic) to the tune of Rs. 65,000 crores (US$ 10.08 billion) had been finalised by the Airports Authority of India with Rs. 17,500 crore (US$ 27.13 billion) for the next five years, and around Rs. 22,000 crores (US$ 3.41 billion) for brown field expansion in Delhi, Mumbai, Hyderabad, and Bengaluru by private operators and around Rs. 21,000 crores (US$ 32.55 billion) for greenfield airports. Because of COVID-19 there can be a delay in implementation of this plan. The post Covid scenario is also very encouraging. With high foreign capital inflows and share market boom in 2021, the likelihood of disposable money with middle class Indians is very optimistic. Once Covid based restrictions are relaxed, the hesitancy by air travellers will go away we could expect a boom in domestic travel. This has started to happen.

The International Scene

On the international front India's outbound traffic overtook the growth in inbound traffic. As Mr. Akbar Al Baker, CEO of Qatar Airways notes, "India's middle class is 100 million more than the entire population of United States." This middle class found international travel very popular and India outbound grew very fast. A major reason is that for tourism/marriage celebration purposes some Indian's find going abroad cheaper than travelling within the country. India's Inbound, especially inbound tourism traffic grew but was lacklustre compared to outbound.

Protest Letter by Dominant Private Airlines of India: 2011

The dominant Indian airlines, in a joint position paper 20 in February 2011, the representatives of three major airlines—Jet Airways, Kingfisher Airlines and Air India—put forth their views on the bilateral rights exchanged in the recent past. The main findings of the three airlines were as follows:

Joint Position Paper:

1. The traffic rights exchanged under bilateral agreements are already far in excess of the true 3rd/4th freedom market requirements in respect of several countries. As a result, in most of the cases, the capacity deployed under the bilateral is also in excess of the market requirements.
2. The capacity entitlements under various bilateral agreements during the period from January 2004 (pre-liberalisation) till March 2010 had increased by 282 per cent. Further, many foreign carriers had also been granted access to a large number of interior points in India, resulting in negating the home country advantage for Indian carriers.

3. Since the available entitlements are far in excess of the true 3rd/4th freedom traffic potential, this has encouraged the mega carriers to carry significant volume of 6th freedom traffic to/from India. The grant of access to interior points has further increased the 6th freedom component of the carriage by these mega carriers, as the 3rd/4thfreedom potential from these interior points is generally quite low. These interior points with low potential should ideally be served by the home country carriers over their hubs.
4. The grant of access to a large number of interior points in India, coupled with the grant of capacity entitlements far in excess of true 3rd/4th freedom has resulted in a situation where the foreign carriers are funnelling Indian traffic over their hubs outside India. This has adversely affected the growth of strong hubs in India to the detriment of the Indian carriers (both for domestic and international operations), Indian airports and other agencies involved in the civil aviation industry.
5. In terms of volume, the 6th freedom carriage to/from India by Emirates (EK) is the highest—2.4 million passengers (59 per cent of its traffic). Even Air Arabia, a low-cost carrier which is supposed to work on the model of point-to-point sale, had 43 per cent 6th freedom traffic.
6. Since the increased entitlements were granted even before the Indian carriers had a proper hub airport, foreign carriers' operations from most of their countries are already much more than the Indian carriers' operations, pre-empting the Indian carriers from expanding their operations in these markets. It is because of such pre-emption and excess entitlements exchanged that the utilisation of entitlements by the Indian carriers appears to be low.

Consequently, they recommended the following measures:

1. Entitlements should be rolled back, commensurate with true 3rd/4th freedom market requirement for the Gulf (Bahrain, Qatar, Abu Dhabi, Sharjah, Dubai), Asia (Hong Kong, Malaysia, Singapore, Thailand), Russia, and Europe (France, Germany and Netherlands).

2. Entry to a foreign carrier to interior Indian points should be restricted, and access to numerous points under bilateral be withdrawn. In other cases, no increase in capacity entitlements/traffic rights should be exchanged for the next five years, except where entitlements are less than the 3rd/4th freedom market requirement (based on Origin/ Destination data).
3. Even if there is significant traffic potential from a point of call in India to another country, before granting access, it must be considered if the Indian carriers are already providing enough capacity.

Comptroller and Auditor General of India (CAG)[6] has also added his own comments on the above as follows:

The position paper of February 2011 of the three leading Indian international carriers—Air India, Kingfisher and Jet Airways— only serves to confirm the serious problems with huge expansion of bilateral entitlements in respect of several countries (notably in the Gulf, SE Asia and Europe). This has facilitated several foreign airlines (predominantly Emirates) in tapping the vast Indian market and funnelling such traffic over their hubs (Dubai, etc.) to various destinations in the USA, UK, Europe and elsewhere, through what is termed as '6th freedom traffic'. Although the bilateral agreements do not explicitly provide for exercise of 6th freedom rights, the entitlements exchanged are vastly in excess of 'genuine' or point to point flying requirements between the two countries (termed as 3rd/4th freedom traffic based on Origin-Destination data) and implicitly allow 'mega-airlines' with giant hubs to exploit 6th freedom traffic. In fact, the advertising campaigns run by many of these airlines make this intent clear. The noting on MOCA files while processing proposed entitlement liberalisation referring to the demand from the 'labour class/working class' Indians for more seats to/from India (as projected by several agencies—MEA, Ministry of Tourism, MoCI), are, in a sense, misleading, since the 'labour class/ working class' Indians would be interested only in point-to-point connectivity (largely to the Gulf/Middle East), and not 6th freedom traffic (i.e., flights to UK/USA/ Europe, etc.). While it is expected that the Indian scheduled carriers would try to protect their commercial interests to the extent possible (and lesser competition from foreign airlines would help them), the clear issue is one of a lack of a level playing field for Indian Airlines due to bilateral rights with a large number of points in India being given to certain countries who do not have reciprocal points to offer in their country. It is certainly not our case that Indian Airlines should benefit from a protected environment, cloistered from competition from foreign airlines, especially in the current era of economic liberalisation. Further, the timing of the liberalisation of bilateral entitlements (notably the Gulf/SE Asia/Europe) from 2004-2005 onwards left much to be desired:

"The delivery of Air India/ Indian Airline new fleet acquisitions (approved by GoI in later 2005) was scheduled only between 2006 and 2010. Giving a reasonable time frame of 2 or 3 years post-aircraft delivery for stabilisation of the expanded 'footprint' could have provided them a 'level playing field' for competition.

"It is only since November 2010 onwards that India finally had an international class airport at Delhi (Terminal 3) capable of large-scale hub and spoke operations (domestic/international and international/ international); large scale development of other international airports in India facilitating hub and spoke operations (at the minimum where domestic and international terminals are co-located) have also come up in Bengaluru and Hyderabad. Again, giving a reasonable time frame of 2 to 3 years after full-scale operationalisation of Delhi T-3 would have provided a level playing field to all Indian airlines (not just AIL/IAL) to take on the mega carriers specialising in 6th freedom traffic."

The conclusion from the above is that India has unnecessarily indulged some foreign carriers by giving them unwarranted bilateral rights into interior points when our own airlines could not provide an equal response. Further, we did not have any airport worthy of becoming a hub till 2010 when T3 in IGI Airport in Delhi came up and, subsequently, Bengaluru and Hyderabad have also come up. Meanwhile, not only did we give away too many seats/flights to these carriers but we also allowed them into a large number of interior airports, as a result of which our airlines lost the opportunity of first mover advantage in their home turf. The time has come to make this correction. In our chapter on ICS we will endeavour to suggest corrections to this aberration.

Code Share

In the case of erstwhile Jet Airways, which was partially owned by Etihad Airways of UAE, it adopted a code share model for long distance flights. As an example, Jet Airways offered a choice of 64 nonstop weekly flights between India and Europe. Jet Airways together with Air France-KLM enhanced connectivity to Europe with 64 destinations via Paris and 84 destinations via Amsterdam. With Air France, it offered 33 weekly flights between Mumbai, Delhi, Bengaluru, Chennai and Paris and with KLM, it offered 31 weekly flights between Mumbai, Delhi, Bengaluru and Amsterdam. One could fly from any of our 44 cities in India via Mumbai, Delhi, Bengaluru or Chennai to 106 destinations in Europe via Amsterdam or Paris. Further, connections to over 200 North American destinations with Jet Airways code-share partners Air France, KLM and Delta Air Lines were also available. Because of code share the time tables are kept such that with transfer times are sometimes as low as 50 minutes at Amsterdam and 60 minutes at Paris. Air India, in the meantime, has joined the Star Alliance which will enable it to offer similar facilities.

However, with direct non-stop flights to Washington or Chicago from India, the concept of connecting at European or Gulf Hubs will change over time. Not only do direct flights save time, the hassle involved in changing aircraft in a short time is cut down. With new small single aisle aircraft coming into the market and providing longer endurance of 7 or 8 hours, direct connectivity between Tier II and Tier II towns to towns abroad is possible and will provide a much greater comfort as the hassle of transfer from a hub airport will no longer be required.

Is our existing Air Service Bilateral Agreements sufficient to serve our existing and future foreign policy needs? Yes, and No.

Anticipating Future Potential in Connectivity: Case ASEAN

Mr. Sham Saran, former Foreign Secretary, in his Foreword to ASEAN India Air Connectivity Report as Chairman, Research and Information System for Developing Countries, says:

With the implementation of India-ASEAN Free Trade Agreement in Services and Investment, ASEAN and India would likely benefit from an extended market. Air connectivity will play a pivotal role not only in expanding trade and investment between them but also in strengthening services trade. The ongoing negotiations for ASEAN Single Aviation Market (ASAM), which is the region's major aviation policy geared towards the development of a unified and single aviation market in Southeast Asia, would create a huge potential for India to integrate with ASEAN. For the present the Regional Comprehensive Economic Partnership is off the block for the time being, but the free trade agreement with ASEAN remains. It is high time we should vigorously pursue it. This should involve direct flights between many Indian cities to many cities of the 10 nation ASEAN, even if there is a subsidy involved in the initial years.

NCAP[7] & Deepening the Aviation Infrastructure: The UDAN[8] Scheme: A timely intervention

The National Civil Aviation Policy (NCAP) was announced in 2016. It is a detailed document covering all aspects of India's Aviation Sector. This policy document is approved by the cabinet and is the direction which the Ministry of Civil Aviation has to follow. New legislation has to be in conformity with this policy. As India's air travellers are still a very small percentage of rail and bus travellers, this document serves also as a road map for the future.

NCAP spells out the details of the UDAN Scheme, which is expected to be a game changer for aviation and growth of smaller towns/regions with regional air connectivity. With huge growth of middle class in these towns the likelihood of UDAN scheme being a success is high. Under these circumstances, the UDAN scheme is timely as it will be able to bring into operation another 100 airports in India, who in turn will become feeders to the existing routes and, thereby, increase the overall throughput of passengers and belly cargo. Such a boost will increase traffic to Tier II and Tier III including city-to-city direct connectivity.

NCAP 2016: Regional Connectivity Scheme (RCS)/UDAN[9]

The NCAP 2016 introduced a new concept of Regional Connectivity. This was in addition to the existing Route Dispersal Guidelines (RDG) meant to connect remote regions of island territories, J&K and some other inaccessible areas . The Regional Air Connectivity Scheme (RCS), also called UDAN (Ude Desh Ka Aam Naagarik), has been launched to provide connectivity to unserved and under-served regional aviation routes by means of a reverse auction method.

The RCS/UDAN Scheme is a key component of the National Civil Aviation Policy (NCAP) of June 2016. The scheme is being jointly funded by the central government and state governments, and several states have come on board by signing a "Memorandum of Understanding" with the union government. UDAN/RCS will connect a large number of new regional routes, by operationalising 100-plus regional airports by the end of 2018-2019 financial year, with a target of 13 lakh (1.3 million) annual passenger seats, requiring annual INR.200 crores Viability Gap Funding (VGF). The frequency of flights must be minimum 3 and maximum 7 per week from the same airport. This target date has been missed mainly due to COVID-19. The new routes will be given by reverse auction based on least subsidy. The main features of this scheme, therefore, are:

1. The regional connectivity scheme will be applicable on route length between 200 to 800 km with no lower limit set for hilly, remote, island and security sensitive regions.
2. The Central government will provide concessions to the tune of 2 per cent excise on Value Added Tax (VAT) and service tax at 1/10th the rate and liberal code sharing for regional connectivity scheme airports.
3. A Regional Connectivity Fund (RCF) will be created to fund the scheme via a levy on certain flights. States are expected to contribute 20 per cent to the fund.
4. For balanced regional growth, allocations will be spread equitably across 5 regions - North, West, South, East and North East with a cap of 25 per cent.

5. Market-based reverse bidding mechanism to determine least VGF to select the airline operator with the right to match to the initial proposer. The government said VGF will be reduced if passenger load factor remains high and will be discontinued after 3 years when route becomes self sustainable.

India has a total of 468 airports available[10] but many of these are non-functional as many were constructed during Second World War and then abandoned. A budget allocation of Rs. 4,500 crores was approved in the 2016-2017 union budget to revive and develop 50 airports in the smaller regional towns between 2017 and 2020 with 15 airports during 2017-2018, another 15 airports during 2018-2019, and 20 more airports during 2019-2020. While a total of 75 civil airports were operationalised for civilian flights in India since independence, during 2016-17, an additional 36 regional airports were made operational for civilian flights, including 3 civil enclave within military airports, with regular scheduled flights and the targets. However, there has been slippage mainly due to Covid related issues. The latest dates and figures are that by 2024 100 additional airports will be ready.[11]

According to well-known political analyst, Sanjeev Ahluwalia regional air connectivity initiative can bring export markets closer. The recently-launched progressive policy of regional air connectivity offers an opportunity for embedding export orientation even in hitherto inland, poorly connected locations. Air connectivity adds value to the local economy by kick starting business around newly serviced airports which are logistic nodes, connected to hubs in metros.

RCS/UDAN is, therefore, an innovative scheme to develop the regional aviation market and the economy of the region. Under this scheme, half of the seats on the plane will be priced capped at Rs. 2,500 per hour's flight determined by a process of reverse auction with a three-year exclusive right on the route to the selected operator. Government will subsidise the losses incurred. Eighty per cent of the subsidy will be collected by charging a levy of up to Rs. 5,000 on each departing flight of domestic airlines (with some exceptions) and the rest 20 per cent will come from other sources. Government will provide subsidy to airlines for the first three years of operations when they will also have exclusive flying rights on the selected routes. This is to give an assurance to the operator to build up the route. Once the market in these routes stabilises, it will operate on a commercial basis as per market forces of supply and demand.

RCS/UDAN is first-of-its-kind scheme globally that aims to create affordable yet economically viable and profitable flights on regional routes as distinct from remote routes. There are many features to this scheme. It provides subsidy to operators based on a reverse auction, but it obliges them to give half the seats at a subsidised rate. While they have exclusive right to the route for three years, they have to operate a minimum of three flights a week. The subsidy fund is partially filled up by airlines running on main routes by giving Rs 5000 into the fund for each regular flight.

This scheme will strive to make flying affordable to the common man even in small towns. The scheme will also help to stimulate growth and employment in the region. The routes under the scheme will connect pre-defined unserved or under-served routes on existing airports in India. India is lucky to have so many such airports lying unused largely with the Airports Authority of India, and some State Governments generally, built during World War II which can be put to use now.

One of the interesting features of RCS/UDAN is the creation of Regional Connectivity Fund under the Airports Authority of India. As normal commercial flights under the scheme contribute Rs. 5,000 per flight to this Fund as a part of their contribution, State Governments and Airports Authority of India also contribute. This is somewhat similar in nature to the Universal Obligation Fund of the Telecom Sector where all telephone calls contribute a small amount to this Fund which in turn funds telecom companies prepared to go to remote and difficult areas of the country.

After three successful auctions of routes under the UDAN Scheme, the Government has operationalised 235 new routes and 56 airports, including five heliports and two water Aerodrome s for amphibious aircraft. The participation of airlines in the bidding shows that the scheme is viable and generating interest amongst the airline operators. More such auctions are coming up.

Has UDAN Scheme been a success? So far it has been a halfway house. A few airlines collapsed like Jet Airways and Zoom. Some airlines like Deccan never took off. Another inference was that small regional airlines cannot easily survive while bigger national airlines do but they need smaller aircrafts. It a mixed bag but one should give it more time to be fully successful. Demand is yet another factor which takes time to generate. Routes in the south of India did better than other regions. Based on experience the Scheme has been modified in places and expanded to include seaplanes also. Even if the scheme is 50 per cent success it fine. But in some cases the demand was too weak for it survive.

NCAP 2016 & International Aviation: Bilateral Air Service Issues

NCAP 2016 has given a direction to bilateral air service policy. It has protected a radius of 5,000 km from Delhi and has talked in terms of Open Sky for countries in the SAASC region as well as beyond 5,000 km. What could be the reason for this? Any serious student of aviation in India will understand that the Gulf and Singapore have a heavy traffic from Indian cities. This is so because these two city states of Singapore and Dubai adopted aviation growth as an essential part of their economic growth model. As they encouraged their airports and airlines to grow, Indians found that they were convenient hubs in the East and West of India for them to change aircraft to a wide number of destinations. They had the first mover advantage. However, Indian airports have now become internationally acceptable, and there is no reason why India cannot create its own hub. But Indian airlines are as yet not at an advantage as these two countries have a better aviation infrastructure both in terms of airlines and airports. When India did not have any worthwhile airports, these countries were able to use India's outbound traffic to hub at and connect with at their airports for destinations beyond and vice-versa. These countries continue to ask for more traffic rights and Indian airlines were not able to match them due to our policy of 5/20 which disallows an Indian airline to go on a foreign route unless it has completed 5 years of domestic flying and has 20 aircraft (the 5-year embargo has been lifted but the 20 aircraft requirement remains). As more landing points are given in India, they are able to connect directly from Tier II and III cities to their hubs.

Committing a self-goal

But here lies the dual and conflicting nature of Indian aviation policy. At one end, India wants to protect its airlines against more aggressive and bigger carriers in the Gulf in the west and Singapore/Thai and Malaysian airlines in the east by following the 5,000 km policy; and, on the other hand, it discriminates between its own airlines by following the 5/20 policy, now modified to 0/20 policy. Further, it has also given out more interior locations in India to Gulf airlines and airlines in the ASEAN countries without any reciprocal advantage.

What is 5/20 policy? In 1994 when Air Corporation Act[12] was repealed and private airlines were allowed to work in the domestic sector, Air India was given protection by a devious means—a rule was introduced by DGCA vide a NOTAM that no airline will be allowed to go on an international route unless it has completed 5 years of service and has 20 aircraft. This was used to block private airlines like Jet or Kingfisher from going abroad. Now, these airlines, through their association called Federation of Indian Airlines, were blocking removal of this NOTAM so that younger airlines will have to follow the same practice. This NOTAM has no relevance anymore and should be removed. However, the Ministry in the Civil Aviation Policy 2016 has removed the 5-year restriction but retained the requirement of 20 aircraft. The modified policy is referred to as 0/20 policy. This policy still inhibits younger airlines from going abroad.

The Ministry of Civil Aviation (MOCA), Government of India released the National Civil Aviation Policy in November 2016 (NCAP 2016). One of the objectives of NCAP 2016 is to "enhance regional connectivity through fiscal support and infrastructure development". As per an ICAO study, "Economic benefits of civil aviation: ripples of prosperity", the output and employment multipliers of aviation are 3.25 and 6.10 respectively. This implies that every Rs. 100 spent on air transport contributes to Rs. 325 worth of benefits, and every 100 direct jobs in air transport result in 610 jobs in the economy as a whole. In fact, the study attributes over 4.5 per cent of the global Gross Domestic Product (GDP) to civil air transport.

India's Skewed International Aviation Coverage

While the coverage of international destinations from India is limited, the share of Indian Airlines within this is also adverse. The share of Indian and Foreign carriers in the total international passenger traffic in and out of India during the first quarter (January-March) of the year 2017 stood at 38 per cent and 62 per cent respectively. In the same Quarter (Q1) of the year 2016, the share of Indian and Foreign carriers was 36 and 64 per cent respectively. This shows the skewed nature of international flights from India. It also reflects the impact of bilateral ASAs carried out in the last 15 years resulting in tremendous growth of India's external Hub airports like Singapore, Bangkok and Kuala Lumpur in the east, and Dubai, Abu Dhabi and Qatar on the west. These airports abroad take a big chunk of Indian outbound air traffic and distribute them over their hubs to other countries.

The top ten international carriers accounted for almost 60 per cent of the international passenger traffic in India during the first quarter of the year 2017. Jet Airways, after having sold 24 per cent of its equity to Etihad Airways in April 2003, carried the maximum number of international passengers followed by Air India and Emirates airlines. All the 5 Indian Carriers, namely, Air India, Air India Express, Indigo, Jet Airways and SpiceJet operating on International Routes, find a place in the top 10 list. However, after the sudden collapse of Jet Airways it is already under a revival plan this ratio has become worse for Indian carriers, albeit temporarily. All the foreign carriers in the top 10 list originate from Gulf Countries. There is, therefore, a skewed relationship between Indian carriers and international carriers. While the bilateral Air Service Agreements provide for equal passenger/aircraft capacities for each country, in actual practice this may not be the case as utilisation may differ. There is also a notion that these Agreements should serve the actual requirements of the two countries concerned. However, this is also not always the case. If we look at Gulf traffic or Singapore traffic, there is a high percentage of transit/connecting passengers from India as well as other countries who prefer to change flights at these hub airports. A good airport is an essential requirement for creating a hub. India did not have any good airport till 2010, but now it does have a few and, therefore, if direct flights are available from India, the need to hub at these airports for Indians will go down and major Indian airports can become a hub for outbound Indian passengers as well as for international passengers, provided we increase direct outbound flights to many more countries. The government has taken cognisance of this fact and has started to look at restricting the number of landing points in India. The Free Press Journal in their article, "Foreign Carriers may not get landing rights on demand" dated December 25, 2015 has stated that they are looking to restrict the ports of call of foreign airlines coming into India. City States like UAE or Singapore have a dozen landing points in India when they can offer only one. This means they are able to collect traffic from multi-points in India, take it to their Hub and redistribute this traffic to a large number of countries. The result is that India is positively helping them to develop a hub in their country hub at the cost of our own airport hub. The UAE in 2007 (based on MoU and ASA of May 10, 2007) had 9 points of call in India, whereas Indian carriers had only one (Dubai), and there also landing slots at prime time were not being given easily by them . That is another good reason why Dubai received 2.1 million Indian tourists in 2017. In 2013 Singapore had air services to 12 Indian cities while India had only one—Singapore. In 2006 Thailand was given landing rights to 18 stations in India. This is not in the spirit of bilateral Air Service Agreement in which both countries should get equal opportunities. As a matter of fact, the government should insist with countries during negotiations, especially countries that have only one airport, to provide a landing slot at a time of our choosing. Airports like Heathrow in London, Dubai or Singapore have limited slots and prime time slots are not available. The availability of a convenient slot should be made a precondition to giving more rights.

Undoing the Previous Wrong

The answer to this skewed international relationship with foreign carriers is the need to provide direct flights to more international destinations from India by Indian carriers only from more regional cities. It is fortunate that the National Civil Aviation Policy 2016 has taken cognisance of this issue. However, more work needs to be done on this issue by the government.

Connecting People in India's Neighbourhood: need to enhance India' aviation connectivity

Ministry of Civil Aviation has already floated a draft scheme in August 2018 for International connectivity as there was demand from some state governments for direct connectivity from their states to an international destination on a subsidy basis in case the particular flight was not viable[13]. This scheme is similar to the UDAN scheme and states,

"However, certain State Governments of India also felt that facilitating/stimulating international air connectivity would be desirable from a public policy perspective and may need financial support, at least in the initial period, to trigger participation of airlines. Such State Governments desire to have direct scheduled flights between their respective states and select international destinations to promote socio-economic growth. It is in this context that the subsidy scheme (the Scheme) was envisaged for promoting international air connectivity between select destinations in the state and international destinations, as decided by the State Governments ("International Air Connectivity Scheme"), hereinafter called "IAC Scheme or the Scheme".

There is a need to take more proactive decisions in this direction. There is no need to leave this scheme to State Governments. There is a need to strategise our aviation policy to encourage our own airlines, as some countries do, and at the same time meet our foreign policy requirements. This is possible by encouraging our airlines to go to as many countries as possible even if required, with incentives, especially from Tier II and III towns. With new type of single-aisle long-endurance (upto 7-8 hours) aircraft now available, some emphasis should be laid on direct flights from our Tier II and III towns to not so popular foreign destinations in East, West and Central Asia in order to build them up for future as destinations for the ever growing Indian outbound traffic. Here another subsidy scheme to be operated by Ministry of External Affairs is needed. Such a scheme would put India in the International aviation map as a place to hub and connect also. It will give an impetus to our outbound passenger to visit certain countries which are desirable but not popular by Indian tourist. It will give a chance to residents of that country to visit India. For example, we could connect Andaman (Port Blair) and Nicobar (Great Nicobar Island) to close by International destinations like Bangkok or Singapore by a subsidised flight and see the international reaction. Similarly, we need direct connectivity from Indian towns to say Angkor Watin Cambodia or Bali in Indonesia or even places of archeological importance in Central Asia which have significant Buddhist monuments written text in Pali and Sanskrit. We also need to connect Kushinagar airport in Bihar with towns abroad which have Buddhist pilgrimage traffic like Bangkok etc. there is an urgent need to arrange subsidy with an UDAN like scheme to make India's neighbourhood well connected.

The Inbound

More than half of the total passengers coming to India are accounted for by the countries in the region of the Middle East. The same pattern is observed in the number of India's outbound passengers, that is, more than half of the total outbound passengers are accounted for by the countries in the region of the Middle East. If we look at the specific countries within the region, the maximum number of passengers are carried to and from the United Arab Emirates (33.2 per cent), followed by Singapore (6.6 per cent) and Saudi Arabia (5.7 per cent). This is so because Dubai and Singapore have emerged as the two hubs for Indians taking connecting flights and for foreigners to come to India. Like London, Heath row is a major hub nurtured by the UK towards the Atlantic Ocean, Dubai and Singapore are hubs for going westwards and eastwards for Indians till such time India develops its own hub—in all probability, in Delhi. To develop a hub, we need a good and friendly airport and plenty of connections.

Delhi Airport tops the position in this category with a share of 27.6 per cent of passengers, followed by Mumbai (21.4 per cent share) and Chennai (8.3 per cent share). Domestic and foreign carriers connect India to 58 countries through more than 300 routes. Out of these routes, 10 routes accounted for approximately 20 per cent of the total international passenger traffic during the first quarter of the year 2017. The maximum international passengers were carried on the Dubai-Mumbai sector, followed by Dubai-Delhi and Dubai-Kochi. While there is no doubt that there are many Indians working in the Gulf region, which reinforces the need for good connectivity to Tier II cities also, permitting Gulf-based airlines to pick up passengers from Tier II cities has lead to growth of sixth freedom traffic. The biggest mistake made by the government in the Indian civil aviation sector was in restricting the growth of airports or airlines till 2000. Delhi's IGI airport became functional in 2010 and private airlines of India were allowed to go abroad by March 2004. This delay gave our neighbours the first mover advantage, both in our East and West, and they went ahead full steam using Indian traffic to create their hubs. This correction can still take place when we allow our airlines to make direct connections to locations abroad in smaller long-range aircraft now available. It is up to India to encourage its airlines to take off from smaller Tier II or even Tier III towns and not give similar rights to foreign airlines unless it is reciprocal. This will bring greater connectivity to not so popular routes and reduce dependence on foreign hubs.

The policy of 5/20

Another issue which impedes growth of our airlines to go abroad is the 5/20 policy described earlier. Under this policy no airline was allowed to go abroad unless it had completed 5 years of flying in the domestic sector and had 20 aircraft. This inhibited the newer airlines to take flights abroad. Since introduction of NCAP 2016 the limit of 5 years has been taken away but the requirement of 20 aircraft exists. This continues to be a dampener on new airlines and has no justification except the older airlines feel that since they waited for 5 years, this should apply to newer airlines also. Further, this rule has no similarity in any other country and is a hindrance to our outbound growth story. It gives advantage to foreign airlines and thereby does not give a level playing field to airlines of India.

Air Freight is yet another important aspect of air operators' profits and viability. Freight in the belly of a modern jet can bring in about 20 per cent of the revenue. India is about the only country in the world which declared a unilateral 'open sky' for freighter aircraft a couple of decades back. This means a full freighter aircraft with no passengers does not have to seek government bilateral ASA rights and can apply to the DGCA by simply submitting a flight plan. However, it has not brought about any significant advantage of creating a cargo hub in India as other conditions like quick customs clearance are absent in our country.

As regards freight, the share of Indian and Foreign carriers is about 21 per cent and 79 per cent respectively. Out of the total number of scheduled international carriers, the top ten carriers accounted for almost 70 per cent of the international freight traffic during the first quarter of the year 2017. Emirates carried the maximum freight with 13.7 per cent market share followed by Qatar airways (10.9 per cent market share) and Jet airways (10.6 per cent market share) during the first quarter of the year 2017. Jet airways and Air India are among the top five scheduled freight carriers with market shares of 10.6 per cent and 8.1 per cent respectively during the first quarter of the year 2017. Other Indian carriers carry approximately 2 per cent of the total international freight. As far as India's inbound freight traffic is concerned, Middle East tops the position with a share of 28.7 per cent followed by Europe (27.5 per cent share) and Asia-Pacific (23.7 per cent share) during the first quarter of the year 2017. If we look at India's outbound freight traffic, Middle East tops the position with a share of 52.8 per cent followed by Europe (22.7 per cent share) and Asia-Pacific (16.6 per cent share) during the first quarter of the year 2017. India, however, may not be attractive enough to become a cargo hub as we are unable to improve our downtime and other bureaucratic issues.

India's Bilateral Civil Aviation Agreements Policy

India followed a tight bilateral air service agreement policy till about 2000. India was very conservative in giving bilateral rights and Air India, the sole carrier going abroad, generally opposed giving away the rights or negotiated with the other airlines a deal beneficial to them. The unfortunate aspect of this was that Air India and airports remained a victim of the rules and disadvantages of the Indian public sector. As a result, Air India was reluctant to compete and airports remained shoddy, unattractive with poor infrastructure for an international hub creation. Things have changed over time. Since 2010 private airports have come up, the first one being in Cochin followed by Delhi, Bengaluru, Hyderabad, Mumbai and now a new one in Goa is coming up. Some are new greenfield like Cochin, Bengaluru, Hyderabad and some are brown field like Delhi and Mumbai. AAI has also modernised many of its airports.

With liberalised air service agreements starting in 2000, the Indian airlines found they were not able to keep pace with some of the better airlines of the Gulf and South East Asia. As a result, it was seen that while these foreign airlines have managed to keep their portion of the bilateral rights fully utilised, India could not. This is the more so because as more private Indian airlines were permitted to travel abroad, more road blocks were put for newer airlines. Initially Air India was granted the right of first refusal for a new route abroad and the Ministry introduced the policy of 5/20 to protect it. This implied that no Indian Airline could go abroad on a route until it had completed 5 years of domestic service and had a minimum of 20 aircraft. This stopped Jet Airways and Kingfisher from competing with Air India for few years. Thereafter when India changed its FDI policy to allow up to 49 per cent of Foreign equity, the two new airlines, namely, Air Asia and Vistara were kept from going abroad by the 5/20 rule. In the NCAP 2016, the five-year requirement has been removed but the requirement of 20 aircraft remains. These self-imposed restrictions by India for its own airlines are not reciprocal when air service agreements are drawn. As a result, a new foreign airline without this requirement can come into India, but Indian airlines cannot go abroad unless they complete 5 years of domestic flying and have 20 aircraft (the 5-year restriction has been removed in NCAP 2016 but the restriction of 20 aircraft has been retained).

The Economic Survey of 2016-2017[14] of the Ministry of Finance and the comments of Comptroller and the report of Auditor and Comptroller General of India (CAG)

Air Service Agreements (ASA) provide the right of each country's designated airlines to fly a fixed number of passengers in seats or capacity between them and are equal and reciprocal.

Post 2004 large increases took place in capacity entitlements under bilateral Air Service Agreements especially with some Gulf countries but this led to under-utilisation of Indian entitlement. The Economic Survey 2016-17, while calling the sector a sunrise sector of growth, has been critical of the policy followed by Ministry of Civil Aviation and has suggested liberalising the flying abroad rule for airlines to bolster India's share in international air traffic, and advocated some protection for domestic carriers while negotiating air traffic bilateral rights. Similarly, second volume of the Economic Survey 2016-17 has stated that the expansion of capacity entitlements under bilateral Air Service Agreements with foreign countries has hurt the Indian carriers as foreign airlines dominated the international traffic to and from India:

"Indian domestic airlines have a very lower share in international traffic to and from India," the Survey said. "Factors like foreign airlines utilising the sixth freedom of the air, expansion of capacity entitlements under bilateral air service agreements with foreign countries, lower utilisation of India's own capacity entitlements, the 0/20 rule and fleet constraints are responsible for the same." Sixth freedom is the bilateral air traffic right to fly from a foreign country to another foreign country while stopping in one's own country. For instance, Emirates operates flight between India and the UK while stopping at Dubai, its home state. The sixth freedom traffic would be the passengers flying from India to England on Emirates Airlines of Dubai without stopping journey at Dubai but only transiting through it. Their ticket will be all the way to the UK and boarding passes will be split into two—India to Dubai and Dubai to UK. This kind of 6th freedom traffic reportedly constituted 61.14 per cent of the total international traffic in 2015-2016, up from 59.15 per cent in 2014-2015. However, no firm figures of 6th freedom traffic are available. While 3rd and 4th freedom traffic mean the actual traffic between the two countries, 6th freedom traffic means an airline carrying traffic from one country to its home and taking it further to a third country. Therefore, a country seeking bilateral rights on behalf of its airlines for its 6th freedom traffic, while acceptable, should not be encouraged on mutual advantage basis unless that country also grants 5th freedom rights to the other country. It could also be stated the there is no need to lament over 6th freedom being utilised by efficient airlines like the Emirates. In many cases India also has the 6th freedom right at airports like Dubai or Singapore but are not able to take advantage of it as Indian airlines are weak. "Round tripping of passengers via international hubs of Dubai and Singapore, utilisation of the 6th freedom of the air and increase in capacity entitlements under bilateral ASAs" have been cited as reasons for low share of Indian airlines in India origin international traffic. The 6th freedom of air allows overseas airlines to fly from a foreign country to another while stopping in one's own country. "The 6th freedom has to a large extent been responsible for reducing the share of direct long-haul flights for Indian carriers from 25 per cent in 2011-12 to 20.5 per cent in 2015-16," the Survey, tabled in Parliament, stated that a large increase in capacity entitlements under ASAs and under-utilisation of India's own entitlements are responsible for the country's lower share in international traffic to a large extent while India remains one of the fastest growing aviation markets.

Policy Issues

Suggesting 'policy prescriptions', the Survey said that besides privatisation/disinvestment of Air India (which has been achieved in

October 2021), the government may consider identifying major cities as aviation hubs—since India is as advantageously placed in terms of geographic location as Dubai or Singapore—and reconsider the 0/20 rule so that all private airlines could fly abroad. It has further stated that, in return, private airlines can be encouraged to fly to under-served airports in Tier II and Tier III cities and mentions UDAN scheme as a possible place where they can be used.

On the issue on 5/20 or 0/20 pointed out by the Economic Survey, it may be said that this policy has created three types of airlines in India: the government-owned airline like Air India, the old full service private airlines, like Jet Airways or LCCs like Indigo, and third, the newly registered airlines like Vistara and Air Asia India. Perhaps, as a response to the Economic Survey of 2016-17—the National Civil Aviation Policy released in November 2016—the Ministry of Civil Aviation diluted the contentious '5/20 rule' that required an Indian airline to have five years of domestic flying experience and 20 aircraft in its fleet before it can fly to overseas destinations. According to the present norm, known as the 0/20 rule, a domestic airline needs to have at least 20 aircraft on the domestic sector before getting the right to fly on international routes from India. However, this is still a hindrance to newer airlines as getting a fleet of twenty aircraft takes as much time. Unfortunately, the incumbent airlines, including IndiGo, SpiceJet, Jet Airways and GoAir that are eligible to fly on international routes had opposed any move to dilute the 5/20 rule while the new airlines Vistara and AirAsia pleaded with the government to do away with the decade-old restrictive norm. With a new airline Aakash as ultra low LCC coming in post Covid, revival of Kingfisher and sale of AirIndia's100 per cent equity, there will be a lot of action on the airline front. What is left to imagine is the boost in consumer demand. Even after government has removed all the restrictions imposed due to COVID (seat and price caps) what needs to be monitored is the reluctance on part of consumer to take flights and the change in business travel as video conferences have become common. Further, would Government agree to reduce the tax/ levy burden on passengers? Now that with LCCs coming in a big way, democratisation of civil aviation is taking place. Would the government bring parity between taxes on airlines to railway and roadways?

Covid-19 and Indian Aviation: Gloom

Covid-19 has been the worst traged for Aviation and Tourism Industry. With total and partial lockdowns both domestic and international the losses of airlines kept mounting . Airlines in India are likely to post a consolidated loss of $4.1 billion in financial year (FY) 2022, forecasts aviation consultancy CAPA.[15]

However, besides the lockdown, the revival has been marred by restrictions imposed DGCA based on medical advice. When the total ban on domestic aviation was lifted, it was conditional. There were seat restrictions as well as ticket price restrictions. As a result the aviation sector's revival was stymied. However, we notice that consumer confidence is returning to air travel. With July-September 2021 GDP growth at 8.4 per cent the economy will revive fast which will reflect in growth of passenger traffic.[16]

Impact of COVID-19 on Aviation

The impact of COVID-19 on Aviation has been disastrous. Airlines around the world have suffered huge losses. Somehow airlines managed to survive in spite of severe lockdown which meant no domestic flights for two months. However, with the opening of lockdown, restrictions were put on airlines. Airlines were allowed to fly a third of their pre-Covid flights with seat restrictions. By third week of October 2021 all restrictions on domestic airlines were lifted. With lifting of restrictions on Airlines the years 2021-22 will, hopefully, bring back a semblance of revival. Statistics for the period impacted by Covid are an aberration and cannot be taken into trend analysis. The issue we now face is the revival of the aviation industry. The lifting of restrictions by DGCA has been slow and in stages. By end of October 2021 one can say that DGCA restrictions have been removed but passenger hesitancy still remains.

On international flights the government went in for bubble arrangements i.e. bilateral point to point agreements with many restrictions due to Covid. By December 2021 the normally in international flights had not returned. Government declared normalisation of international flights by December 15th.

Post Covid Revival: issues of government intervention and reaching for Regional Domination

The government needs to looks into the many hurdles put in place due to Covid to make the aviation sector come back to its double digit growth. The domestic air passengers are not more than about 5 per cent of the population. As economic growth takes place there is no reason why the first time air travellers will not grow. However, it has a caveat. The growing passenger traffic is low income and sensitive to ticket prices. There is a relative price sensitivity between low ticket prices and railway tickets. The moment air tickets go down to a level when the compete with say 2 tier railway ticket that the switch over from rail travel to air travel takes place. It may be added that railway tickets are not taxed and often are kept below even running cost. The railways provide a cross subsidy with their freight tariff. If the government intervenes to bring a parity on taxation between railways and aviation, especially between Air Turbine Fuel (ATF) and diesel or electricity for railways things can change for the better for both. There will be a massive shift to air travel by the low income travellers which will bring profitability to airlines, and there will be some relief to railways. However, no examination of this aspect has been done so far. But with this policy prescription one can expect revival of the aviation sector. Once domestic airlines get revived the airports sector and other affiliated sectors also get revived.

According to Mint as capacity restrictions are lifted (which has happened) a rebound in air travel will follow. Domestic air traffic has been increasing every month since May-end in 2021. In July it was 5.02 million passengers and it increased to 6.7 million passengers in August. With removal of all restrictions on seat occupancy and ticket pricing but keeping Covid protocol in place, it looks as that the rebound would bring it back to preCovid time. As the hesitancy in taking a flight by common citizens gives way tourism and visiting friends and relatives domestically will go up. As far as corporate travel is concerned it will take longer. With the introduction of digital platforms like Zoom and others the business has got used to virtual meetings which saves time and costs.

On the issue of International travel the dependence on policies adopted by each country regarding opening of their airports to passengers of another country will matter.

Extending UDAN to international routes

On the International sector revival is also very much desired. However, much depends upon the policies of other countries. For the present the bubble arrangements with many countries continue with Covid based restrictions like quarantine. Multi country travel remains a problem. However, there is scope for yet another scheme which may be linked to our foreign policy and yet revive our airlines going abroad. Therefore, if India introduces an external subsidised scheme for international connectivity to some countries less connected where commercial airlines find poor viability it will give a boost to both India outbound in that direction as well as inwards tourism and will also promote business.

Aircraft manufacturers [17]already have in their offer single aisle long range aircrafts with endurance of up to 7-8 hours. This should change the method of flying from two and three tier towns of India direct to destinations abroad without using any hubs. This can change the way Indians fly abroad and can be encouraged to fly to neighbouring countries as a political strategy to enhance people to people contacts. This should enable a policy to extend our exiting UDAN scheme to international destinations directly from our smaller two and three tier towns, with subsidy, if necessary.

We propose that in order that since India's objective to reach a $5 trillion economy in near future, we should go for another innovative subsidised scheme- an international travel scheme to supplement our domestic subsidised scheme UDAN.

While 0/20 rule implies that domestic carriers can fly overseas only if they have at least 20 aircraft it will, however, serve our purpose if the 0/20 rule is relaxed for those airlines which are ready to fly abroad on routes designated our proposed International Connectivity Scheme (ICS). Both 5/20 and 0/20 rule are anti-competition. Later in the book it has been proposed to relax this rule under International Connectivity Scheme, or UDAN international.

Conclusion

Aviation offers a sunshine sector to India. With less than 5 per cent of the population flying currently the scope is huge. However, the sector has been impacted very harshly by Covid-19. It needs government support, not by grants , but proper fiscal support so that profitability of airlines is maintained. It should not become a milch cow for unnecessary taxation/cess. It's not only supporting tourism both domestic and international, it offers great opportunities for job creation, something much needed in India. The government support post-COVID could be in the form of fiscal support like reduction of taxation on fuel and other charges, or increasing subsidised UDAN like schemes to widen the aviation infrastructure. It should also be by extending UDAN to locations abroad in the region as a foreign policy objective and helping India becoming a hub for the region.

Notes

1. This essay forms a part of a book (with modifications) written by the author which is being published by KW Publishers. Dr Sanat Kaul is Chairman, International Foundation for Aviation, Aerospace and Drones. He was with the Ministry of Civil Aviation, on Boards of Air India and Airports Authority of India. He was also India's Permanent Representative to International Civil Aviation Organisation.
2. Business Today May 9th ,2019 quoting an IATA report : business today.in
3. business today.in August 31, 2018 businesstoday.in/industry/aviation./story/india-fastest- growing-aviation-market-IATA-108907-2018-08-31
4. Air travel on certainAir travel on certain routes is cheaper than travelling by train: Times Travel Editor|TRAVEL NEWS: Jul 23, 2018,
5. https://www.hindustantimes.com/ October 17, 2021 based on a report a report of November 13, 2016
6. CAG report on Ministry of Civil Aviation Chapter 6, Report 40 of 2016 https://www.google.co.in/url?sa=t&rct=j&q=&esrc=s&source=web&cd=

&ved=2ahUKEwi79eSFqeLzAhWSSH0KHc_xBt0QFnoECBAQAQ&url= https%3A%2F%2Fcag.gov.in%2Fuploads%2Fdownload_audit_report %2F2016%2FChapter_6_Management_Union_Government_Report_40_of_2016_ Commercial_Civil_Aviation_PA.pdf&usg=

7. https://www.civilaviation.gov.in/sites/default/files/Final_NCAP_2016_15-06-2016-2_1.pdf
8. see Regional Connectivity in the NCAP 2016 https://www.civilaviation.gov.in/sites/default/files/Final_NCAP_2016_15-06-2016-2_1.pdf
9. www.aai.aero REGIONAL CONNECTIVITY SCHEME - RCS UDAN
10. quora.com
11. Upcoming /New airports in India and it's impact on real estate- Housing: 7th October 2020: http://housing .doc>news>upcoming
12. blog.ipleaders.in : The Air Corporations (Transfer of Undertakings and Repeal) Act, 1994
13. Draft Scheme for enhancing air connectivity between Indian states and international destinations August 2018 : AAI.aero https://www.aai.aero/system/files_force/rcs_news_notifications/UDAN%20Intl%20Placing%20on%20MoCA%20Website.pdf?download=1
14. indiabudget.gov.in https://www.google.co.in/url?sa=t&rct=j&q=&esrc=s&source=web&cd=&ved=2ahUKEwjfh4PO39PzAhWPbisKHWnFBxgQFnoECAYQAQ &url=https%3A%2F%2Fwww.indiabudget.gov.in%2Fbudget2017-2018 %2Fes2016-17%2Fechapter.pdf&usg=AOvVaw3seajKbiuYQgPjq26At2Sc
15. CAPA is a leading Consultancy Service on Aviation. INDUSTRY
16. GDP expands at 8.4% in Jul-Sept quarter:Mint 1st December 2021: livemint.com
17. Airbus reveals the world's longest-range single-aisle jetliner by Amit Malewar:www. tech explores the.com

3
India's Foreign Policy and Allied Issues

Although there are many aspects to India's foreign policy, this chapter will look into issues of our foreign policy only in the neighbourhood. We have divided it into East of India which will come under the 'Act East Policy' and West of India under 'Look West Policy' in which we will discuss the Gulf region and Iran-Afghanistan and Central Asia as one and, finally, the Indian Ocean Region (IOR), more specifically the Bay of Bengal region.

Act East Policy (AEP)

A1. The Minister of State for the Ministry of External Affairs, Gen. V. K. Singh (Retd.) provided the following information in December 2015 in reply to a question in Lok Sabha:[1]

> India's Act East Policy focusses on the extended neighbourhood in the Asia-Pacific region. The policy which was originally conceived as an economic initiative, has gained political, strategic and cultural dimensions including establishment of institutional mechanisms for dialogue and cooperation. India has upgraded its relations to strategic partnership with Indonesia, Vietnam, Malaysia, Japan, Republic of Korea (ROK), Australia, Singapore and Association of Southeast Asian Nations (ASEAN) and forged close ties with all countries in the Asia-Pacific region. Further, apart from ASEAN, ASEAN Regional Forum (ARF) and East Asia Summit (EAS), India has also been

actively engaged in regional fora such as Bay of Bengal Initiative for Multi-Sectoral Technical and Economic Cooperation (BIMSTEC), Asia Cooperation Dialogue (ACD), Mekong Ganga Cooperation (MGC) and Indian Ocean Rim Association (IORA). Act East Policy has placed emphasis on India-ASEAN cooperation in our domestic agenda on infrastructure, manufacturing, trade, skills, urban renewal, smart cities, Make in India and other initiatives. Connectivity projects, cooperation in space, S&T and people-to-people exchanges could become a springboard for regional integration and prosperity.

The Objective of 'Act East Policy' should be to promote economic cooperation, cultural ties and develop strategic relationship with countries in the *Asia-Pacific region* through continuous engagement at bilateral, regional and multilateral levels thereby providing enhanced connectivity through the States of North Eastern Region including Arunachal Pradesh with other countries in our neighbourhood. The North-East of India has been a priority in our Act East Policy (AEP). AEP provides an interface between North-East India including the state of Arunachal Pradesh and the ASEAN region. Various plans at bilateral and regional levels include steady efforts to develop and strengthen connectivity of Northeast with the ASEAN region through trade, culture, people-to-people contacts and physical infrastructure (road, airport, telecommunication, power, etc.). Some of the major projects include Kaladan Multi-modal Transit Transport Project, the India-Myanmar-Thailand Trilateral Highway Project, Rhi-Tiddim Road Project.

A Major Policy Lacuna: Andaman and Nicobar Islands

The policy statement is, however, silent on Andaman and Nicobar Islands whose strategic importance is brought out in chapter 5 of the book. The two archipelagos of Andaman and Nicobar Islands, consisting of 572 Islands, islets and rocks connect south of Myanmar with Malacca Strait. About 30 per cent of India's EEZ is because of these islands. This book will endeavour to fill in the vacuum left unmentioned in the strategy statement. Further, these islands form a chain from the southern tip of Myanmar to the western entrance of the Malacca Strait. The Great Nicobar Island is near the mouth of the western entrance of the Malacca Strait. The importance of these islands from hard and soft power point of view is immense and has not been tapped to India's advantage. A proposal to declare the Great Nicobar Island as a Free Port has also been suggested. This issue will be discussed in greater detail in chapter 5. India's not getting archipelagic status for the Andaman and Nicobar Islands at the United Nations Convention on the Law of the Sea in 1982, resulted in the 10-degree channel between the two archipelagos remaining an open sea and not under Indian control, was our first diplomatic failure in this region. The second failure was not getting into the Malacca Strait Patrols (MSP) due to Indonesia's objection. Both these need to be corrected.

The purpose of the above analysis is also to show that while South China Sea is under tension and turmoil because of the aggressive stance of China in claiming the entire South China Sea under some fictitious 'Nine-Dash Line', the Bay of Bengal is an area of peace as all maritime/littoral countries of India, Indonesia, Thailand, Malaysia and Myanmar have no disputes and have legally settled borders. The disputes on maritime boundaries between India and Bangladesh and Bangladesh and Myanmar have been settled amicably by international arbitration. China, on the other hand, has refused to accept the Award of the International Tribunal in a case between the Philippines and China, resulting in raised tension. The lack of appreciation in our foreign policy of leveraging the advantage of having these archipelagos will be brought out later in this book.

China and the Indo-Pacific

China also supports the United Liberation Front of Assam (ULFA). This terrorist group in Assam operates across the border in Myanmar and seeks the help of China. Myanmar and Indonesia both broke off diplomatic relations with China earlier. In both cases it was interference in internal affairs of the country. It is also ironic that China tried its best in 1971 to stop the birth of Bangladesh and then tried to deny it membership of the UN. It has claims over Indian territory and objected to a visit by India's Prime Minister to Arunachal Pradesh, a state of India also claimed by China. A Report called "Non-Alignment 2.0" issued by an Independent Group of "Eminent" Experts states:

> China will, for the foreseeable future, remain a significant foreign policy and security challenge for India. Skirmishes and incidents have occurred along the LAC. The Strategy of India should be to "hold the line" on the Sino-Indian land frontier but maintain and, if possible, enlarge India's current edge in the maritime south. This strategy takes into account both the superiority of current Chinese deployment and the posture on the land boundary, and the unlikelihood of the border issue being resolved in the near future.[2]

The recent encroachment by stealth by China in Ladakh in 2020 is a reminder of China's muscular approach to India. This is the second time in the history of independent India that China has used its armed forces to encroach Indian land. The first time was in 1962 and again now in 2020.

Indian defence forces appear to have already adopted a Forward Policy in 2001 in the Indo-Pacific Region starting with a concept of Tri-Service Command or Indian Far Eastern Command in the Andaman and Nicobar Islands. This is the first Tri-command in India with the three forces coming under it. This command has a full-fledged Air Force base in Car Nicobar, a Naval base in Port Blair and Kamorta Island of the Nicobar group and a small Naval airbase in Campbell Bay in Great Nicobar Island called Baaz, and another in the north near Diglipur called INS Kohassa. With this the strategic emphasis is getting implemented. While the Kamorta-Nancowry, the deep sea and safe harbour in the Nicobar, is considered one of the best natural harbours in the world but is yet to be fully utilised. Its future development will be watched with interest. The strategic location of these islands needs to be developed as a springboard for power projection in the region using both hard and soft power to complement each other. India needs to convert the Malacca

Dilemma of China into the Malacca Advantage of India and, therefore, there is a need for a shift in policy for an integrated civil-defence projecting both for hard and soft power in the maritime domain.

ASEAN AND SAARC: 2003 Aviation Policy on Connectivity with East of India

The issue of connectivity with east has been under consideration for a long time. The first attempt was made by Prime Minister Atal Bihari Vajpayee in 2003. A unilateral aviation policy for SAARC and ASEAN was announced. A policy for Open Sky for SAARC countries was announced in October 2003. He announced an "open skies" arrangement with the ten-member ASEAN group to allow their designated carriers to fly into designated Indian metropolitan cities. "There is a need for increased connectivity between India and ASEAN. The open skies arrangement is a unilateral move by India", Vajpayee told the ASEAN leaders at the second India-ASEAN summit at Bali. The Prime Minister also offered flights from ASEAN member nations to 18 tourist destinations in India to improve people-to-people connectivity. In continuation he also said that ASEAN members could start daily flights from Delhi, Mumbai, Kolkata and Chennai (7 flights a week) subject to reciprocal rights. These 18 other destinations of India were: Patna, Lucknow, Guwahati, Gaya, Varanasi, Bhubaneshwar, Khajuraho, Aurangabad, Goa, Jaipur, Port Blair and Cochin, Thiruvananthapuram, Calicut, Amritsar, Visakhapatnam, Ahmedabad and Trichy, but subject to reciprocal rights. It was also decided to allow private airlines to operate to SAARC countries against unutilised Indian entitlements. However, the result was that not a single country started a flight then but the existing airlines of Singapore, Malaysia and Thailand increased their flights.

Prime Minister Vajpayee's unilateral offer in 2003 was really to encourage airlines of all ASEAN countries to come to India and not just to the Metro cities but also to the smaller cities, and develop a mutual appreciation. This incentive, however, was taken up only by the big few airlines in the neighbourhood. Since there was no incentive or promotional scheme with this to follow up, the smaller airlines did not find it worth their while. This was, probably, the cause of its failure. In order to build traffic between two little known destinations, starting a flight is not enough, but providing incentives is important. A lot of hard work goes into it. FAM or familiarisation tours rearranged and travel trade is involved. But nothing of this kind was done. The countries that took advantage were those that already had good services to India and were hubs for taking Indians further east beyond their airports. However, countries like Cambodia, Vietnam or Indonesia did not take the bait as it was not viable.

Prime Minister Atal Bihari Vajpayee also announced a similar policy for SAARC countries unilaterally. It was also decided to allow private airlines to operate from SAARC countries against unutilised Indian entitlements. The only country who took advantage of this offer was Sri Lanka. Sri Lankan Airlines operates 126 flights a week from 14 cities of India to Colombo. They are the second largest airline to operate into India after Emirates. A large part of their traffic is 5th/6th Freedom Traffic. Sri Lankan Airlines had a tie-up with Emirates Airlines of Dubai.

Bay of Bengal and India: India's Forgotten Archipelagos of Andaman and Nicobar Islands

In the Bay of Bengal India's relations with all its littoral states in the east are excellent and it is necessary that this is maintained and improved. It may be pointed out that while the South China Sea is an area of turmoil with conflicting sovereignty issues with China, the Bay of Bengal in the Indian Ocean is an area of peace and harmony because India has signed up maritime agreements with all its littoral neighbours, that is, Myanmar, Thailand, Malaysia and Indonesia. It has also settled its maritime dispute with Bangladesh through an international arbitration. Myanmar and Bangladesh have also settled their maritime boundary dispute through international arbitration. China, on the other hand, in the South China Sea refuses to accept the award of an international arbitration with the Philippines.

Bay of Bengal is not only a zone of peace but full of promise. The hydrocarbons potential cannot be denied. Yadana and Yetagun in Myanmar and Arun in Indonesia have oil. The exploration activities in the Andaman Basin commenced in 1959 by the Oil and Natural Gas Commission (ONGC) Ltd. of India with about 4,533 sq. km. of the islands covered by reconnaissance survey. The Andaman Basin should be considered as the frontier area for hydrocarbon exploration. So far 21 wells have been drilled and some gas has been discovered which was considered sub-commercial. Geological formations of Thermogenic and Biogenic nature were found, similar to Yadana and Yetagun gas fields in Myanmar and Arun gas field in Sumatra. It is generally felt that continued exploration activities will definitely prove availability of commercial hydrocarbons in the Andaman. Bay of Bengal has the advantage of having member countries from ASEAN, SAARC and BIMSTEC groupings.

Following is a report on the Prospects of Oil and Gas in the Andaman Sea which falls into India's EEZ based on a report by Larry Prado in 2020.[3]

"Wet gas prospect spurs resource development in Andaman Sea Development for Southeast Asia looks promising with exploration programs planned for 2021 and 2022.

Other exploration

ONGC also is focusing on the unexplored deep waters of the Andaman Nicobar Basin, the Indian frontier zone that lies between hydrocarbon producing fields in south Myanmar and northwest Indonesia. The company will be targeting the Andaman Nicobar deep waters because of the potential for hydrocarbon reserves. Studies indicate the Andaman Nicobar Basin has potential to produce oil and gas like the adjoining basins in south Myanmar and southwest Indonesia, as the geological structures of the three are same.

According to ONGC, the Andaman Nicobar Basin, spread over an area of 47,000 sq km—including deep waters in southeastern part of Bay of Bengal—is part of the Island Arc System that extends from Myanmar in the north to Indonesia in the south. The giant Yadana and Yetagun gas fields in Myanmar are located on the north side of Andaman Basin, while Arun, Kuala Langsa and NSO in North Sumatra Basin (Indonesia) are in the south.

ONGC plans to launch a new exploration campaign to drill as many as 18 wells in six deepwater blocks in the Andaman Basin. The exploration program includes drilling three exploratory wells in each of the six blocks that are located in water depths between 9,170 ft and 11,221 ft on the east and west sides of Andaman and Nicobar islands.

ONGC has submitted a proposal to India's federal environment ministry to drill each of the 18 wells in six blocks to a depth about 19,685 ft.

The first four are located in water depths of 2,875 m to 2,980 m on the west of the Andaman Islands. The remaining two are in water depths of 2,320 m to 3,420 m.

The geophysical and 2D seismic surveys by ONGC in the deepwater blocks have shown the presence of hydrocarbons and the prospects for large hydrocarbon reserves, similar to the ones in the neighboring oil and gas fields in Myanmar and Indonesia."

The above analysis is to show the economic potential of India's Exclusive Economic Zone around the Andaman and Nicobar islands. There is a need to protect it with a proactive policy because countries like China would be very happy to get a hold of it and with it control the Malacca straits as well as the potential oil and gas.

In the Act East Policy we have many combinations of nations and regional groupings which we need to consider separately and together. The main ones are as follows:

SAARC[4]

Founded in 1985 and consisting of eight countries, that is, India, Bhutan, Bangladesh, Pakistan, Nepal, Maldives, Afghanistan and Sri Lanka, the South Asian Association for Regional Cooperation (SAARC) consists of our immediate neighbours. However, relations with Pakistan being what they are, this group has not quite taken off.

India has proposed an air connectivity scheme linking towns in Bangladesh, Myanmar, Sri Lanka, Thailand, Bhutan and Nepal, which are part of the Bay of Bengal Initiative for Multi-Sectoral Technical and Economic Cooperation.[5] But nothing as yet has happened.

Bay of Bengal Initiative for Multi-Sectoral Technical and Economic Cooperation

BIMSTEC[6] is a group of 7 countries consisting of India, Bangladesh, Myanmar, Sri Lanka, Thailand, Bhutan and Nepal with a combined population of 1.5 billion people and a combined GDP of $ 2.5 trillion. BIMSTEC states are dependent upon Bay of Bengal. Fourteen priority sectors have been identified for cooperation which includes transport and communications.

BIMSTEC was established on June 6, 1997 through Bangkok Declaration. It is headquartered at Dhaka, Bangladesh. Six priority sectors of cooperation were identified at the 2nd Ministerial Meeting in Dhaka on November 19, 1998. Out of the 14 key sectors identified for cooperation, India would lead the group in transportation & communication, tourism, environment & disaster management, and counterterrorism and transnational crime.

During the course of the pre-Conference curtain raiser India proposed an air connectivity scheme linking towns in Bangladesh, Myanmar, Sri Lanka, Thailand, Bhutan and Nepal. There was apparently no follow-up on it. It could become an extension of India's UDAN scheme of bringing in cheaper air connectivity to cities of BIMSTEC.

India's Minister of State for Civil Aviation has stated during a curtain raiser to mark the 20th anniversary of BIMSTEC in June 2017:

> "It is worth considering whether we can work with countries that are in the BIMSTEC to see whether we can create a policy package that will enable us to connect smaller towns across the entire BIMSTEC region," Jayant Sinha, India's Minister of State for Civil Aviation, said in New Delhi.[7]

According to him the proposed scheme will be based on India's RCS/UDAN scheme which provides a ticket for an hour's flight for approximately US$ 38. RCS/UDAN is considered one of the cheapest air connectivity schemes aimed to bring smaller cities on aviation route for the economic uplift of a region.

Although the proposal has not been formally offered to BIMSTEC, the Minister suggested an agreement with various countries to provide financial aid to roll out the scheme. "We can sign an MoU with different countries to be able to provide support for an RCS/UDAN-type scheme across the BIMSTEC community. Of course, we will have to couple that with something like an Open Sky Agreement so that airlines can fly freely."

India expects such air connectivity will encourage high-value travellers and allow free movement for business persons. Over the last two years, India has started favouring BIMSTEC in place of the South Asian Association for Regional Cooperation (SAARC) in a bid to isolate Pakistan.[8]

While the Minister for Civil Aviation did propose such an air connectivity scheme linking towns in Bangladesh, Myanmar, Sri Lanka, Thailand, Bhutan and Nepal, which are part of the Bay of Bengal Initiative for Multi-Sectoral Technical and Economic Cooperation (BIMSTEC), there was no response from other countries and the scheme did not materialise. The proposed scheme was to be based on India's UDAN scheme which provides a ticket for an hour's flight for approximately US$ 38. UDAN is considered one of the cheapest air connectivity schemes aimed to bring smaller cities on aviation route for the economic uplift of a region.

BIMSTEC and North-East India

India conducted the first ever international conclave on BIMSTEC from November 2 to 4, 2017, in Guwahati under the overarching theme of "BIMSTEC: An Enabling Architecture for Growth, Prosperity and Partnerships".

India is already developing North-East railways and roadways network to reach out to countries in Southeast Asia via Myanmar. India had already planned a Southeast Asian connectivity project connecting Moreh in India to Mae Sot in Thailand via Myanmar in 2002, years ahead of China's One Belt, One Road (OBOR) Initiative.

ASEAN: Association of Southeast Asian Nations

Kishore Mahbubani[9] has stated:

> The ASEAN-India relationship is not just 25 years, it's a few thousand years old, and it's important that the leaders draw from this deep well of history to build ties. Nine out of ten ASEAN countries, all except Vietnam, have Indian cultural base. Even when the Philippines, a 90 per cent Catholic country hosted the East Asian summit in November last year, it opened with a Ramayana performance. Most Indians are so ignorant and unaware of these links, however. The second thing to push for is more flights between ASEAN and Indian countries, to facilitate people-to-people exchanges.[10]

As Kishore Mahbubani has stated India and ASEAN countries have a shared but forgotten history. The exception of Vietnam mentioned above is also not fully correct. The famous Champa kingdom in central Vietnam was a Hindu kingdom with much in common with India. Neither India nor ASEAN seem to emphasise this issue.

ASEAN is a 10-Member group consisting of Singapore, Malaysia, Thailand, Indonesia, Cambodia, Lao PDR, Vietnam, Brunei, the Philippines and Myanmar. It is, therefore, not a Pacific or South East Asian grouping, as the name suggests, but surely an Indo-Pacific Group as Myanmar, Thailand, Malaysia and Indonesia also have their maritime boundary in the Bay of Bengal. The present combined GDP of this group has risen from $95 billion in 1970 to $2.55 trillion in 2016 and $3.08 trillion in 2020 and further is expected to be $6.44 trillion by 2027,[11] while India currently has a GDP of $2.7 trillion (at pre-Covid level) and expecting it to grow to $6 trillion by 2027, making it the third largest economy, according to a Morgan Stanley report.[12] ASEAN as a group would be the sixth largest economy today after the US, China, Japan, Germany and the UK. ASEAN's success has today transformed the fundamentals of geopolitics of South East Asia in the Indo-Pacific Region. India celebrated in 2018 twenty-five years of partnership with ASEAN. India and ASEAN became Sectoral Dialogue partners in 1992. Thereafter in 1996, they became Full Dialogue Partners. Then, in 2002, Summit Level Partners and by 2012, Strategic Partners. In 1916 ASEAN for India was the fourth largest partner accounting for 10 per cent of India's trade while India was ASEAN's seventh largest partner. In 2018 India's trade with ASEAN stands at US$ 81.33 billion, which is approximately 10.6 per cent of India's overall trade. India's export to ASEAN stands at 11.28 per cent of our total exports. Investment flows are also substantial both ways, with ASEAN accounting for approximately 18.28 per cent of investment flows into India since 2000.[13]

India was in the process of joining ASEAN-led Regional Comprehensive Economic Partnership (RCEP), which when implemented would cover 40 per cent of the world's population, 40 per cent of world trade and 33 per cent of Global GDP. So, ASEAN, as a block, is most important to India.[14] However, the issue of India joining RCEP has been postponed by India as India does not find it advantageous at present. The issue is still alive.

The ASEAN-India Plan of Action for the period 2016-2020 was adopted in August 2015 which identifies concrete initiatives and areas of cooperation along the three pillars of political-security, economic and sociocultural. India continues with stepped up efforts to forge closer partnership with concerned regional and Multilateral organisation such as ASEAN, ARF, EAS, BIMSTEC, ACD, MCG and IORA. On the Civilisational front, Buddhist and Hindu links could be energised to develop new contacts and connectivity between people. On Connectivity, special efforts are being made to develop a coherent strategy, particularly for linking ASEAN with our North East. Measures, including building transport infrastructure, encouraging airlines to enhance connectivity in the region, contacts between academic and cultural institutions are underway. Our economic engagement with ASEAN has been stepped up—regional integration and implementation of projects are priorities. The ASEAN-India Agreement on Trade in Service and Investments has entered into force for India and seven ASEAN countries from July 1, 2015. The ASEAN-India Trade Negotiating Committee has been tasked to undertake a review of the ASEAN-India Trade in Goods Agreement. India has also invited ASEAN member states to participate in the International Solar Alliance which it has co-launched with France on November 30, 2015. On strategic issues, we have increasing convergence on security interests with key partners both in bilateral and multilateral format. Closer cooperation in combating terrorism, collaborating for peace and stability in the region and promotion of maritime security based on international norms and laws are being pursued.

Though ASEAN-India economic engagements are moving forward in the desired direction, there are certain challenges that call for policy interventions. With signing of the ASEAN-India Agreement in Services and Investments, ASEAN and India are likely to benefit from an extended market, where the air connectivity aims to play a pivotal role. ASEAN-India summits have been taking place since 2003. In the 8th Summit held in October 2010 in Hanoi, it adopted ASEAN-India Plan of Action 2010-2015.

Over time ASEAN-India Summits have led to meetings in Telecom sector, Digitalisation and Connectivity. In physical connectivity much attention has been on, and the main focus has gone to, maritime and road connectivity, *but not much on air connectivity except that it is kept as a desirable goal.* The ASEAN-India connectivity initiative in specific has taken the initiative for India-Myanmar-Thailand trilateral Highway, and the Kalandan project which involves sea and land and river connectivity between India and Myanmar including building a Kolkata to Sittwe port sea link.[15] In a ASEAN-India Connectivity Summit held in Delhi on December 11-12, 2017 various issues were discussed like roads and highways connecting India to Myanmar and Thailand-INSTC—International North-South Transport Corridor by India-Myanmar-Thailand Trilateral Highway which will extend to Lao PDR, Cambodia and Vietnam. They also spoke of Andaman and Nicobar Islands as a 'Strategic Hub' in the Bay of Bengal. It also mentioned that ASEAN-India island connectivity has gained momentum and there is vast scope of cooperation including in Tourism, Maritime and Security, especially in Tourism promotion with Thailand, Malaysia and Indonesia. There is also scope for other items and other related industries. ASEAN has redesigned Master Plan for Connectivity (MPAC) 2025 which they have adopted at the ASEAN summit in Vientiane, Lao PDR in 2016. This Master plan has updated design and strategy for connectivity improvement in ASEAN as well as for Dialogue Partners such as India. While this MPAC 2025 focuses on five strategic areas—sustainable infrastructure, digital innovation, seamless logistics, regulatory excellence and people mobility—air connectivity as a specific topic has been left out.

Over the past few years India's Developmental Assistance has provided a Line of Credit of $ 1 billion for physical and digital connectivity between India and ASEAN countries and has also set up a Project Development Fund of $ 77 million to support manufacturing units in Cambodia, Lao, Myanmar and Vietnam (CLMV countries). On top of this India has also been providing Lines of Credit on a Bilateral basis to ASEAN member countries also.

For Myanmar besides the Road connectivity, India is also developing Dawei Port in Myanmar along with Sittwe Port, Sittwe to Paletwa inland waterway and a connecting road to Mizoram. The construction activities in Sittwe started in 2010. The work on Kaladan Project is complete. In this way India has been giving funds for development of projects abroad as part of its foreign aid and as a part of its Line of Credit to enhance trade and to establish industries abroad. For example, Ministry of External Affairs together with Ministry of Shipping had advised Shipping Corporation of India to launch a direct India-Myanmar Container Shipping Service which was launched in October 2014 to strengthen the bilateral relations between the two countries. The Port rotation for this purpose was Colombo-Chennai/Krishnapatnam-Yangon-Colombo. The reason for adding Colombo was due to abundant opportunities of

Commercial Trade between Colombo, Chennai and Krishnapatnam. For this purpose, Ministry of External Affairs granted a subsidy of Rs. 14.33 crores to SCI on July 28, 2014 for running the service for six months. The subsidy had to be continued and enhanced and was finally Rs. 18.08 crores. Subsequently, Ministry of Shipping decided to run through SCI two separate services: India-Bangladesh-Myanmar and India-Sri Lanka-Maldives on a pilot basis.

In addition, an East-West Economic Corridor is also coming up connecting India to Thailand via Myanmar and extending up to Cambodia, Lao PDR and Vietnam—a distance of 3,200 km or 2,000 miles by road from India all the way up to Vietnam.

A task force on ASEAN-India Maritime Connectivity has also been set up for Shipping and Logistics. This force is examining the viability of Coastal linking India with ASEAN nations (Brunei, the Philippines, Indonesia, Malaysia, Singapore, Cambodia, Myanmar, Vietnam, Laos, Thailand) Shipping Network. India has also proposed signing of an India-ASEAN Maritime Agreement similar to the China-ASEAN Maritime Transport Agreement.

All this above has been brought out to show how MEA is directly funding transportation projects to enhance the trade between India and certain countries where we have a strategic interest. There is, therefore, no reason why this fund cannot be used to boost air connectivity between India and ASEAN countries without spending anything on capital costs but, perhaps, subsidising initially for a few years. It is a moot question whether the political dividend would be higher in providing subsidised aviation to connect business and tourism or in construction of roads and ports. This is not quantifiable and there cannot be an answer to it.

China Factor in South China Sea Compared to India factor in Bay of Bengal

Since 1974, when a swift naval operation saw China grab the Paracel Island from the waning South Vietnamese regime, China has steadily expanded maritime areas under its control through surprise attack and stealth. These include the Spratly Islands (from Vietnam) and Mischief Reef (from the Philippines). While claiming indisputable sovereignty over all of the South China Sea,[16] Beijing proposed postponing resolution of the dispute and instead wanted to discuss, from a position of strength, the joint development of undersea resources. To ease regional concerns, China signed in 2002 a standstill agreement, a so-called Declaration on the Conduct of Parties in the South China Sea with a promise that a formal code would follow. However, so far, China is avoiding to sign one. It has now deployed anti-ship cruise missiles and surface-to-air missiles in the artificially created islands and does not permit oil exploration by other countries. Already seven or more artificial islands with airstrips for military planes have been built. This is causing immense tension amongst its neighbours—mainly the ASEAN member countries.

China's military build-up with shock and horror symbolism says more about the unchallenged position that Beijing has built and the submissive compliance it has come to expect from ASEAN countries. However, the fact that the US has offered to help find a multilateral solution to a vexing international problem strikes at the heart of China's tried and tested strategy of "talk, take and hold". In the meantime, China has already started to land its military jets on the newly built reclaimed islands' airstrips.

China does not like to deal with ASEAN as a group but prefers to deal bilaterally. It has treated those ASEAN members not having sea borders with China differently from those that do, then seeks only bilateral agreements with the disputants. This leads to countless futile meetings to divert attention from China's continued effort to strengthen its military control over its possessions and expanding its de facto boundaries by barring its neighbours from fishing in disputed waters or drilling for oil in waters far away from China. In 2007 and 2008, it even stopped BP and ExxonMobil from drilling in waters offshore Vietnam.

India, on the other hand, has been in the forefront of developing multilateral organisations in the East. As Shashi Tharoor points out in his book, *Pax Indica*, "India has played a crucial role in developing multi-lateral organisations in the region, notably the Mekong

Ganga Cooperation (MGC), the IOR-ARC and BIMSTEC",[17] besides SAARC.

China has told senior US officials that its sovereignty over the South China Sea was undisputed and one of the core issues that brooked no compromise. China took its expansive claim to the South China Sea a notch higher by challenging in 2009 a US Navy survey ship, the *Impeccable*, some 75 miles from the shore of China's Hainan Island, effectively extending its 12 nautical miles territorial waters to a 200-mile Exclusive Economic Zone (EEZ). The US maintains that under the UN Convention on the Law of the Sea, its naval vessels have the right of free passage through the EEZ.

After assuming chair of ASEAN, Vietnam made a sustained effort to draw US attention to the danger of China's rising power in the South China Sea. Malaysia, Indonesia and the Philippines too have raised concerns with Washington. When the Philippines won the UNCLOS Arbitration case against China over South Chine Sea islands, as Hague-based international tribunal ruled that China's nine-dash line claim over the disputed waters is invalid,[18] the new President of the Philippines surrendered to China claiming that China is too big to take on and it's better to collaborate with them.

The recent growth of Chinese economic power has caused a lot of distress in South East Asia. After taking over Tibet militarily in the 1950s, the take-over of South China Seas in 1974 under the fictitious nine-dash line is the second biggest show of military strength by China which has led to a state of shock for the ASEAN countries, Japan as well as South Korea. It has created an atmosphere of fear coming from a giant and growing power. India is the only country in the region which can offer a semblance of opposition.

While India does believe in territorial expansion as an objective, it must protect its own and contain the growth of China in its neighbourhood lest we find China our neighbour once again, this time in the Andaman Sea. India has already signed up peacefully agreements of its maritime borders with its neighbours in the East like Bangladesh, Myanmar, Thailand, Malaysia and Indonesia. The Bay of Bengal is an area of peace. Maritime disputes between India and Bangladesh have been settled by International Arbitration and so also the dispute between Bangladesh and Myanmar. While the military challenge needs to be met, the people-to-people contact between India and its neighbours is still very poor. Tourism is a major soft power that needs to be mobilised to garner public support. Chinese Government, on the other hand, tries to make up with ASEAN by promising them aid and sometimes grants on a bilateral basis. China is, nevertheless, wary of dealing with ASEAN as a multilateral group. The Chinese have already signed projects worth $ 1 trillion in the region bilaterally of which ASEAN countries are a major beneficiary.

India decided to invite all the ASEAN Heads of State as Chief Guests on the occasion of India's 69th Republic Day on January 26, 2018 and preceded by the 25th Anniversary of the India-ASEAN partnership on January 25. Many Heads of State came and the rest were represented by Senior Representatives. This show of solidarity developing between ASEAN and India has a political significance.

The Singapore Prime Minister, Lee Hsieng Loong, and son of former PM Lee Kuan Yew, commented that while India alone or ASEAN alone might not be a significant global player, together they can "look China in the eye".[19] Together with 1.8 billion people and a GDP of $ 4.5 trillion, "India and ASEAN combine can certainly aim high. ASEAN as a group is of world's seventh largest economy and hosts to more than 200 of the world's largest companies. While Singapore is one of the main sources of investment in India, Vietnam holds the record for incoming foreign direct investment. If New Delhi's hope of pioneering a huge new trade block, the Regional Comprehensive Economic Partnership (RCEP) to include all 10 ASEAN nations materialises then it will comprise almost 30 per cent of global GDP and facilitate India's access to key supply chains as well as natural gas and oil".[20] However, Niti Aayog, Government's Think Tank, the Chief Economic Advisor and even the former Foreign Secretary have a word of caution against India moving ahead with RCEP as it might affect India adversely and warned against India joining RCEP. Presently, India's export to

RCEP accounts for 15 per cent of our total exports and 35 per cent of our total imports. India's trade deficit with China is $ 52 billion and accounts for half the trade deficit of India. However, in 2020-2021 it has dipped to $44 billion. Had India joined RCEP the trade deficit might balloon.[21] Joined RCEP India will open up its market to China with whom it had an unsustainably high trade deficit of $ 63 billion in 2017-2018.[22] While we should observe caution, RCEP does offer a decisive opportunity to further engage with our eastern neighbours economically. It has been decided in 2020 that for the time being India will not be joining RCEP. While this decision has been criticised by many eminent economists, it is, perhaps, prudent to err on the side of caution, rather than be taken in by China which does not honour its commitments like the one above on Code of Conduct in South China Seas.

The successful "Delhi Declaration" (of 2018) reaffirms in para 6 the importance of maintaining and promotion of "peace, stability and maritime safety and security, freedom of navigation and over flights in the region and other lawful uses of the seas and unimpeded/maritime commerce." It further goes on to emphasise peaceful resolution of disputes in accordance with universally recognised principles of international law, including UNCLOS, ICAO, IMO and effective implementation of Declaration on the Conduct of Parties in the South China Sea and early conclusion of Code of Conduct in the South China Sea. As pointed out by Surendra Kumar, a retired Indian diplomat, "The Delhi Declaration will also have reverberations in China and Pakistan as there are certain references, which directly point out to them without naming them."[23]

At the invitation of H. E. Mr. Nguyen Xuan Phuc, Prime Minister of the Socialist Republic of Vietnam, the Prime Minister of the Republic of India H. E. Mr. Narendra Modi paid an Official Visit to the Socialist Republic of Vietnam from September 2 to 3, 2016.[24] They shared the view that Vietnam-India relations have been built on a firm foundation, with close links in culture, history and civilisation, mutual trust and understanding as well as the strong mutual support in international and regional fora. The Vietnamese side reaffirmed Vietnam's support for India's Act East Policy and welcomed a greater role for India in the regional and international arena. Prime Minister Narendra Modi reaffirmed that Vietnam is an important pillar of India's Act East Policy.

Based on the current excellent relations, in order to meet the expectation of the Leaders and people of the two countries, and with the desire to contribute to regional peace, stability, cooperation and prosperity, Vietnam and India agreed to elevate the current Strategic Partnership to Comprehensive Strategic Partnership. The two Prime Ministers agreed to assign the two Ministries of Foreign Affairs to be the focal points, in collaboration with other ministries and agencies of both sides, to build the Plan of Action to bring the Comprehensive Strategic Partnership to reality in all area. The Comprehensive Strategic Partnership cannot be without a good relationship between the peoples of the two countries. However, the people to people connectivity between the two countries remains poor. Direct air connectivity is erratic. The need for direct air connectivity between Indian cities and cities of ASEAN has been felt. In the case of India and Vietnam, both sides reiterated the importance of connectivity between Vietnam and India. They urged airlines of both sides to soon open direct flights between major cities of Vietnam and India. They sought acceleration of the establishment of direct shipping routes between the sea ports of Vietnam and India. Both sides agreed on the need to further strengthen physical connectivity between India and ASEAN. The Indian side urged Vietnam to utilise various initiatives of India for Cambodia, Laos, Myanmar and Vietnam (CLMV) countries and the India-ASEAN Line of Credit for physical and digital connectivity.

Vietnam Air announced a direct flight from Ho Chi Minh City (Saigon) to Delhi. Their service has since commenced on a thrice-weekly basis. However, this is not satisfactory as again this service may not last long if it looks at pure profitability. India's Jet Airways had a service to Ho Chi Minh City for one and a half years. While this service was via Bangkok and not non-stop, it had to be closed down due to lack of profitability.

Vietnam's special geographic position and its keenness to look towards India for both security and economic issues makes it a special country for India. Security issues for both countries are mutually reassuring. Their offer of Naval facilities to India as well as Oil Blocks are both something that India should not refuse. It is time India makes its presence felt in South China Seas in a manner similar to China making its presence felt in Indian Ocean through their String of Pearls strategy.

Asean-India Dialogue Relations

ASEAN-India dialogue relations have grown rapidly from a sectoral dialogue partnership in 1992 to a full dialogue partnership in 1995 and subsequently to a Summit level interaction, with the First ASEAN-India Summit being held in 2002, all of which took place in a decade. This reflects the confidence both ASEAN and India have in the dialogue partnership which is reflected by the expanding and intensifying dialogue and cooperation in many sectors.

ASEAN-India cooperation covers the economic, political and security, and development cooperation dimensions with a number of mechanisms established to promote dialogue and cooperation in these areas. In recent years, sectoral cooperation has been gaining strength with the establishment of working group level meetings in science and technology, transport and infrastructure, and small and medium-scale enterprises.

Political and Security issues

India has been an active member of the ASEAN Regional Forum (ARF) since July 1996. It views the ARF as valuable in promoting stable relationships between the major powers, and as a useful complement to the bilateral alliances and dialogues which are at the heart of the region's security architecture. ASEAN and India committed themselves to jointly contribute to the promotion of peace, stability and development in the Asia-Pacific region and the world, and respond positively to the challenges of a dynamic regional and international environment.

ASEAN and India are now intensifying their political and security dialogue to add a new dimension to a mutually beneficial economic and commercial relationship.

In embarking on concrete initiatives to step up cooperation mechanisms between ASEAN and India in the international fight against terrorism, India has proposed the signing of an ASEAN-India Joint Declaration for Cooperation in Combating International Terrorism. India presented a draft text for the consideration of ASEAN during the Fifth Meeting of the ASEAN-India JCC on April 22-23, 2003 in New Delhi. The Meeting agreed that the draft would be considered by the ASEAN Senior Officials on Transnational Crime and the ASEAN-India SOM.

India's accession to the Treaty of Amity and Cooperation (TAC), further adds significantly as a key instrument in ensuring peace and security, stability and development in Southeast Asia.

Trade

Volume of trade and investment flows between ASEAN and India remained relatively low compared with other dialogue partners of ASEAN. Between 1993 and 2001, two-way trade between ASEAN and India has more than doubled from US$ 2.9 billion to US$ 9.9 billion, which is equivalent to a compounded annual growth rate of 16.5 per cent. Although trends in economic interaction are positive, the volume of trade and investment remains low. India accounts for less than 2 per cent of ASEAN's total trade and 0.2 per cent of FDI in the region. An area of concern that needs attention is the fact that over the past five years, India's trade with ASEAN has witnessed moderation from US$ 75 bn in 2012 to US$ 64.6 bn in 2016, with both India's exports and imports slowing down over the period. The slowdown in India's exports to ASEAN, and thereby overall trade, has been especially consistent since 2013. India stands as ASEAN's 11th largest trading partner in the year 2016. There is immense potential to enhance India's trade relations with ASEAN, and in the process to correct the trade imbalance between India and ASEAN.[25]

Acknowledging this trend and recognising the economic potentials of closer linkages, both sides started economic consultations at the ministerial and senior official levels. As a result of these consultations and the recommendations of the Joint Study on AFTA-India Linkages for the Enhancement of Trade and Investment, both sides are now working on an ASEAN-India Framework Agreement on Comprehensive Economic Cooperation. The Framework Agreement is being drafted by the ASEAN-India Economic Linkages Task Force (AIELTF). The volume of trade and the trend of investment are expected to improve when initiatives under the Framework Agreement are eventually implemented.

Cooperation between India and ASEAN trade and investment relations have been now growing steadily, with ASEAN being India's fourth largest trading partner in 2018. India's trade with ASEAN stands at US$ 81.33 billion, which is approximately 10.6 per cent of India's overall trade. India's exports to ASEAN stand at 11.28 per cent of our total exports.[26]

Development Cooperation

Since the establishment of the ASEAN-India dialogue relations, development cooperation activities/areas have grown in strength and number. In terms of sectors, ASEAN-India cooperation covers the following: trade and investment, science and technology, human resources development, tourism, transport and infrastructure, health, small and medium-scale enterprises and people-to-people contact. Science and technology has been one of the most prolific areas with significant outputs. However, there have been delays in implementing cooperation activities and both sides are now actively working through the ASEAN-India Working Group to take stock and improve project formulation, coordination and implementation.

The ASEAN region as a whole is characterised by the presence of strong production networks and Regional Value Chains (RVCs) both within and outside the ASEAN. On the other hand, India is almost left out of any significant regional value chains in its neighbourhood. Such endeavours unleash a dynamic process that creates positive developmental pressures on forging better infrastructural linkages. India and ASEAN could thus explore opportunities to cooperate and partner in mutually beneficial Regional Value Chain networks. Other areas of collaboration between India and ASEAN could include improving connectivity network, cooperation in SME sector in the CLMV region, cooperation in ITES, and developing stronger linkages with investment promotion agencies in the region, among others. Closer economic and trade linkages among the economies of Asia could prove to be a mutually rewarding association. In this regard, it is important to note that India had contributed US$ 2.5 million in October 2002 to the ASEAN-India Cooperation Fund to further enhance cooperation. However, a few activities have been identified to utilise the funds and India has expressed its strong desire to see the effective utilisation of the Fund by undertaking new cooperation activities. Here, again, direct air connectivity will enhance the chances of improved production networks. This is so because direct connectivity helps business between unknown groups to also come up.

India-ASEAN Relations

As already stated by Kishore Mahbubani, India has a history of relationships with ASEAN region and, therefore, ASEAN cannot be considered to be just a Pacific/South China Group but an Indo-Pacific Group. With Thailand, Malaysia, Indonesia and Myanmar having a maritime opening in the Bay of Bengal, it is an Indo-Pacific group. It is a fact of geography that India is in the immediate neighbourhood of ASEAN. It shares a land border with Myanmar, and maritime border with Malaysia, Indonesia and Thailand. Further the 572 islands of Andaman and Nicobar archipelago of India makes India a close maritime neighbour of ASEAN also. India's relations with ASEAN have grown considerably over the last decade, but a vast potential still remains untapped. Apart from economic cooperation, there is much more that the two sides can work for together.

With the convening of the First ASEAN-India Summit, the dialogue relations have been elevated to the highest level. While it demonstrated the commitment of ASEAN and India to work closely in the areas of mutual interest, both sides must now increase the level of cooperation.

In order to facilitate a more balanced and comprehensive cooperation, ASEAN and India have developed a mechanism for it.

To give greater visibility to cooperation, both sides should embark on a programmed approach with clear strategic thrusts. Such programmes would comprise a number of projects to meet the objectives of the relations and could be multi-year in nature thereby having high impact on ASEAN-India development cooperation. Such programmes will tap on the strengths of the relations and the synergies within the programmes. The programmes could focus on Science & Technology (including IT, HRD) and capacity building and people-to-people contacts. It is, however, the people-to-people contact which will bring ASEAN and India closer to each other. This requires better air connectivity.

Two-way trade and investment between ASEAN and India remains low, although both sides are of the view that opportunities for collaboration are yet to be fully tapped. The ASEAN-India Framework Agreement on Comprehensive Economic Cooperation, once agreed and implemented, could facilitate greater flow of trade and investment. In addition, ASEAN and India should encourage their respective private sectors to tap on the huge market potential that both sides have to offer. The current international situation also presents a case for ASEAN and India to collaborate more closely.

Combating international terrorism is another point of cooperation. At the initial stages, both sides could focus on exchange of information and best practices as well as training. Seminars and workshops on counterterrorism and related areas could be initiated to better appreciate the situation on the ground, and how both sides are tackling the problem as well to identify possible areas for joint cooperation and action. The Malacca Straits have been an area of piracy. While piracy is well under control in this region, it can reoccur. Singapore, Indonesia, Thailand and Malaysia are involved in the control in the Straits. India being on the western entrance of Malacca Straits with Great Nicobar Island right there, should actively participate in the anti-piracy operations. Somehow, this has not happened as India has not been able to project itself in the eyes of ASEAN countries as a player in the region as they do not display its presence in the Bay of Bengal.

ASEAN has no objection to India's interest to develop a network of relations with ASEAN through other means of cooperation frameworks as it would complement the larger goal of enhancing ASEAN-India ties. In this regard, India's active participation in the Mekong-Ganga Cooperation and the five-member subregional grouping of Bangladesh, India, Myanmar, Sri Lanka and Thailand Economic Cooperation (BIMSTEC) also enhances India's Act East Policy. But a major opportunity which India is losing is in not projecting itself as a major player in the Bay of Bengal by not opening the Andaman and Nicobar group of islands. This issue will be discussed in chapter 5 on the Missing Link.

Security: Importance of Malacca Straits

Security from an ASEAN perspective—unlike the western perspective—it is not just military cooperation but more holistic and inclusive. Noting that ASEAN was "central" to the future of Asian security itself, India's former National Security Advisor, Shivshankar Menon, had pointed out that the ASEAN countries and India had already achieved success in tackling piracy in the Malacca Straits, and called for replicating the cooperation model for promoting the new security architecture too for the region.

"If you look at our record in dealing with piracy along the straits of Malacca, our power—as ASEAN and neighbouring countries—I think we can claim to have been more successful example. Look at the Horn of Africa, the efforts there are not quite successful," he said. However, what was not said is that India should be treated as a participant stakeholder of Malacca Straits along with Singapore, Malaysia, Indonesia and Thailand due to the strategic position of Great Nicobar Island on the western entrance of Malacca Straits. India has not yet been able to join the Malacca Strait Patrol (MSP).

Established in 2004, the Malacca Strait Patrol is a quadrilateral arrangement between Indonesia, Malaysia, Singapore and Thailand for intelligence exchange, coordinated air (eye-in-the-sky) and sea patrol through the vital straits.

The narrow channel of water, which stretches for around 600 nautical miles, accounts for 25 per cent of world trade. It is also one of the world's energy choke points, with a transit volume of over 16 million barrels per day of crude oil and petroleum products. About 40 per cent of India's trade also goes through the straits.

Finally, in 2018 Indonesia has agreed to let India develop a port at the island of Sabah in Sumatra only 80-90 km from Great Nicobar Island.[27] However, a highly-placed diplomatic source said that whenever India had brought up the issue of joining the Malacca Strait Patrol with Indonesia in the past, Jakarta had stated that New Delhi did not either understand or delineate its role clearly.[28] However, it would be of greatest importance to India if it can join the Malacca Strait Patrol. This will give a great leverage to Indian security to check any Chinese designs in this region.

On account of India's critical absence in the Great Nicobar Island and because of the utter underdevelopment of these islands, ASEAN member countries do not consider India as a stakeholder in the Malacca Straits. India needs to correct this impression and show its presence here much more. This aspect is also reflected in our Act East Policy statement. This will be discussed in chapter 5.

From its inception, ASEAN has emphasised the concept of comprehensive security. This means not just threat from outside but also from within like tensions, economic and social disparities, etc. This comprehensive approach has been further enhanced by the view that inclusive regionalism and multilateralism are complementary approaches to managing security.

In this context India needs to reformulate its regional cooperation policies in order to strengthen its engagement with the Association of Southeast Asian Nations (ASEAN) and the general region. Despite ASEAN concerns about India's recent military build-up, India signed the Treaty of Amity and Cooperation (TAC) and endorsed the Southeast Asia Nuclear Weapons Free Zone concept. Expansion of TAC to include countries such as India indicates the region's willingness to enlarge the institutional framework for security. ASEAN would like to use India as a counterweight in its relations with China.

The ASEAN-India Framework Agreement can lead to further increases in trade between the regions within a win-win situation. India should not subject development of economic relations to political changes. It should try to minimise bureaucratic hurdles that challenge multilateral arrangements.

With the proposed establishment of the India-ASEAN Free Trade Area, there is a need to develop adequate infrastructures that connect both regions. *This calls for better person-to-person connectivity which is possible if we have better air connectivity—point-to-point.* In this concept there is a need to promote tourism between India and all the ASEAN countries. While east of Malacca Straits is the South China Sea, which China is determined to take over and has become a major point of conflict, west of Malacca Straits is the Bay of Bengal—a region of peace. All littoral states of Indonesia, Malaysia, Thailand, Myanmar and India are at peace with each other, having tied up all maritime boundaries.

India-ASEAN Air Connectivity: The Disconnect

The issue of enhancing air connectivity between ASEAN Countries does not find any mention in the Indian Press Note on December 23, 2015 on Act East Policy. Similarly, the National Civil Aviation Policy of 2016 also does not have a specific mention of Act East Policy of 2015. This lack of coordination needs to be corrected. If the Act East Policy needs to be implemented in full the Civil Aviation Policy 2016 needs to take into account a comprehensive view of our trend in foreign policy. Can the Act East Policy—as enumerated in the Press Note of December 23, 2015—be fulfilled without direct air connectivity with more than half the Asian countries? This anomaly needs to be corrected. Further, while policy pronouncement has been made in December 2015, there has been little follow-up on the air connectivity issue. While it may be desirable, commercial compulsions of viability may not be favourable. This brings us back to a chicken and egg situation. Do we build a connecting road first to encourage industry to come up in a certain region or let the industry come up first before we build a road? The same logic applies to aviation. It is well established that we build the infrastructure first to attract the investors, and not the other way around.

As pointed out by Harsh Pant, "*With China having three times more commercial flights than India into South East Asia, improving air connectivity between India and ASEAN should also be high on the agenda.*"[29] However, this is yet to find a proper place in the Indian Civil Aviation Policy or in the Foreign Policy.

As India has not joined RCEP, it will mean greater stress for India with ASEAN countries. As India's annual trade deficit with ASEAN approaches $ 24 billion it is the added vulnerability of opening up its economy under RCEP deal that has led to the decision not to join RCEP at least, in the near future. However, some feel that by sealing off its economy from trade deal, India is undermining not only its economic influence in Southeast Asia, but also its political clout.

Poor Air Connectivity between ASEAN Countries and India

India's Skewed Civil Aviation Outbound Market with ASEAN

While ASEAN constituted about 16 per cent of international passenger flow from and to India in 2015, the distribution of passengers between ASEAN countries and India is skewed. Flow of ASEAN passengers coming to India has been much lower than the Indian passengers going to ASEAN or transit through ASEAN. Hubs like Bangkok, Singapore and Kuala Lumpur equipped with bigger and better connected airlines continue to attract passengers and air cargo from India. Today, out of 10 ASEAN countries, only five ASEAN countries like Malaysia, Myanmar, Singapore, Vietnam and Thailand have direct flights with India. Even direct connectivity with Myanmar and Vietnam remains poor. For the rest five ASEAN countries (Cambodia, Indonesia, Lao

PDR, the Philippines, Brunei), there is no direct flight but there are interconnections from other ASEAN countries, of which Indonesia and the Philippines are two prominent ASEAN countries with which India has substantial business and tourism interests. With Indian arrival figures to the Philippines touching the 100,000 mark in 2017, the Department of Tourism in the Philippines is focusing strongly on Indian travellers, and they are also doing roadshows in India. However, direct connectivity between India and the Philippines or Indonesia remains elusive or intermittent.

At the same time there appears to be a lack of enthusiasm on the part of ASEAN countries to visit and holiday in mainland India. One reason could be that it has not been promoted well.

India's Skewed Civil Aviation outbound market with ASEAN could have many reasons. It could be wrong publicity in the Indian and International Press regarding treatment of women in India. It could be non-promotion by Bollywood and other films from India. There could also be a lack of promotion of Buddhist pilgrimage sites in India.

As *Cruising Heights*,[30] an Indian magazine dedicated to aviation, points out in an article on ASEAN air connectivity:

> The Air connectivity issue has been raised time and again but there has been little action on the ground. Way back in 2003, the then Prime Minister Atal Bihari Vajpayee had advocated an open sky arrangement between ASEAN and India. Five years later, in 2008, the ASEAN-India Aviation Cooperation Framework was adopted (but remained a non-starter).
>
> The Result: Not only has tourism between ASEAN and India (not) gone up, neither has trade.[31] India has been recording the highest number of air travellers but Indians accounted for only 3 per cent of all tourist arrivals in ASEAN. As for trade between ASEAN and India, it was at a low... With the signing of ASEAN-India Agreement in Services and Investments, ASEAN and India are likely to benefit from an extended market, where air connectivity plays a pivotal role. The issue of direct air connectivity between countries is

one of them. The major issue and challenges relating to promoting air connectivity between ASEAN countries and India pertain to growing demand for air cargo services; facilitating business and leisure tourists by having more direct flights connecting Tier II and Tier III cities of India.

In addition to the *Cruising Heights* views, it may also be pointed out that in a recent newspaper report[32] even after the Indian Prime Minister's offer of a $ 1 billion line of credit at the Kuala Lumpur summit of November 2015, for both digital and physical connectivity in ASEAN countries, it has really not taken off. Only Laos had sent a request for this line of credit. As a result, India has decided to give a grant of $ 40 million for a pilot project in Cambodia, Laos, Myanmar and Vietnam (CLMV) countries to help kick start the credit line.

All these issues need corrective action. In addition, for many reasons, the Andaman and Nicobar Islands have remained closed and expensive to foreign travellers. While they offer fantastic potential for creating a tourism paradise comparable to resorts of Phuket in Thailand, Hainan island in China or Vietnam's Phu Quoc island, it needs proper planning and development. This could be the Soft Power projection by India for these countries. This issue is discussed further in chapter 5.

North-East India: Gateway to Act East Policy

North-East India comprises 7 States, namely, Assam, Manipur, Tripura, Arunachal Pradesh, Nagaland, Mizoram and Meghalaya. Arunachal Pradesh has a 1,400 km border with Tibet which China claims, and in 1962 a war between the two countries has been fought. Arunachal, Manipur, Nagaland, Mizoram share a border with Myanmar, while Tripura and Mizoram share a border with Bangladesh. Arunachal Pradesh was under the administrative control of the Ministry of External Affairs for about ten years due to the sensitive border with China. However, being on the eastern side of India it has the potential for a gateway to Myanmar, Thailand and other ASEAN countries by road and rail, which are under various stages of construction. Besides this aspect, the air connectivity between this region and ASEAN countries is missing. Once established it could be a great integrating force, and also for business development.

Advantage Assam Seminar December 15, 2017

The Statement by Indian Minister of State on Act East Policy on December 23, 2015, mentioned earlier, had specifically mentioned promoting cooperation between North-East India and ASEAN region. Government of Assam has taken up the challenge. In a seminar held on December 15, 2017 in Delhi on "Advantage Assam—An interactive Session with Aviation Industry" with Chief Minister of Assam along with Chief Secretary, Secretary Civil Aviation and Aviation industry leaders present, the Chief Secretary made a detailed presentation on how Assam, and in particular Guwahati, can become a region international hub for the North-East. He further stated that Guwahati is within two hours flying time from Dhaka, Kathmandu, Bangkok, Yangon by modern jets. He was of the view that Guwahati should come up as a regional international Hub to support Act East Policy implementation just as Kunming in Yunnan province of China has become. He was supported by Secretary, Civil Aviation who stated that a subsidy may be required to start these flights and the state of Assam/North East Council should provision for about Rs. 100 crores for it. The Chief Minister thereupon announced a subsidy of Rs. 100 crores per year for three years for this purpose. This matter has been referred to Ministry of Civil Aviation and is under their examination. Making Guwahati the hub, both domestic and international, for North-East India is an excellent idea as this area has tremendous tourism potential. The representative of Fly Dubai, who was also present at the meeting, was of the view there is enough potential traffic between Assam and Dubai and his airline is willing to fly provided Ministry of Civil Aviation gives them the rights.[33]

There is much merit in what was stated by the Chief Secretary, Assam. North-East India can become a Hub for entry into India. It is a maximum of two hours from Bangkok, and less from Dhaka, Yangon,

Kathmandu and other cities of ASEAN countries. If direct flights are made available the traffic will grow and North-East India will evolve in terms of economic activity and tourism. As one tour operator stated, tourists are always looking for new locations. The last new location was Rajasthan and it was getting saturated with tourists. It was now the turn of the North-East.

In a statement the Chief Minister of Assam, Mr. Sarbananda Sonowal, stated that Government of Assam is determined and committed to upgrade Guwahati airport as an international airport connecting at least ASEAN countries. He stated that:

> We aim to turn Guwahati Airport as an international airport mainly connecting South East Asia. Expansion work for the current airport has already begun and work on new terminal will begin soon. We look forward to enhancing the coverage of RCS/UDAN putting Guwahati as a hub and cover South East Asian and ASEAN countries.[34]

This was further confirmed by Mr. R. N. Choubey, Secretary, Ministry of Civil Aviation who stated:

> Travelling to Southeast Asia is likely to get cheaper for those who are ready to fly out of Guwahati, as Assam has made a proposal to subsidise the airfare.

The Secretary, Ministry of Civil Aviation[35] also confirmed that Assam has offered to make available a subsidy bill to the extent of Rs. 100 crores a year for three years to flights from Guwahati to South East Asian destinations. He has also stated that the central government is working on a request from Assam Chief Minister to launch a subsidy programme for air travel between the state's largest city and destinations in Southeast Asia.

The State of Assam is the first state of India which has offered to foot the subsidy bill to the extent of Rs. 100 crores annually for three years, as it stands to benefit from higher economic activity that an international travel airport/hub would bring with it. The RCS/UDAN will then connect with IAC/ICS at Guwahati to make Guwahati the hub for outbound flights for North-East India, similar to what Kunming in Yunnan in China has already become. Therefore, Guwahati will emerge as a hub for both UDAN and UDAN-International.

It is a pity that North-East India as well as Andaman and Nicobar Islands, which are so close to ASEAN countries, still do not have direct international connectivity. Consequently, passengers from this region would need to fly to Kolkata to fly abroad eastwards. Tourists from abroad also have to come via a metro city, Kolkata or Chennai. Guwahati had a direct flight to Bangkok but it closed down. Andaman and Nicobar Islands which are closer to ASEAN countries still do not have any direct flights abroad and all passengers and tourists have to go via mainland airports of Kolkata and Chennai.[36]

It may, however, be pointed out that while the desire of North-East India to connect with ASEAN by air has become vocal, there is no response from the Foreign Ministry.

The Importance of Straits of Malacca

"Peace, Stability and Freedom of Navigation in the Pacific Ocean are inseparable from Peace, Stability and Freedom of Navigation in the Indian Ocean", said Shinzo Abe, Prime Minister of Japan.

Why Is Strait of Malacca the Preferred Option?

The Strait of Malacca, being 900 km in length, is the longest international navigational route, better known as Sea Line of Communication, or SLOC, to connect the Indian Ocean to the South China Sea and beyond. The Strait provides the shortest route for ships to reach between East Asia and Europe. With the narrowest point being 11 miles wide, at certain parts of the Strait with the navigable route being less than one nm, and in some parts less than 30 metres deep. At a particular point on the Strait, the maximum draught recommended by the International Maritime Organisation (IMO) for passing ships is

19.8 metres. However, even with such limiting navigational constraints, the Strait is still an attractive and preferred navigational route for international shippers, compared to other alternative routes like Sunda or Lombok-Makassar Straits in the Indonesian archipelago. The first alternative is the 80-km long Sunda Straits. It is 15 miles wide on its north-eastern entrance but the strong currents and limited depth has prevented deep-draft ships of over 100,000 Dead Weight Tons (DWT) from transiting this strait. Moreover, the Sunda Strait is unsuitable as it has highly irregular bottom topography and the presence of rip tides render it unsuitable for vessels drawing over 18 metres of water to use the Straits. In addition, there are hazards posed by the numerous oil drilling platforms to the north of Western Java. The Sunda Straits has yet no available detailed navigational map. The second alternative is the Lombok Strait. With a minimum passage width of 18.5 km and depth of more than 150 metres, the Lombok Strait, on the other hand, is the safest route for supertankers because it is wider, deeper and less congested than the Strait of Malacca. Lombok Strait does not feature serious navigational hazards along the navigational channel but the routes require an additional three and a half days navigating at full commercial speed of 14-16 knots, an extra mileage of 1,600 nm, which adds to transportation cost. In the long term, it is not profitable for tanker operations.

Closure of Straits of Malacca will cause a major economic disaster. The blockage and bombing of the Suez Canal in 1956 was a crisis of international dimensions. It was done when President Nasser of Egypt nationalised the Suez Canal Company after the refusal of US and Britain to finance the construction of Aswan High Dam in Egypt. He felt that tolls from Suez Canal could help build the dam. This was then a major international economic crisis as the Suez Canal was closed with 46 shipwrecks after its bombing by the British. The Suez Canal was also a major choke point like the Straits of Malacca when at that time 10 per cent of global oil passed through it.

The blockage of Suez Canal in 1956 is a reminder of what could happen to Straits of Malacca. The present Iranian threat of blocking the Strait of Hormuz, through which one-fifth of the world's traded oil passes, could become a reality if the US and Iran are not able to come to an understanding over the Iranian Nuclear Programme. During World War II, the Malacca and Singapore Straits were mined. The battle of Malacca Straits led to sinking of the Japanese ship Hugaro around the end of World War II. Currently, the three states of Singapore, Indonesia and Malaysia maintain submarines in the straits. India and Thailand are not known to have deployed submarines in this region. According to Michal Jarocki, no nation can control the traffic through the Strait relying on military strength alone. Developing and maintaining a dominant position in the region also requires strong and positive relations with the regional straits. According to the *Eur Asian Times*[37] the fact that India enjoys a strategic advantage over China because of Malacca Straits has forced Beijing to look for alternatives. It has invested heavily in Gwadar port in Baluchistan in Pakistan along with a road to Khaitan in Xingjiang, and also from Kyaukpyu port in Myanmar to Kunming in Yunnan, China, with Chinese construction and funding.

China's Malacca Dilemma and India's Advantage

The Chinese have referred to the Straits of Malacca as their "Malacca dilemma". This is so because this Strait is perhaps the world's most important waterway linking the Persian Gulf with South China with about 40 per cent of world trade passing through it. It is the shortest route between India and the Pacific Ocean and carries a very large part of the Gulf oil. Between the Straits of Hormuz and Malacca there is a huge value of the world trade flowing. In so far as the Chinese are concerned their oil imports from the Middle East are about 50 per cent of their total import and will become 75 per cent by 2015. More than 80 per cent of China's oil imports are carried by tanker ships through the Straits of Malacca. Any blockage of this route will derail their economic growth. The Strait is about 900 km long but, around Singapore, where it is called Philips Strait, it is barely 2.4 km wide. Daily nearly 12 million barrels of oil in supertankers pass through it. In a war scenario the Straits of Malacca can easily be a target and blocked.

Further, the question being raised is whether the Straits of Malacca is getting congested and overused with over a hundred thousand ships passing through annually. The most pressing problem for China is the over-reliance on oil from Middle East sources which comes through Straits of Malacca. China would like to have a say in the administration of the Straits of Malacca. They presently feel that while piracy in the Straits can be controlled the saturation of this sea lane is going to cause deep problems for trade especially for them. While China seeks to have a greater say in the administration of this sea lane, the littoral countries do not want its participation, especially in view of its dubious claims and show of force in South China Sea. Further, the US, it is claimed, has managed to get a foothold with an airbase at Banda Ache, the Sultan Sikander Muda Air Force Base, on the northern-most tip of Indonesia. In the meantime, China has stepped up its engagement with Myanmar with millions of dollars of military assistance, has made the Myanmar Army the second largest army after Vietnam in South East Asia, from 180,000 to 450,000 men and vastly more sophisticated technologically. With the latest military coup d'état on February 1, 2021 the Chinese influence will grow in Myanmar. Uncertainty over Malacca Straits is forcing China to build an alternative route for oil and goods via Gwadar Port in Pakistan and another through Myanmar's Kyaukpyu Port.[38]

Andaman and Nicobar Islands: The Strategic Reach. The two archipelagos of Andaman and Nicobar Islands consisting of 572 Islands, islets and rocks connect south of Myanmar with Malacca Straits. About 30 per cent of India's EEZ is a result of its sovereignty over these Islands. This issue is not fully appreciated by Indian policymakers. There is a need to leverage this great asset and the locational advantage of these islands. It may also be emphasised that Indian borders do not end with Indian peninsula but go right up to Sumatra with these maritime assets deep in the Bay of Bengal. India's not being able to join the Malacca Strait Patrol (MSP) in spite of proximity of Andaman and Nicobar Islands, especially the Great Nicobar Island, remains a great disadvantage for India and a failure of its diplomacy in a strategic sense.

India Losing Malacca Advantage

Having stated the obvious above, India needs to capitalise on its advantage. How can it do so? Does India have the will and the imagination to turn these islands to our advantage not just from the point of view of economics but also from foreign policy angle? India can do it using the Andaman and Nicobar Islands as a Soft Power. More of this in chapter 5.

China Factor in South China Seas

China is upsetting all its littoral countries by claiming sovereignty over South China Sea and East China Sea with its imaginary "Nine-Dash Line", which has no legal basis, and use of its military power. China is already in deep dispute over Paracel and Spratly Islands as well as over Mischief Reef and Scarborough Shoal and other locations with Taiwan, Vietnam, the Philippines, Malaysia and Brunei. It has already lost the Arbitration to the Philippines under UNCLOS in 2016.[39] Further, Indonesia's claims of EEZ overlap with China's claims. Vietnam has rejected China's historical explanation and claim over these islands. Historical claims do not have much legal standing. In such a background India needs to take all its littoral neighbours into confidence and come to a mutually acceptable arrangement. At present Cambodia, Laos and Thailand do not have any boundary dispute with China and therefore do not have a problem with China.

With the growing influence of China in all these countries, it is important for India to take stock of its position and see the ground realities. It is felt that while we may increase our political dialogue, it is most necessary to improve people-to-people contact also and create the goodwill and fill the vacuum created by China's muscle showing gestures by use of India's soft power. While we had excellent relations with Indonesia in its early days of independence when Biju Patnaik rescued President Sukarno and others by an airlift, all that has been wasted. Today Indonesia is denying India the honour to join the Malacca Strait Patrol (MSP).

While the Straits of Malacca is getting congested and overused with over a hundred thousand ships passing through annually, the most pressing problem for China is the over-reliance on oil from Middle East sources which comes through the Straits of Malacca. China would like to have a say in the administration of the Straits of Malacca. They presently feel that while piracy in the Straits can be controlled the saturation of this sea lane is going to cause deep problems for trade, especially for them. While China seeks to have a greater say in the administration of this sea lane, the littoral countries do not want its participation, especially in view of its dubious claims and show of force in South China Sea. Further, the US, it is claimed, has managed to get a foothold with an airbase at Banda Ache, the Sultan Sikander Muda Air Force Base, on the northern-most tip of Indonesia. In the meantime, China has stepped up its engagement with Myanmar with millions of dollars of military assistance, has made the Myanmar Army the second largest army after Vietnam in South East Asia from 180,000 to 450,000 men and vastly more technologically sophisticated. It is for this reason that China is building an alternative route for oil and goods via Gwadar Port in Pakistan and another through Myanmar's Kyaukpyu Port.[40]

An enigma in our Act East Policy is the overlooking of Bay of Bengal and the missing role which Andaman and Nicobar Islands could play for foreign policy objectives. This issue will be discussed in chapter 5.

The recent Chinese military occupation of Paracel Islands in South city of Sansha, with their flag and supported by their navy, is a case in point of having actual jurisdiction over one's own claimed territory. Besides this they have created seven to nine artificial islands with airstrips and fortified within the fictitious nine-dash line of claim over South China Seas. Therefore, the need for proactive policies showing India's physical presence in these islands is very important. This can be best achieved by opening these islands to international tourism directly from the ASEAN countries.

India's Look West Policy[41]

India has a Look West Policy also which was announced by Prime Minister Dr. Manmohan Singh in 2005 and reconfirmed by Prime

Minister Modi. These policies can be divided into two parts: our relations with Gulf Countries and with Iran. While we have multiple relations with Iran, we have three important needs from them: oil procurement, bypassing Pakistan to reach Afghanistan through Chabahar Port, and finally our approach to Central Asia and Russia and Europe by a land route through Chabahar port in Iran for trade which will be cheaper and also avoid the Suez Canal shipping route.

Gulf

As far as the Gulf region is concerned, it is important for India because of increased cooperation in the fields of trade including oil, business, politics and security. In the recent past several high-level visits have been exchanged and important agreements signed between the two sides on a number of issues. Bilateral engagement has also gathered momentum because of common perspectives on terrorism and piracy. India's endeavours for deeper engagement with the region has been well accepted by the Gulf countries that realise India's potential as a large, stable, democratic country and an emerging political and economic power in Asia and the world.

Trade and Investment. The Gulf remains a favourite trading partner for India and the trade figures have been consistently going up especially with countries like the UAE, Saudi Arabia and Iran. The UAE is India's foremost non-oil trading partner in the world and Saudi Arabia is the fourth largest non-oil trading partner? The Gulf countries look at India as a fast-growing economy which holds the potential to compete with the major world economies. Realising the trade potential of the Gulf countries, India has entered into negotiations with the GCC to finalise a Free Trade Agreement. Both the sides have already met for four rounds of negotiations on it.

India and the UAE are two fast-growing economies from Asia. It is estimated that UAE investment in India is around US$ 10-11 billion.[42] Both countries are seeking to increase innovation and entrepreneurship in sectors of mutual interest.

The UAE-India relationship has now entered a vibrant growth phase with bilateral trade on track to exceed $ 100 billion by 2020 according to key speakers at the "2018 Dubai Global Convention".[43] However, because of COVID-19 there is a setback on this issue.

"India is an important demographic and economic powerhouse in Asia and investments between the 2 countries exceed billions. This convention will take the India-UAE relationship a step further as both countries explore ways to enhance business ties, intensify economic cooperation and increase innovation and entrepreneurship in sectors of mutual interest," Abdulla Al Saleh, Under Secretary, Foreign Trade & Industry, Ministry of Economy, said in his inaugural address.

"India is the first trading partner for the UAE. In 2017, trade relations between the UAE and India reached $ 53 billion, of which $ 35 billion is non-oil trade. The UAE is the third largest foreign trade partner to India after China and USA," said Al Saleh.

He further said the UAE invested over $ 5 billion in India through foreign direct investment stock until the end of 2017, which makes the UAE one of the top investors in India. Additionally, India is the second largest direct investor in the UAE at the end of 2016 with $ 6.6 billion. "In the beginning, foreign trade and oil and gas were the focal point of the India-UAE relationship. But today, this has diversified to include many new sectors following the recent high-level visits of UAE and Indian leaders," Al Saleh said.[44]

Attracting Foreign Direct Investment from the cash rich Gulf region is also a priority for India. The Gulf countries have huge potential for investing in different sectors in India for mutual benefit. According to the Department of Industrial Policy and Promotion, from April 2000 to October 2010 the UAE was the top investor in India from the region with investments worth US$ 1,815.29 million, followed by Oman which has invested US$ 326.55 million. During the same period, Saudi Arabia invested US$ 31.59 million, Bahrain US$ 26.78 million, Kuwait US$ 15.70 million and Qatar US$ 1.13 million. India offers the foreign investors opportunities in various sectors such as infrastructure development, science and technology, information technology, biotechnology, healthcare, higher education, etc. The Gulf is also a major source of employment of Indian workers, and a good source of inward remittances by them.

Forging Strategic Ties.[45] While the oil and energy trade dynamics define India's relationship with the Gulf countries, there is a growing realisation that it is time to move beyond the traditional buyer-seller relationship. India is looking forward to enhance strategic ties with the region. India needs to engage the Gulf countries to further its own influence in the region as well as the world. India has already discussed its intention of joining the United Nations Security Council (UNSC) as a permanent member with the Gulf countries. By forging ties in sectors other than energy and trade with the Gulf region, India is developing a close relationship with the Gulf world. This would help in building up India's engagement with organisations like the Organisation of Islamic Cooperation (OIC) and the Arab League.

Particular attention has been paid to military cooperation to deal with common security threats. The growing threats of Islamic extremism, terrorism and maritime piracy have become concerns for both India and the Gulf countries, and there is a growing concern over the rise of criminal activities, money laundering and illegal arms trade between the two regions.

Accelerating India's "Look West Policy" in the Gulf

India has signed defence cooperation agreements with the UAE, Oman, Qatar and Saudi Arabia. The defence agreements are aimed at providing military training, cooperation in military medical services, joint exercises, joint development and manufacture of sophisticated military hardware, cooperation in product support, services, defence science and technology, etc., and jointly combating pollution caused by the military at sea.

The Indian Navy has been at the forefront of conducting military exercises with the Gulf region. The Indian Navy has conducted exercises with the navies of Kuwait, Oman, Bahrain, Saudi Arabia and UAE. Besides, the Indian Air Force has also come forward to conduct aerial exercises with their counterparts. In September 2008, India conducted its first joint air force exercise with the United Arab Emirates at the Al Dhafra base in Abu Dhabi. In October 2009 the Indian Air Force conducted a joint exercise with Oman code-named "Eastern Bridge" at the Royal Air Force of Oman (RAFO) base at Thumrait. The exercise, though ostensibly conceived to increase interoperability between the RAFO and the IAF, also served to underline the strategic reach of the Indian Air Force. India is also seeking strategic port facilities at Duqm, on Oman's southern coast.[46] As per reports, the details of the Indo-Omani agreement over Duqm are generous for New Delhi. The Indian Navy will be able to use the port for logistics and support, allowing it to sustain long-term operations in the western Indian Ocean, a hotspot for piracy. Further, a dry dock will be available to the Indian Navy at Duqm as well, allowing for maintenance without returning vessels to India-based shipyards.[47]

Fighting Piracy. The recent spurt in piracy activities off the Gulf of Aden in the Indian Ocean has affected both India and the Gulf countries. For India, the security of the Indian Ocean is important as a large number of oil tankers pass through these waters. Cooperation with the Gulf countries in fighting piracy would also strengthen India's presence in the strategic waters of the Indian Ocean. India has already deployed its naval ships to deter the pirates.

Strengthening Soft Power. India has emphasised strengthening the soft-power relationship with the countries of the region. There is a conscious effort on the part of India to bring back Indian cultural influence in the region, which India enjoyed in the past. In recent years, India has attempted to strengthen cultural ties with the Gulf countries by signing and renewing the existing cultural exchange programmes. India signed an Executive Programme for Cultural Cooperation for 2007-2010 in 2007. An Executive Programme for the Cultural and Information Exchanges between India and Kuwait was signed for the years 2009-2011 in April 2009. India signed an MoU on Cultural Cooperation with Oman in July 2010 for a period of five years.

Unlike ASEAN countries where people to people contacts are weak, India has excellent people to people contact in Gulf countries and this is complimented by excellent air connectivity with a large number of countries of the Gulf.

Gulf Policy

The Look West policy has certainly accelerated India's engagement with the Gulf region. As India has huge stakes in the region, the policy should be supplemented with more proactive Indian involvement in the various sectors. With the rapid economic growth and rising profile of India, devising such policy of engaging with the extended neighbourhood has become imperative for India.

The focus of the Indian interest in the Gulf region remains in the fields of trade, energy supply and protecting interests of Indian workers there. India is robustly pushing its soft power in the form of education and culture in the region, emphasising exchange and cooperation. India has adopted a cautious approach while dealing with political and military issues. India is careful so as not to be blamed as an interventionist big power in the region. India has been looking at the Gulf as a region to augment its economic and political power and not to exercise it. Strengthening the relationship in the areas of education and culture is intended to maintain India's soft power dominance by spreading Indian culture and contributing to human resource development in the region, while the defence and strategic partnerships have been driven by the need to tackle the increasing threats of terrorism and piracy, and to deal with the changing political and strategic environment in the region and in the neighbourhood. By attempting to forge strategic ties, India has expressed its desire to engage the Gulf region in all possible new sectors, while strengthening the all-important energy and trade ties between the two.[48]

However, on issues of air connectivity we are more than adequately connected. The Gulf countries have one airport per country, except for the UAE and Saudi Arabia. There are concerns within India of our over liberal bilateral Air Service Agreements at the cost of our airlines and creation of hub in India. Gulf countries have robust airlines and India has a great traffic outbound westward, but there is always a demand for more. Utilisation of bilateral traffic rights is always better for the Gulf carriers than Indian carriers because they are able to carry 6th Freedom traffic from India. This remains a sore point with Indian carriers and has been objected to by CAG also.

Iran and Central Asian countries

Iran: Building a Land Air Route to Afghanistan, Central Asia and Russia

Iran, in a number of ways, is an important country for India in the present context. Iran has been defined as a part of India's "proximate neighbourhood". Its geopolitical and strategic location, long coastline along the Gulf, and its influence over the Straits of Hormuz make it an important country in the region. For India, Iran is an important source of energy to cater for our growing energy needs. Iran has the third largest proven oil reserves and second largest proven gas reserves in the world. Iran's close geographical location with India would be beneficial for transporting oil and gas at relatively low cost. Iran is of primary importance for India in the region. India is currently the fourth largest energy consuming country in the world, and it may go up to third position in the next couple of decades. India's annual GDP growth at the rate of eight per cent would require further industrial growth, which in turn would demand more energy supply for the country. Iran oil supplies to India were third highest after Saudi and the UAE (under US sanctions this has come down drastically). The Gulf countries are the main crude suppliers to India, with Saudi Arabia at the top followed by Iran and the UAE. The growing energy necessity has undoubtedly dictated India's initiative of building up a "strategic energy partnership" with the region to secure long-term energy supply for the country. With the sanctions by the US imposed in August of 2018, the situation for India becomes more difficult.

Another potential area of cooperation between India and Iran is in maritime security. The Indian interest in the Indian Ocean region and the proximate neighbourhood focuses on the need for regional peace and stability, mutually beneficial relations with littoral states, accessibility of oil and gas resources, the freedom of navigation through the Gulf and the Straits of Hormuz, and access to regional markets for Indian goods, technology, investment, labour and services. The four-day visit of the Indian Navy Chief to Iran in April 2018 is significant.[49] With the deteriorating relations between Gulf States and Qatar, the possibility of a blockade of Straits of Hormuz cannot be ruled out. Iran is, therefore, a hedge of our oil supplies and the land route to the west and Afghanistan. Further, with a potential blockade of Straits of Hormuz, the Iranian port of Bandar Abbas will decline and Chabahar will become more sought after.

Chabahar Port

Under the current situation where Pakistan does not permit trucks to cross from India to Afghanistan through its territory (Pakistan has allowed India to send Food to Afghanistan through Pakistan as a sudden gesture in late 2021. It is not clear whether this permission will last), the most urgent and important "work in progress" with Iran is the Chabahar Port and its implications for Indian Foreign Policy in the next decade or so. It is a gateway to Afghanistan, Central Asian Countries and Russia and Europe by the land route, both railways and roadways. With Pakistan not permitting Indian trucks to go to Afghanistan through their country, Iran's Chabahar Port has provided the answer.

Map 1: India's Alternative Routes to Afghanistan

As a background, the ancient traveller El-Beruni believed Chabahar—or Tiz as it was called then—to be the starting point of the Indian subcontinent. The people here speak fluent Hindustani, which they call 'Urdu'. This may have to do with its proximity to Pakistan as well as the popularity of Bollywood films in these parts. The people around here are known as Baluchis.

Russia also does not have a port in warm water of Indian Ocean and had always desired it. Chabahar was always a part of Tsarist Russia's quest for a warm water port in the Indian Ocean. British diplomat and author, Olaf Caroe, in his book, *Wells of Power*,[50] wrote about the Russian government sending officials of the ministry of roads and port at the turn of the century to scout for a port. They found Chabahar climate mild. Thereafter, its successor state, the Soviet Union, invaded Afghanistan to prevent an imperial Iran from enlarging its influence in Kabul. Shortly thereafter, in 1979, the Shah of Iran, Reza Pahlavi, was ousted in an Islamic Revolution in Tehran—an epochal event that sharpened the sectarian divide amongst Muslims and also changed the balance of power in the region. Also, Russia never got the warm water port in the Indian Ocean.

Background to Development of Chabahar Port

Discussions on building the Chabahar port began during the era of the Shah of Iran, who wanted to bring in some US companies to establish the infrastructure.

The Islamic Revolution of 1979 stalled the development, but this port was used by the Iranian Navy to keep its fleet protected from Iraqi threat. Even now, Chabahar's strength remains its distance from the troubled waters of Strait of Hormuz, where Bandar Abbas is located. The Strait of Hormuz sits between the Gulf of Oman and the Persian Gulf from where some 14 oil tankers pass every day. The UAE contests Iran's ownership of the Strait and there are always fears that this contestation could trigger another oil crisis. Chabahar is, therefore, outside the UAE threat.

Is Chabahar India's answer to China's China-Pakistan Economic Corridor (CPEC)? While the main purpose of China is to seek an entry into the Indian Ocean through CPEC, Chabahar Port will be India's answer to entry into Afghanistan, which Pakistan is blocking, as well as entry into Central Asian countries and Russia and Europe. Afghanistan's willingness to accept China's offer to join its ambitious China-Pakistan Economic Corridor (CPEC) and the possibility of Russian support to Chabahar lends a new nuance to the contestation brewing between India, China and Pakistan. Chabahar Port remains critical to India's foreign policy.[51]

Afghan President Ashraf Ghani, Indian Prime Minister Narendra Modi, and Iranian President Hassan Rouhani signed the trilateral transit agreement between the three countries in May 2016. Along with this India also signed a series of twelve memorandums of understanding with Iran which centred round the Port of Chabahar. The trilateral transit agreement signed by India, Iran and Afghanistan allows Indian goods to reach Afghanistan through Iran. It links ports in the western coast of

India to the Chabahar port and covers the road and rail links between Chabahar and the Afghan border.

This has been described by the Afghan Ambassador to India, Shaida Abdali, in April 2016 as:

> This is a very, very crucial agreement for Afghanistan. The opening of this corridor will help us to fully reach our potential, give us a new trade route. This is a completely new chapter.

India-Iran-Afghanistan MoU and plans have included $ 21 billion worth of works like Chabahar-Hajigak corridor, including $ 85 million for Chabahar port development by India, $ 150 million Line of Credit by India to Iran, $ 8 billion India-Iran MoU for Indian industrial investment in Chabahar Special Economic Zone, $ 11 billion Hajigak iron and steel mining project awarded to seven Indian companies in central Afghanistan, and India's $ 2 bn commitment to Afghanistan for developing supporting infrastructure, including the Chabahar-Hajigaj railway, with potential for several times more trade via connectivity to 7,200-km-long multi-mode International North-South Transport Corridor (INSTC) connecting to Europe and Turkey, R297 Amur highway and Trans-Siberian Highway across Russia, and planned Herat to Mazar-i-Sharif railway providing access to Turkmenistan, Uzbekistan, Tajikistan and Kyrgyzstan.

Chabahar Port also provides direct land access to India's Farkhor Air Base in Tajikistan.[52] Chabahar route will result in 60 per cent reduction in shipment costs and 50 per cent reduction in shipment time from India to Central Asia.

The berths will be developed at a cost of $ 85 million. Under the agreement, India Ports Global will refurbish a 640 metres (2,100 feet) long container handling facility, and reconstruct a 600 metres (1,970 feet) long container handling facility at the port. India Ports Global will modernise ancillary infrastructure by installing four rail-mounted gantry cranes, sixteen rubber-tire gantry cranes, two reach stackers, two empty handlers, and six mobile harbour cranes. Upon completion of upgrade works agreed to in the May 2016 agreements, Chabahar's capacity will be increased to 8 million tons from the current 2.5 million tons capacity.

The investment is supplemented with a $ 150 million credit line to Iran through the Exim Bank of India. India has also offered to supply $ 400 million worth of steel towards the construction of a rail link between Chabahar and Zahedan.[53] Indian commitments to Iranian infrastructure could total $ 635 million as per the twelve memorandums of understanding signed in May 2016. India will also be developing various industries, including aluminium and urea production plants, in the Chabahar economic zone attached to the port.

While the Zahedan-Bam-Mirjaveh railway is already complete and operational, India is finalising a plan to construct a 900-km Chabahar-Zahedan-Hajigak railway line that will connect Port of Chabahar in Iran, being built with Indian help, to the mineral-rich Hajigak region of Afghanistan. However, India is not a part of the Chabahar-Zahedan railway at present, but as Iran begins the second phase of the 628-km project, Tehran hopes New Delhi will help it procure equipment to run the rail line from the Chabahar port to the Afghan border.[54] In 2011, seven Indian companies acquired rights to mine central Afghanistan's Hajigak region, which contain Asia's largest deposit of iron ore. The Government of India has pledged to spend $ 2 billion in developing supporting infrastructure.

In May 2016, a memorandum of understanding was also signed for financing of the planned Chabahar-Zahedan railway section of Chabahar–Zahedan-Hajigak railway, as part of North–South Transport Corridor, by Indian Railway's public sector unit IRCON International. India has already built a 240 km of road connecting Afghanistan with Iran.

India has offered to supply approximately $ 400 million worth of steel towards the construction of this railway and also offered to finance construction of the Chabahar to Zahedan rail line at a cost of $ 1.6 billion. India began shipping rail tracks worth US$ 150 million in July 2016 and in December 2016 Iran also allocated US$ 125 million for this rail route.

A rail link between Chabahar and Zahedan, when completed, can connect Chabahar to the Kerman-Zahedan Railway and further to the Trans-Iranian Railway going all the way to Russia.

Chabahar port, sitting on the coast of the Gulf of Oman, was inaugurated by Iran's President Hassan Rouhani in early December 2017. Chabahar port construction was offered to India by Iran much earlier than China's offer of CPEC to Pakistan. China has since offered to Afghanistan a connectivity of its CPEC during a trilateral summit of China, Pakistan and Afghanistan in Beijing in late December 2017. Chinese Foreign Minister Wang Yi offered to link Afghanistan with CPEC. CPEC aims to connect Gwadar with Kashgar in China through an area disputed by India and, therefore, India has refused to join CPEC. Meanwhile, Wang announced that Kabul was willing to join the CPEC.

Although China has also said that the CPEC offer made to Afghanistan was not directed at any country (read, India), Iran's President Rouhani has tried to put the fears of Pakistan and China to rest when he was flagging off the Chabahar port by offering them to join the Chabahar Port development. Their anxieties stemmed from the Indian investment in the development of the strategically significant Iranian port and how it could not just make Gwadar unviable, but also threaten its security. Therefore, both China and Iran may be giving the impression that all is well with the two projects. Yet that is hardly the case. Both countries and their neighbours are aware of the strategic importance of these ports; they are conscious of how the waters of the Oman Sea could be the stage for future power contests in the region.[55]

While China has been looking to an access port in the Indian Ocean to avoid their "Malacca Dilemma", so was also Russia looking at a warm water port in the Indian Ocean. Chabahar in Iran offers Russia a similar advantage. So Chabahar Port also presents an opportunity to Russia to fulfil its objective of accessing the all season part in the Indian Ocean. As a result, it will activate its North-South Corridor which provides a road and sea route between Europe and India. In many ways, the viability of Chabahar Port would be determined by its ability not only to restore

India's trade links with Afghanistan, but also explore cheaper and quicker trade routes to West Asia, Russia and Europe. A test run of an Indian shipment from Kandla port in Gujarat to Bandar Abbas port of Iran and then beyond by land route saw a reduction of 21 days of travel compared to taking the Suez Canal route. Both Russia and Iran, ravaged by economic sanctions, give great importance on revenue earned through transhipment. In 2016, Iran earned more from goods being transhipped through its country than the sale of oil and gas.

Both Iran and Russia see the economic value in opening up new land routes and waterways. Iran is surrounded by seven countries, and Russia by fourteen. Both provide a compelling logic for creating land and sea corridors that can safely provide passage to trade consignments to many countries.

During a visit to Delhi, Russian Foreign Minister Sergey Lavrov, in reply to a question on joining China's CPEC said, "Russia has its own corridors and has large territory for such corridors and connectivity initiatives." Russia, which is largely bypassed by the Belt and Road Initiative (BRI), has signed a cooperation agreement with China as part of the Eurasian Economic Union (EEU). It is hoping that it will gain from the various corridors being promoted by different countries. Indeed, the possibility of Russian support to Chabahar port lends more complexity to the contestation brewing between India, China and Pakistan. Further, in February 2018 during the visit of Iranian President to New Delhi, Iran signed an accord to lease operational control of Chabahar Port for 18 months. With this India's effort at creating a strategic trade route to Afghanistan, Central Asian Republics and also to Russia and Europe bypassing Pakistan is complete. Prime Minister Modi of India has described Chabahar Port as a "Golden Gateway" to Afghanistan.

The first shipment of wheat to Afghanistan was flagged off from the Indian port of Kandla on October 27, 2017 to Chabahar Port for onward passage to Afghanistan by land route and on October 29, 2017 this shipment of wheat from India to Afghanistan was again flagged off via Chabahar as part of 1.1 million tonnes of wheat to be sent by India to Afghanistan. The Indian Ambassador to Afghanistan Manpreet Vohra tweeted:

> 1st Indian wheat shipment via #Chabahar welcomed into Zarang #Afghanistan with traditional song, dance and joy! Proud moment.

While the Iranian Foreign Minister could not be present at India's Kandla Port, he made his presence felt by video conference. His message, however, sent out loud and clear that Chabahar was ready for business. In fact, the port and its free zone have been ready for quite some time before that.

The announcement of shipment of wheat through Chabahar Port to Afghanistan took both Pakistan and China by surprise as they thought that India did not have the courage to move fast on Chabahar lest they antagonise the US.[56] They drew solace from reports that Iran had put on hold various deals with India, including oilfield Farzad-B, due to. They saw far too much in Russian President Vladimir Putin's one-day visit to Tehran in November 2017 without reading the fine print of the $ 20-billion worth of oil deals that he had signed. Iranian officials have taken pains to explain that President Rouhan was clear that Chabahar Port and Farzad-B should go to India as long as Iran was not seen as giving away too much or incurring losses on Farzad.[57]

The dispatch of wheat consignment through Chabahar to Kabul two days after US Secretary of State Rex Tillerson's visit to Delhi was seen by Pakistan as the US' nod of approval and an assurance that the country would not come in the way of the business ties between India and Iran. Moreover, New Delhi's engagement with Kabul neatly fits in with US President Donald Trump's new Afghan policy that demands more from India in stabilising the war-torn country. As Brahma Chellaney, a geostrategist and author, points out,[58] "Afghanistan is already becoming a major beneficiary of Chabahar-transport corridor. It has shifted its bulk cargo traffic away from Karachi to Chabahar and Bandar Abbas. Chabahar is set to turn into a vital trading hub—a sprawling, modern port. He goes on to say that India's biggest challenge would be to counter US sanctions on Iran.

Chabahar's activation worried Pakistan, who sent its Army Chief to Kabul with an offer of a new trade and transit treaty that they are refusing to negotiate to come to their border. Pakistan does not allow Indian trucks to transit through their territory to Afghanistan.

Map 2: India's Alternative Routes to Europe: Via Sea and Land

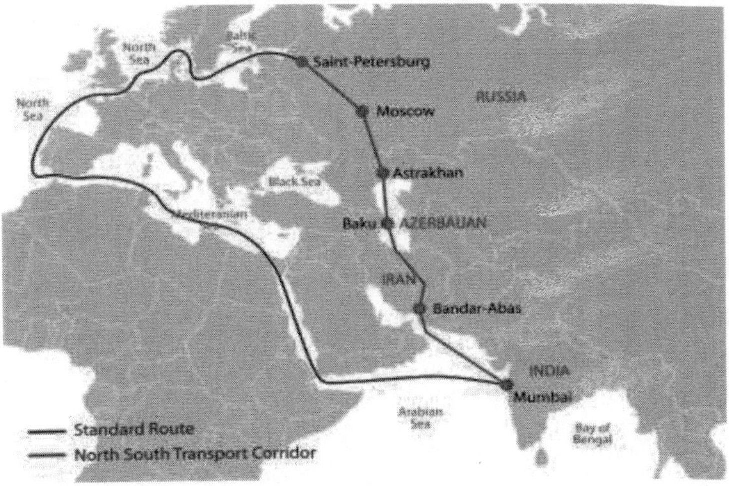

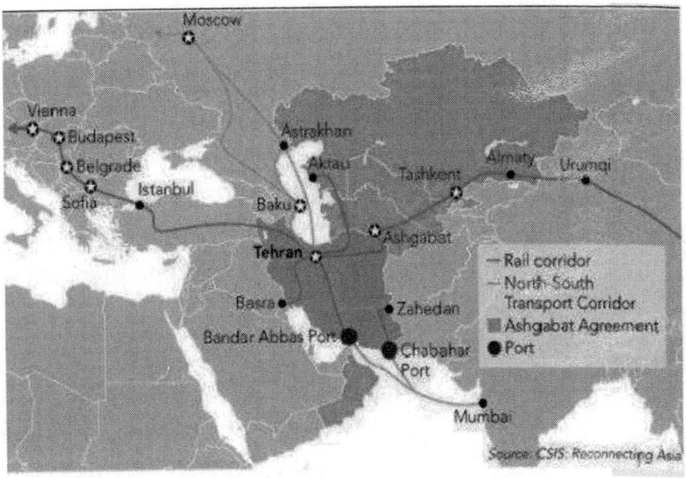

On February 24, 2019 President Ghani of Afghanistan flagged off the first consignment of Afghan exports to India through Chabahar route. He also stated that the route via Chabahar will help double his country's exports to India to $ 2 billion from the current level of $ 1 billion. The 570 tons of cargo includes Afghan carpets, dry fruits, cotton, talc, stones and other items. Confederation of Indian Industries is also sending a delegation of 30 companies to Chabahar to celebrate Chabahar Day on February 26, 2019 and Secretary, Shipping of Government of India will lead an official delegation to the event.[59] There is, therefore, an increasing use of Chabahar Port for Indo-Afghan trade. During the Presidency of President Donald Trump in the United States, there was pressure on India to reduce our oil import from Iran as more sanctions were put on Iran by the USA. However, some exemptions were given to India on Chabahar port issues.

Russia, through its 7,200 km long International North-South Transport Corridor, provides the additional justification for India to remain invested in Chabahar and Iran even if Pakistan allows India direct road transit facilities to Afghanistan. This route cuts down the travel time to Europe by 40 per cent, thereby reducing costs. It holds clear economic logic to use the road route for those who are shipping their goods. Iran, for instance, claims that it has fulfilled not even 10 per cent of the transhipment potential.

Russia is cognisant of India's problems with CPEC as it passes through the disputed area near Karakoram Highway and will not want to get caught in the crossfire between India, Pakistan and China. Russia is suggesting some corrections in CPEC to take care of India's concerns; it will mean connecting India through Lahore. This scenario seems impossible at the moment, but China would not like its investment to be compromised by India-Pakistan tensions. Therefore, there are various suggestions within diplomatic circles about what it would take for India to join BRI. With activation of Chabahar Port, which will connect to Afghanistan, Central Asian countries and up to Moscow in Russia and beyond, there is a need to provide air connectivity on an immediate basis to many locations in its transit route. At present Delhi is connected by an Iranian airline to Tehran. No other city of Iran, including Chabahar Port with an existing airport called Konarak, is connected. This needs urgent rectification.

Ashgabat Agreement 2018 and International North-South Transport Corridor (INSTC) 2002

India has been admitted to Ashgabat Agreement in 2018[60] which establishes an International Transport and Transit Corridor between the Governments of the Islamic Republic of Iran, the Sultanate of Oman, Turkmenistan and the Republic of Uzbekistan.

Signed on April 25, 2011 and known as Ashgabat Agreement, this will give further justification for the Indian investment in Chabahar Port and SEZ.

With Phase 1 of the India-funded Chabahar Port in Iran becoming operational, India's entry into Iran, Oman, Turkmenistan and Uzbekistan led transport and transit corridor can be considered as a smart move by India to enlarge its footprint in Central Asia, which has so far not been possible due to Pakistan's non-cooperation.

International North-South Transport Corridor (INSTC)

India, Iran and Russia are busy executing another project called International North-South Transport Corridor (INSTC).[61] India, Iran and Russia signed the INSTC Agreement on May 16, 2002 much before the Chinese Road and Belt Initiative. It provides the shortest multimodal transport route linking the Indian Ocean all the way up to St. Petersburg. This project, which is 7,200 km long, is also expected to become operational by the end of 2018 or early 2019. INSTC will connect India, through Iran, Turkey, Armenia, Belarus Azerbaijan, Turkmenistan, Kazakhstan, Tajikistan, Kyrgyzstan, Oman, Ukraine, and Syria to Russia. RITES, India's Rail India Technical and Economic Services, was offering consultancy for the 165 km of missing rail link between Rasht in Iran and Astana in Azerbaijan. This missing link has become operational and the first train with Russian timber arrived in Iran through Rasht-Azerbaijan rail link. With this the time reduced from Kandla port in India to Russia by 50 per cent and the cost by 30 per cent in comparison to the traditional routes via the Suez Canal.

Map 3: Routes Available with Ashgabat and INSTC Agreements

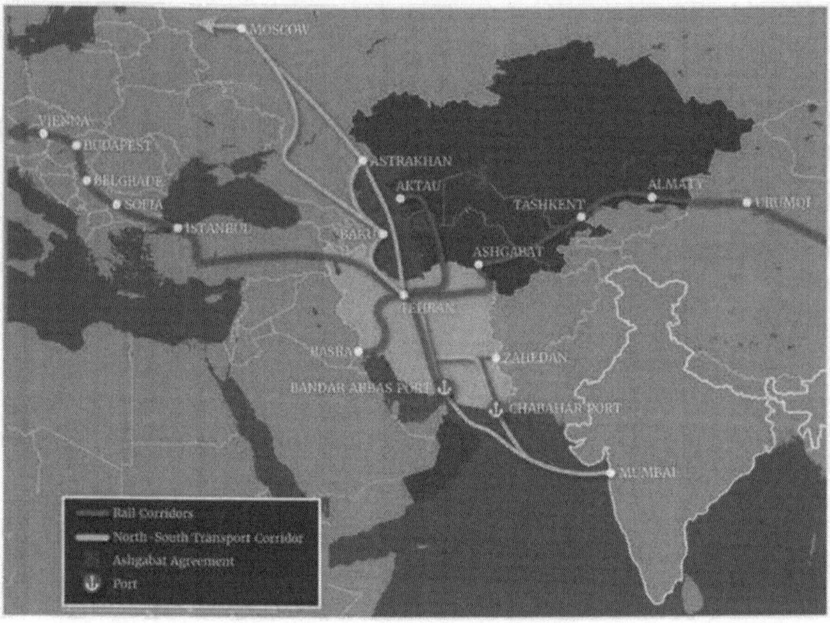

Ashgabat Agreement envisages facilitation of transit and transportation of goods between Central Asia and the Persian Gulf. Accession to the Agreement would diversify India's connectivity options with Central Asia and have a positive influence on India's trade and commercial ties with the region. Turkmenistan, as the depository State of the Ashgabat Agreement, informed India on February 1, 2018 "that all the four founding members have consented to the accession of India (to the agreement)."

India has good relations with all the Central Asian countries. India has been imparting hundreds of young professionals training in areas like Banking, Agriculture, remote sensing, rural development, information technology and English-language speaking courses.[62] This has left a lot of goodwill for India in these countries.[63]

Once all the three corridors—starting from Chabahar Port to Afghanistan and beyond—are integrated through INSTC, it will be easy for Indian businessmen to spread out to Afghanistan and Central Asia up to Russia. According to estimates, once Chabahar Port is linked to INSTC trade between India and Central Asian region is estimated to go up to $ 170 billion. This is apart from the advantages of Ashgabat Agreement which involves India, Iran, Oman, Uzbekistan and Turkmenistan.

With INSTC, Ashgabat Agreement and Iran-India-Afghanistan corridors coming up there will be a need for an increase in air connectivity. To begin with, we need immediate connectivity with Chabahar airport called Konarak, a well-established airport. If India is interested in improving the use of Chabahar it must operate a flight from somewhere in India, preferably Mumbai to Konarak Airport of Chabahar. This will be a master stroke even if the flight is not viable. This will give a boost to developing commercial relations between the two countries. We will also need to connect to Turkmenistan. We also need direct air connectivity with other countries coming in the INSTC route mentioned above.

India and Central Asia: Building an Air Corridor: Indian Foreign Minister

Another important region is the Central Asian Region with which India has good relations but poor connectivity. Our trade with the region has been languishing below $ 2 billion for years. *This issue was stressed by the Indian Foreign Minister late Sushma Swaraj in a speech at the first India-Central Asia Dialogue in Uzbekistan in January 2018.* She noted that "India wants to build up a modern and comprehensive partnership on strong foundation."[64] She further stressed that in spite of their being landlocked, there are several ways to get over it. She mentioned the joint efforts of India, Iran and Afghanistan in creating the Chabahar Port route in Iran to connect India to Afghanistan and potentially to Central Asia. She urged these countries to participate in a Conference on Chabahar to be held very soon. She also mentioned that India would like to forge closer links with Central Asia and "*to organise a dialogue on air corridor with participation of civil aviation authorities, air freight and aviation companies of India and Central Asia so that goods, including perishable items, can be transported efficiently and swiftly.*"[65] India already had opened air corridors for the transport of goods and perishables between India and several Afghan cities mainly to circumvent Pakistan's refusal to India-Afghanistan trade passing overland through its territory. After takeover of Afghanistan by Taliban this will not be feasible.

With US sanctions threatening Iran's main port of Bandar Abbas, the Iranian government is planning to promote the Chabahar port being developed by India in Iran beyond the original purpose of connecting India for India-Afghan trade alone. India is also interested to achieve the triple aims of trade with Afghanistan, bypassing Pakistan and posing a counter to the China-Pakistan developed Gwadar port nearby.

"The government of Iran wants to build Chabahar as the focal point with the entire coastline of 1,000 kilometres to be developed for oil refineries, petrochemical and steel factories, and other projects," said the newly appointed Iranian Ambassador to India Ali Chegeni to *The Hindu*, in an exclusive interview. "We want to promote Chabahar as a hub where big ships can enter, offload to smaller ships that can go easily to other ports as well."[66]

Indian Ocean Region (IOR)

The Indian Ocean Region (IOR) is a vast region of 66,526 km of coastline. We have already covered the Bay of Bengal Region, SAARC and the Gulf region, including Iran. The Indian Ocean Rim Association is an intergovernmental organisation which was established on March 7, 1997. The Secretariat of the Indian Ocean Rim Association (IORA) is hosted by the Government of the Republic of Mauritius which is based Ebène, Mauritius. It consists of 21 members and 7 dialogue partners. It manages, coordinates, services and monitors the implementation of policy decisions, work programmes and projects adopted by the Council of Ministers. The Indian Ocean Rim Association (IORA)—formerly known as the Indian Ocean Rim Initiative and Indian Ocean Rim Association for Regional Cooperation (IOR-ARC)—is an international organisation consisting of coastal states bordering the Indian Ocean. The IORA is a regional forum, tripartite in nature, bringing together representatives of Government, Business and Academia, for promoting cooperation and closer interaction among them. It is based on the principles of Open Regionalism for strengthening Economic Cooperation particularly on Trade Facilitation and Investment, Promotion as well as Social Development of the region.

The budget of 2018 also announced maritime strategic diplomacy. It announced benefits for the island nations of Seychelles, Mauritius, Sri Lanka and Maldives, all in the strategic Indian Ocean Region. India has signed a revised pact with Seychelles to develop an airstrip and a jetty, with Mauritius an amount of Rs. 350 crores has been earmarked for 'improvement of sea and air transport facilities at Agalega island'. In addition, India is also constructing the Chabahar Port in Iran and Sittwe in Myanmar. However, there have been setbacks at Maldives where the airport construction contract given to an Indian firm was snatched away due to politics; there has been opposition to our efforts in Seychelles as well. While all this is excellent, it needs to be cemented with more direct flights.

It is pertinent to point out that in August 2011 the Chinese government won an approval from the International Seabed Authority—mandated under the UN Convention on the Law of the Seas to regulate and control all mineral-related activities in the international seabed for the benefit of mankind—to explore 10,000 square kilometres in the Indian Ocean for polymetallic sulphide ore. This can be a source of anxiety for India.[67]

India has limited air connections with most of the IORA countries. The island countries need better connections. With more outbound tourism from India it is possible that more flights can take place. Again, the International Connectivity Scheme (ICS) has to step in to give it the impetus required.

Future Trends: Issues of Direct Air Connectivity

Though ASEAN-India economic engagements are moving forward in the desired direction, there are certain challenges that call for policy interventions. In recent years, trade and investment relations between India and ASEAN have continued to improve. With massive growth expected in all infrastructure sectors, myriad opportunities will arise for Indian companies operating in the region.

Under ASEAN-India Free Trade Agreement (AIFTA) that entered into force on January 1, 2010, tariffs on over 4,000 product lines were eliminated by 2016 and sensitive products have been given a longer time frame for tariff liberalisation. Both sides are now consolidating the trade in services and investment provisions. The tariff liberalisation schedule for AIFTA has five components: (i) Normal Track; (ii) Sensitive Track; (iii) Special Products; (iv) Highly Sensitive List; and (v) Exclusion List. The tariff liberalisation schedule began in January 2010 and is to be fully implemented by 2013 and 2016 in respect of the items on the two 'normal tracks'. The trade in goods agreement contains phased elimination/reduction of customs duties on imports from signatory countries. The objective of the agreement is to reach a zero customs duty regime for 'substantially all trade' between India and ASEAN countries. The time frame for phasing out of tariffs varies by country and product grouping. Once the agreement comes into full implementation, tariffs will be eliminated on 80 per cent of traded goods between India and ASEAN countries, that is, about 75 per cent of the total trade. While the progress is not as per schedule, some bilateral arrangements with ASEAN member countries are taking place.

Indian businesses must recognise the opportunities presented by the ASEAN's growth and economic integration. It will be important for Indian businesses to understand their strength in the ASEAN market and to tailor their strategies accordingly. We need to think of ASEAN as a whole with distinctive regions to get a clear sense of perspective, keeping in view the following:

(a) Attractive opportunities require a local business presence. This requires initial and ongoing investment, and well-established organisational competencies.

(b) Invest in relationships. This is the key to the door for most ASEAN markets, but takes time to develop.

(c) Aim to operate in a "harmonious" supply chain in which participants at all stages share benefits out of the venture:

    (i) 15 million barrels of oil transit through the Malacca Strait daily;

    (ii) $ 5.3 trillion of global trade passes through ASEAN waterways each year.

The ASEAN + 6, namely, Brunei Darussalam, Indonesia, Malaysia, the Philippines, Singapore and Thailand, has applied zero tariff rates for intra-ASEAN trade in over 99 per cent of tariff lines since 2010. Progress has also been made in the newer ASEAN Member States, i.e., Cambodia, Lao PDR, Myanmar, and Vietnam (CLMV) where zero tariff rates have been applied to 72.6 per cent of tariff lines in 2013, a significant increase from only 45.9 per cent in 2010. The average intra-ASEAN tariff in ASEAN + 6 has gone down to near zero since 2010, and stood at slightly above 1 per cent in 2013 in CLMV.

Marking a major milestone in the regional economic integration agenda, the ASEAN Economic Community (AEC) was officially launched on December 31, 2015 to create a single market to enable an easier movement of goods, services, investment, capital and people across the region. This will result in a common market of more than 600 million people, dwarfing the EU's 500 million and NAFTA's over 400 million. The removal of tariffs throughout the AEC presents a significant advantage for Indian companies in two ways. First, companies that manufacture in the region will be able to take advantage of the free flow of goods through the AEC when exporting finished goods. Second, Indian companies that rely on ASEAN nations for intermediate goods in their supply chain will benefit from reduced costs not only in goods, but also in simplifying the 'paperwork' necessary to move goods through the region. The consolidation of the AEC represents an important initiative that will have a global impact.

With signing of the ASEAN-India Agreement in Services and Investments, ASEAN and India are likely to benefit from an extended market, where the air connectivity aims to play a pivotal role. Once direct air services between unserved ASEAN cities and various cities of India are established, the belly space of a passenger aircraft will provide relief initially till freighter services become viable.

ASEAN-India Air Connectivity

Prof. Harsh Pant of King's College, University of London, writes in his article, "Future of India's Ties with ASEAN":

Economic engagement will require better connectivity between India and ASEAN than what exists today. Instead of talking about ASEAN-wide connectivity projects, New Delhi now needs to focus on more effective delivery of projects it is already committed to. In this context, prompt completion of the India-Myanmar-Thailand Trilateral Highway, which will run from Moreh in Manipur to Mae Sot in Thailand via Myanmar, is key. The plan is to extend this highway to Cambodia, Laos, and Vietnam in an attempt to project India's role in the emerging transportation architecture in the region. With China having three times as many commercial flights to Southeast Asia as India does, improving air connectivity between India and ASEAN should also be high on the agenda. In the maritime domain, the Bay of Bengal can be used as an exploratory ground for the development of an India-ASEAN maritime framework.[68]

Enhancing direct air connectivity between ASEAN cities and Indian cities should be the major thrust of India's Act East Policy as this will bring out the attitudinal change for business communities and tourists on both sides. Air connectivity is an important mode of transportation to carry tourist and business travellers, high-value fragile goods and perishable products from one place to another in the shortest time. International air passengers to and from India had grown at a CAGR of 9.20 per cent during 2008-2009 to 2013-2014. The Government of India has been supporting the development of the aviation sector and planning to develop 100 low-cost airports in the country under the RCS/UDAN. Further reforms in the aviation sector have also been initiated, including the introduction of National Civil Aviation Policy 2016.

Agreements in Services and Investments has led to a need for a comprehensive ASEAN-India Air Transport Agreement; expanding scope of bilateral air services agreement (BASA); strengthening India's air links with CLMV countries; and establishing an ASEAN-India School of Aviation; greater cooperation in aviation technology, logistics and infrastructure building.[69]

All this can be justified as India has emerged as the fastest growing economy during the last three years. India is expected to become the world's largest domestic civil aviation market in the world in the next 10-15 years according to Mr. Jayant Sinha, Minister for Civil Aviation. According to IATA, India will displace the UK to become the third largest civil aviation market by 2025.[70] Further, India's outbound is growing very fast and was projected by IATA to be 50 million by 2020. In diplomacy, as pointed out by Ambassador Rajiv Sikri, person-to-person contact is also important, besides contacts between governments. Aviation connectivity between countries takes a high priority to enable person-to-person contact. While there is no way to calculate in monetary terms the advantage of enabling air connectivity over building roads and ports, both are of equal importance politically.

Higher aviation connectivity was also important in view of the ongoing Regional Comprehensive Economic Partnership (RCEP) negotiations. The RCEP would have liberalised trade between India and the ASEAN-member states, apart from the other free trade agreement partners of the ASEAN-member countries. However, India's participation in RCEP has been postponed. As civil aviation improves, India, which already has a trade surplus through airborne trade via ASEAN airlines, would be well poised to better connect with regional value chains of appropriate industries and, thereby, reap economic benefits. India's 'Act-East' policy would also benefit through building air connectivity with countries like Vietnam both for tourism as well as for trade in parts and components, as the latter rapidly builds production potential with liberalised labour norms, having been a signatory to the erstwhile Trans-Pacific Partnership.

In conclusion, India's aviation links with the ASEAN member states have not grown significantly and uniformly with all countries since 2015, following the signing of investment and services agreements with the ASEAN-member countries. Singapore, Malaysia, Thailand have emerged as the three aviation hubs for connecting to other ASEAN countries and beyond. Myanmar and Vietnam have limited direct connectivity to India. Direct air connectivity between Indian cities and the other ASEAN-member states needs to be developed. There is no doubt that growth in tourism between India and the Southeast Asian region would gain greater momentum through enhanced air connectivity efforts and would bring in both political and business gains. ASEAN budget airlines have been observed to fly a growing number of passengers to and from India. Freight exports from India to the ASEAN-member countries via ASEAN budget airlines have also experienced impressive growth.

ASEAN constituted about 16 per cent of international passenger flow to and from India in 2015. However, the distribution of passengers between ASEAN countries and India is skewed. The flow of ASEAN passengers coming to India has been much lower than the Indian passengers going to ASEAN, or transit through ASEAN hubs like Bangkok, Singapore and Kuala Lumpur equipped with bigger and performing airlines which continue to attract passengers and air cargo from India. Today, out of 10 ASEAN countries, only three ASEAN countries, Malaysia, Singapore, and Thailand have direct flights with India and vice versa. For other countries direct connections are not regular and stable. Airlines of India also do not go to these seven countries.

As for the rest seven ASEAN countries (Cambodia, Indonesia, Lao PDR, the Philippines, Brunei, Indonesia and Myanmar), there is either no direct flight or no regular and stable service. Indonesia and the Philippines are two prominent ASEAN countries with which India has substantial business and tourism interests but no reliable direct service. While some of the airlines of these countries do attempt direct services, they also close down due to poor load factors. Indian airlines do not do so and restrict their flights to existing routes.

Once a trade route is established, businessmen tend to find new items of perishables like vegetables, flowers or fish or light-weight types like gems and jewellery or computer peripherals for export or import by air. Goods that are high in value and low in volume are most suited to air transport. Besides, goods that are time sensitive, with higher opportunity cost, need air transport.

West Asia and the Need for Air Connectivity

In our Look West Policy described earlier, we can divide look west countries into two regions: the Gulf, and Iran and CIS/Russia.

In the Gulf, air services connecting India to the various Gulf countries are more than adequate. Gulf airlines are extremely well organised and have an excellent coverage of Indian cities. In fact, Indian airlines are protesting against over liberal bilateral rights given to them by the government of India.

Next, however, is an area of concern. This is Iran, Afghanistan and Central Asian Countries where connectivity is inadequate. At present there is only one flight of an Iranian airline connecting Tehran with Delhi, and no other city of Iran is covered. With the Chabahar Port becoming operational the need to connect it by a regular air service is urgent, even if the demand for it is low for the present. Similarly, with countries of Central Asia, as already discussed, the following three Agreements will change the way we look at West and Central Asia:

- India-Iran-Afghanistan Trade and Transit Agreement of 2016 and the operationalisation of Chabahar Port.
- International North-South Transport Corridor (INSTC), India-Iran-Russia-Turkmenistan-Kazakhstan corridor.
- Ashgabat Agreement 2018, India-Iran-Oman-Turkmenistan-Uzbekistan.

As these three corridors get operationalised there will be increasing traffic using them. Air connectivity incentivises the possibilities of business in these areas. If air services are provided, even on a subsidised basis, it will lead to an enhancement of trade and industry ties.

As trade and investments pick up, the need to connect all these stations by air will become important. A trade of $ 170 billion has been projected after operationalisation of these projects. Meanwhile, though the relationship between Iran and India has traditionally been good, in recent times it has gone through many difficult phases. It has now strengthened after a couple of high-level visits exchanged between New Delhi and Tehran, but with new sanctions put up by the US in August 2018, it is becoming tricky for India.

As a favourable development aimed at promoting trade for the war-ravaged country through the Indo-Afghan air corridor, SpiceJet of India planned to transport 1,500 tons of cargo every month. It also signed a Memorandum of Understanding (MoU) with the Afghan Chamber of Commerce in 2018 but the flights had to be closed down after the Pulwama attach by Pakistan as the air space over Pakistan was closed to India.

India and China: India's Land and Sea Connectivity in the East and West Compared to China's Belt and Road Initiative

Bert Lintner has pointed out that "Gwadar in Pakistan and Kyaukpyu in Myanmar—ports located at the end of Pakistan and Myanmar corridors respectively—have become major concerns for India. But the Chinese attempt to secure and defend those two corridors—one to the west of India and the other to the east—are the reasons why India feels it is being encircled by China and therefore has to shore up its defences."[71]

Are Indian Foreign Policy connectivity initiatives able to match China's Belt and Road Initiative (BRI)? India's resources are about one-sixth of China's. China's BRI initiative is much bigger in size and financial outlay. However, as *Economist* magazine states in its analysis of Chinese BRI:

> BRI countries risk piling up dangerous amounts of debt, which some fear is designed to give China a strategic hold over them. Pakistan, one of the most important BRI countries, has just held an election in which candidates vied to take credit for Chinese investment; yet the debts are so large that, before long, Pakistan is likely to need an IMF bailout.

It further says that some other ambassador, political leaders and business bosses "see something less grandiose. They think that China wants to crate up and export surplus cement plants, steel mills and glass works built during the years of stimulus spending and reassemble them abroad—along with pollution and green house gases formerly belched into the skies. More obviously, the BRI has secured contracts from Chinese firms."

It goes on to say, "Needed or not, there are places where BRI has been rejected. Fears of indebtedness and rows over murky payments have led to Chinese funded projects being cancelled, suspended or referred to anti-corruption watchdogs for review in Nepal, Myanmar and most dramatically in Malaysia. In Sri Lanka rows about China's influence in domestic politics helped topple a government."[72]

India's initiatives building the trilateral highway connecting North-East India with Myanmar and Thailand and subsequently all the way to Vietnam by INSTC road. Further, connecting Kolkata with Myanmar by ship through Sittwe port, connecting Sittwe to Patetwa inland waterway and then by road to Mizoram are some of the initiatives in the East. The Chabahar Port in Iran followed by road/rail to Afghanistan, member countries of Ashgabat Agreement and the Russian road/rail initiative called International North-South Transport Corridor all the way to Moscow and beyond are west of India. While Road and Belt initiative of China is much bigger, it is done through loans to countries which is in turn making them bankrupt, leading to resentment against the Chinese Government. By contrast, India's initiatives are peaceful and meet India's requirement. India is lucky in having Indian Ocean, a warm water sea, with plenty of ports and, therefore, India's needs are also less.

Importance of Air Cargo

While the world trade moves by surface/sea transport in terms of volume and weight, in terms of value, trade by air is as high as 35 per cent. As IATA has stated:

> Air cargo is a trade facilitator that contributes to global economic development and creates millions of jobs. The global economy depends on the ability to deliver high-quality products at competitive prices to consumers worldwide. Air cargo transports over US $ 6 trillion worth of goods, accounting for approximately 35 per cent of world trade by value.[73]

High-value goods as well as perishables are transported by air wherever possible. The absence of discussion on air cargo connectivity, except as a passing reference, is indeed surprising as most persons do not realise the high value of air cargo. Indian aviation strength has already been described earlier. As already stated, according to IATA India is expected to displace UK as the third largest aviation market by 2026, and Indian air passenger traffic is poised to grow from around 120 million to 442 million by 2035. With such a powerful aviation industry and a fleet of over 900 aircraft over the next few years, there is no reason why India's various cities cannot directly be connected to various cities of ASEAN group of countries and central Asian countries. Once such services start, perishables, such as vegetables, fruits and flowers will easily find a market in each other's countries and help the bottom line of the air operators. Any new flight that connects India with a new airport in an ASEAN country has a good potential for transport of perishable cargo.

China's second undeclared aggression on India and the world through Wuhan virus, necessitates an urgent need to build closeness with our neighbours to the east and west

> China dealt a body blow to the world in the year 2020. The Wuhan Virus has upset the entire world economy and has badly impacted the aviation and tourism sector. It may be brought out that when China became aware if the deadly virus it stopped all air flights and other means of transport domestically but allowed international flights to leave China thereby spreading the virus abroad. While China has fully revived its economy, other economies are still struggling. The Indian aviation industry is limping back to normalcy. Domestic Aviation is returning faster to normalisation than the international sector. It is time for India to take a proactive view on our external people-to-people relations and introduce an UDAN type scheme for Outbound to countries where we have a political advantage.

Notes

1. "Act East Policy", Press Information Bureau, Government of India, Ministry of External Affairs, December 23, 2015.

2. Centre for Policy Research, New Delhi, "Non-Alignment 2.0: A Foreign Policy and Strategic Policy for India in the Twenty-First Century". This is a report by an independent group of analysts and policymakers, namely, Sunil Khilnani, Pratap Bhanu Mehta, Lt Gen Prakash Menon (Retd.), Nandan Nilekani, Srinath Raghavan, Shyam Saran and Siddharth Varadarajan, available at www.cprindia.org
3. Larry Prado, Activity Editor: www.epplus.hartenergy.com
4. See www.saarc-sec.org>about-saarc
5. "India shares UDAN with SAARC. India seeks to share cheap air travel scheme with neighbours". Published on June 8, 2017.
6. See http://bimstec.org
7. See www.dnaindia.com>business>report, June 6, 2017.
8. See Prashant Jha, "India's SAARC dilemma", in *Hindustan Times*, May 3, 2018, p. 11.
9. Kishore Mahbubani is Singapore civil servant, a career diplomat, academic and Singapore's Permanent Representative to the United Nations, as well as President of the United Nations Security Council (2001-2002).
10. Subhashini Haidar, at thehindu.com, January 23, 2018.
11. Srihari Avuthu, "The pioneer ASEAN: Making a Paradigm Shift", in *The Pioneer*, January 24, 2018.
12. Thehindubusinessline.com, October 2, 2017.
13. MEA.gov.in.aseanindia.20-years
14. See Shrihari Avuthu, "ASEAN: Marking a paradigm Shift", in *Pioneer*, January 24, 2018.
15. See article, "Connectivity a must for boosting India-ASEAN relations—A host of initiatives are in the pipeline for better land, sea and air links in India" (ASEAN supplement of *Indian Express*, January 26, 2018.)
16. See *The Pioneer*, March 4, 2018, p. 12.
17. Shashi Tharoor, *Pax Indica—India and the world of the 21st Century* (Penguin Books: 2012), p. 191.
18. Manila, Philippines (Update 2): "The Permanent Court of Arbitration (PCA) under the United Nations ruled in favour of the Philippines in its arbitration case against China over the South China Sea", Patricia Lourdes Viray at philstar.com. Read more at https://www.philstar.com/headlines/2016/07/12/1602113/verdict-philippines-wins-arbitration-case-vs-china#hmXPxXUtfwxkcAyK.99
19. Sunanda K. Datta-Ray, *The Asian Age*, January 30, 2018.
20. Sunanda K. Datta-Ray, "India, ASEAN: Talk Less, act; keep an eye on China", *Asian Age*, January 30, 2018.
21. *Mint*, April 26, 2018.
22. Elizabeth Rouche, "India urged to seal trade pact with S-E nations", *Mint*, July 20, 2018.
23. Surendra Kumar, *The Asian Age*, January 30, 2018.
24. Pmindia.com
25. "Strengthening Asean-India Partnership: Trends and Future Prospects", a Special Publication Commemorating 25 Years of ASEAN-India Partnership, by the Export-Import Bank of India, in association with the Indian Mission to ASEAN, Jakarta.

26. MEA.gov.in.aseanindia.20years
27. "Why India is developing its maiden deep-sea port in Indonesia", at https://timesofindia.indiatimes.com/india/why-india-is-developing-its-maiden-deep-sea-port-in-Indonesia/articles show/69511228.cms
28. Devirupa Mitra, "Indonesia Told India Its Quest to Join Malacca Strait Patrols Isn't Feasible. This happened at an Indian and Indonesian experts meeting three weeks before Modi landed in Jakarta", in *The Wire*, May 31, 2018.
29. Harish Pant, "The future of India-ASEAN partnership", https://www.orfonline.org
30. "India Reaches Out—The move by India to woo 10 ASEAN Heads of State/ Government is one that will have far reaching consequences- both economically and politically. A report", *Cruising Heights*, April 2018, vol. XII, issue 11, pp. 66-67.
31. *The Indian Express*, April 4, 2018.
32. *The Indian Express*, April 4, 2018.
33. Read more at https://economictimes.indiatimes.com/articleshow/62516636.cms?utm_source=contentofinterest&utm_medium=text&utm_campaign=cppst
34. *The Pioneer*, December 20, 2017.
35. R. N. Choubey at "Wings India 2018" Conference in Hyderabad, *Mint*, March 9, 2018.
36. Mihir Mishra, "North-East India, Assam and Act East Policy: Assam plans to subsidise airfares to Southeast Asia", ET Bureau, January 16, 2018, 07.11 a.m. IST.
37. "India can no longer choke China at the Strait of Malacca as Beijing finds solutions", *The Eurasian Times*, July 11, 2020.
38. *South China Morning Post*, April 28, 2018, at www.scmp.com
39. The South China Sea Arbitration, The Republic of Philippines v. The People's Republic of China, PCA case no 2013-19, at http://academic.oup.com.article
40. *South China Morning Post*, April 28, 2018, at www.scmp.com
41. See Prasanta Kumar Pradhan, "Accelerating India's 'Look West Policy' in the Gulf", IDSA Issue Brief, February 3, 2011. Prasanta Kumar Pradhan is Associate Fellow at the Institute for Defence Studies and Analyses, New Delhi.
42. Embassy of India, Zanuck Dhabi, January 17, 2021, at indembassyuae.gov.in/bilateral-eco-com-relation.php
43. Issac John, *Khaleej Times*, Dubai, April 17, 2018.
44. "2018 Dubai Global Convention", organised by the Institute of Directors (IOD), in association with *Khaleej Times*, in April 2018.
45. Fact Sheet on Foreign Direct Investment (FDI) from August 1991 to October 2010, Department of Industrial Policy and Promotion, Ministry of Trade and Commerce, Government of India.
46. Ankit Panda, "India gains access to Oman's Duqm Port, putting the Indian Ocean Geopolitical Contest in the Spotlight", *The Diplomat*, May 7, 2018, at http://thediplomat.com/2018/02/india-gains-access-to-oman-duqm-port-putting-the-indian-ocean-geopolitical-contest-in-the-spotlight/
47. Ankit Panda, *The Diplomat*, February 14, 2018.
48. August 19, 2015, 02:11 IST. Updated: March 29, 2016.
49. "Navy chief Admiral Lanba begins 4-day visit to Iran", *The Pioneer*, April 23, 2018.
50. Olaf Caroe, *Wells of Power* (Macmillan, 1951).
51. Sanjay Kapoor, Editor, *Hardnews* Magazine for ORF January 2018.

52. Rahul Bedi, "Indian base in Tajikistan 'quietly' operational", August 22, 2002, at irishtimes.com
53. Geeta Mohan, "Real reason why India sits out of Iran's Chabahar-Zahedan rail link project", *India Today App* magazine, July 21, 2020, at www.indiatoday.in
54. Months after starting Chabahar rail project without India, Iran seeks equipment by Suhasini Haidar NOVEMBER 07, 2020 : The Hindu: the hindu.com
55. See Chabahar Port, at http://en.wikipedia.org/wiki/Chabahar_Port
56. *The Hindu*, October 29, 2017.
57. See "A Shadow Over Chabahar's fate", ORF Special Report #55, January 23, 2018.
58. Brahma Chellany, "India must reject the US' Iran policy", *Hindustan Times*, April 26, 2018.
59. *Hindustan Times*, HT Correspondent, February 25, 2019.
60. Dipanjan Roy Chaudhury, ET Bureau, "India admitted to Ashgabat Agreement as Delhi pushes Eurasian connectivity:", February 1, 2018, 10.00 PM IST, at https://economictimes.indiatimes.com/articleshow/62746478.cms?utm_source=contentofinterest&utm_medium=text&utm_campaign=cppst
61. Saarat Hassan ....
62. Mridu Kumari, "Indian Bugbear for China", *The Dayafter Magazine*, February 14, 2018; and Dipanjan Roy Chaudhury, ET Bureau, "INSTC to be operationalised mid-Jan 2018; game changer for India's Eurasia policy", December 5, 2017.
63. Dipanjan Roy Chaudhury, ET Bureau, "India admitted to Ashgabat Agreement as Delhi pushes Eurasian connectivity agenda", at https://economictimes.indiatimes.com/articleshow/62746478.cms?utm_source=contentofinterest&utm_medium=text&utm_campaign=cppst
64. Elizabeth Roche "India seeks better air Connectivity with Central Asia to boost trade", in *Economic Times*, January 1, 2018.
65. *Economic Times*, January 1, 2018.
66. Suhasini Haider, "Iran to promote Chabahar as curbs will hit main port", in *The Hindu*, February 17, 2019.
67 Bert Lintner, *The Costliest Pearl: China's Struggle for India's Ocean* (Madison, MS, USA: Context, 2019), p. 67.
68. *The Diplomat*, January 26, 2018.
69. Deeparghya Mukherjee, "India-ASEAN Air Connectivity: Prospects for Growing Trade and Tourism", National University of Singapore, Institute of South Asian Studies, at as.nus.edu.sg
70. See India Brand Equity Foundation, on Indian Aviation Industry, at www.ibef.org
71. Bert Lintner, *The Costliest Pearl: China's Struggle for Indian Ocean* (Madison, MS, USA: Context, 2019), p. 72.
72. *Economist* Magazine, July 28, 2018, pp. 14-15.
73. See IATA.org home> program>cargo>cargoSustainability>value of cargo

4
Synchronising Aviation Policy with Foreign Policy

Introduction

The desire to have better air connectivity between certain countries and India have been expressed by Indian Prime Minister Atal Bihari Vajpayee in 2003. He even made a unilateral offer to SAARC and ASEAN countries but it did not yield the desired results. In 2019 India's Foreign Minister, Sushma Swaraj, gave a call for an air corridor between India and Central Asian Countries. She stated, "To forge closer trade links with Central Asia", Swaraj said, "India would like to organize a 'dialogue on air corridors' with the participation of civil aviation authorities, air freight and aviation companies of India and Central Asia so that goods, including perishable items, can be transported efficiently and swiftly." India already has opened air corridors for the transport of goods and perishables between India and several Afghan cities mainly to circumvent Pakistan's veto over India-Afghanistan trade passing overland through its territory.[1] Ambassador Rajiv Sikri had also brought out in his book, quoted in chapter 1, the importance of people-to-people contacts, besides diplomacy. This gives adequate emphasis to the need for air connectivity to countries where we feel it is politically advantageous to us. Hence the need for this lengthy analysis. It is not possible to do any quantitative analysis or cost benefit analysis to prove the advantages of incentivised flights. Tangible and non-tangible benefits do come with a time lag. Historically also India has used aviation as a tool of foreign policy so long as our national airline was a public sector monopoly.

Role of Air India as a Monopoly Airline in Helping Indian Foreign Policy

Air India was a private company operating internationally when it was nationalised in 1953. Air India, as the national carrier, has played a significant role in promoting Indian foreign policy, and considered it as part of its monopoly obligations. So long as Air India was a monopoly airline of the Government and was considered the national flag carrier, it performed the very useful purpose of connecting India to various countries based on requests from the Foreign Ministry. Very often, even when a route was not viable, a little nudge from the government was required for it to start operations, which it cross-subsidised. Often such a route had to be closed down after a while due to continued losses, but it did operate for some time. The protection given to Air India as India's only airline permitted to fly abroad, the compulsion that government officials only use Air India while on duty travel, as far as practicable, and the high prestige it had in the market as a carrier of repute, enabled it to operate on many routes even when not viable. This came to an end in 1994 when its monopoly was taken away.

A Second Attempt at Synchronising Aviation with Foreign Policy

According to the Annual Report of the Ministry of Civil Aviation 2003-2004, another attempt towards aligning Civil Aviation to Foreign Policy was made in 2003-2004 when Prime Minister Atal Bihari Vajpayee made an open offer to ASEAN and SAARC countries.

With a view to enlarging our economic cooperation with ASEAN countries, it was decided that designated airlines of 10 ASEAN countries will be allowed to operate up to 7 services a week to/from the four metropolitan cities of New Delhi, Mumbai, Chennai and Kolkata, subject to equal reciprocal rights to the Indian side, and on existing terms of commercial agreement with our national carriers. Designated airlines of ASEAN countries will also be allowed to operate as many services as they wish, subject to reciprocal rights of equal number of flights to 18 other destinations in India, namely, Patna, Lucknow, Guwahati, Gaya, Varanasi, Bhubaneshwar, Khajuraho, Aurangabad, Goa, Jaipur, Port Blair, Cochin, Thiruvananthapuram, Calicut, Amritsar, Visakhapatnam, Ahmedabad and Tiruchi.[2]

Private airlines of SAARC countries would be permitted to operate to India against unutilised Indian entitlements. This meant little to countries who had no flights to India as the route was not considered viable. On the other hand, it was a gift to countries that already had existing airlines services and were able to increase their quota of flights/seats.

In view of the strategic importance of our relations with Sri Lanka, the designated airline of Sri Lanka was allowed to operate daily services to Delhi, Mumbai, Chennai, Bengaluru, Hyderabad and Kolkata and as many services as they wished to 18 other destinations in India, namely, Patna, Lucknow, Guwahati, Gaya, Varanasi, Bhubaneshwar, Khajuraho, Aurangabad, Goa, Jaipur, Port Blair, Cochin, Thiruvananthapuram, Calicut, Amritsar, Visakhapatnam, Ahmedabad and Tiruchi, subject to reciprocal rights of equal flights to Indian carriers. Since Sri Lankan Airlines was an aggressive airline, it utilised this offer and started services connecting many of these locations mainly for taking passengers beyond Colombo, that is, for 5th Freedom traffic.

Further, liberalisation of Bilateral Policy followed. It was decided to permit airlines of all countries having bilateral Air Services Agreements with India to operate 7 flights/week each to any two of the 12 international airports in India, subject to reciprocal rights being granted to Indian carriers.

Availability of traffic rights for operation of air services to/from India was also reviewed as part of the ongoing process of bilateral civil aviation consultations with various countries, namely, South Korea, Malaysia, Turkey, Italy, Gulf States, UAE (Dubai), Thailand, Ukraine, Slovakia, Kyrgyzstan, Bhutan, Germany, Poland, Russia, South Africa, Pakistan, Sri Lanka, Ethiopia, UAE, Tunisia, Italy, Slovak Republic and Germany.

Charter Policy

Tourist charter guidelines were further liberalised by permitting operation of 'Inclusive Tour Charters' with no limitation on frequency, size of the aircraft and points of call, subject to the availability of customs and immigration facilities. Indian passport holders have also been allowed to travel on inbound inclusive tour charters. There was also to be no restriction on frequency of flight and size of the aircraft in respect of outbound inclusive tour charters provided the concerned outbound tour operator also organises inbound charters with 2:1 tourist ratio between inbound and outbound operations.

Open Sky Policy

To take care of the peak season rush into India in the winter season, instead of giving more bilateral rights, India would declare an Open Sky Policy for winter season of 2003-2004, under which designated foreign airlines operated additional services to/from India subject to the existing terms of the commercial agreement with Air India. This only helped the big airlines as they were able to either put in service bigger aircraft or more of the same in a short time.

Results of 2003 initiative remained ineffective. Only countries that had strong airlines like Singapore, Thailand and Malaysia on the East and Gulf Airlines in the West took advantage of it and increased their flights into India. Sri Lanka, which had a strong airline and a collaborative agreement with Emirates, also took advantage of it. However, the rest of the eligible countries of the ASEAN or SAARC countries did not avail of the scheme. The main reason for this offer not being taken up was the non-viability of direct flights from those countries. So, neither did airlines of those countries offer nor did Indian airlines take advantage of the Scheme.

The lesson to be learnt from our 2003 open offer is that commercial viability is important. When an airline is not able to find a route viable it will either not attempt it at all or close down within a short period. For example, Jet Airways ran a flight to Ho Chi Minh City via Bangkok, but was not able to sustain it and had to close it down after one and a half years. Therefore, any future policy to provide connectivity to countries which do not have traffic loads must be accompanied by a scheme of direct or indirect subsidy as is being done in RCS/UDAN for domestic connectivity. Similarly, there are other examples. Direct connectivity with cities like Manila or Jakarta have always been problematic. Attempts to connect directly have failed due to lack of viability of a regular service, and dependence on a hub like Singapore or Bangkok continues. Unless a subsidy programme is provided for, say, three years to allow an Airline to build up traffic, it will not be able to sustain continuous losses beyond six months on a scheduled flight.

While no other attempt was made to bring the aviation policy in line with the foreign policy, however, as has been mentioned earlier, Minister of State in the Civil Aviation Ministry, Jayant Sinha, did offer to extend the Regional Connectivity Scheme known as UDAN to BIMSTEC countries in June 2017 at the 20th Anniversary of BIMSTEC, but no concrete proposal was submitted. This offer did not find any takers either from BIMSTEC members nor from our foreign ministry.

Case Study: China Outbound as a Tool of Foreign Policy

According to a recent report released by the Tourist Research Centre of the Chinese Academy of Social Sciences, China has the highest number of outbound tourists and highest amount of overseas spending in the world.[3] According to a McKinsey Report, "China's tourists are worth getting to know better. In 2017, Chinese travellers took more than four billion trips in-country and 131 million trips overseas. China is already the world's largest outbound travel market, and is set to grow further. By 2020, we expect that more domestic travellers will graduate to overseas trips, pushing annual outbound traffic to 160 million. More than 70 percent of Chinese tourists travel with family and friends; as a result, these groups are the world's highest spenders per single trip. Spending has more room to grow: we expect annual growth of 6.1 percent for the next couple of years."[4]

Consequently, Chinese government has discovered that the large Chinese outbound tourists who also spend an average $ 6,000 per person can indirectly add to their tools of manipulating their foreign policy. The Chinese National Tourism Organisation controls China's outbound tourism through its Approved Destination Status (ADS) list. This list restricts overseas travel by Chinese nationals to an approved list of countries and also forces Chinese nationals to travel in tightly controlled groups.[5] The Government can always manipulate the list to suit its purpose. Reportedly 97 million Chinese travelled abroad in 2013 beating the 2012 mark by roughly 14 million, according to the China National Tourism Administration. The number currently is reported to be about 135 million. According to the United Nations World Tourism Organisation (UNWTO), Chinese tourists overseas spent $ 261.1 billion in 2016[6] up from around $ 10 billion in the year 2000 (the figure for 2017 is likely to top $ 300 billion). Collectively, America's globetrotters parted with a relatively paltry $ 123.6 billion.[7]

Chinese tourists have had the world's strongest purchasing power since 2012. They overtook German and US tourists as the world's biggest-spending travellers in 2012, spending US$ 102 billion overseas, a 40 per cent increase from 2011. The current spending is estimated to be around $ 260 billion.

International traffic for China's three big carriers—Air China, China Eastern and China Southern—has seen the number of international passengers increase by an average of 20 per cent. To meet demand, Chinese Airlines have announced many new non-stop services from many Chinese cities to all over the world.

"Business, leisure and educational travel and trade between the United States and China have been growing dramatically," Liang Pubin, managing director of Hainan Airlines in North America, said at the time of the announcement of a direct flight to Boston. "This wonderful new link will stimulate this growth via the important Boston gateway." These new flights offer access for US visitors to more than 32 Chinese cities via Hainan Airlines' hub in Beijing.

Because of an increasingly competitive domestic market Chinese Airlines are seeking new opportunities abroad. With the nation's outbound travel set to soar, Chinese airlines are banking on brand recognition to capitalise on the population's increasing appetite to travel abroad. At the same time, Chinese Airlines are offering air tickets at the lowest cost on international flights which is, perhaps, due to subsidies which they get from their government.

How are China's airlines able to beat competition in international aviation?

China's Subsidy to Its Airlines

According to Bloomberg News,[8] *China's Airlines are getting subsidies worth $ 1.3 billion in cash or incentives which is worth close to half of 2016 airline profits, and are given through government sources.* Flights hardly make money from smaller cities, if not subsidised. China is, therefore, set to become the world's biggest aviation market thanks in part to hefty subsidies from local governments nudging the airlines to fly mainland tourists overseas. Local governments, especially those outside mega cities like Beijing, Shanghai and Guangzhou, spent at least 8.6 billion yuan ($ 1.3 billion) subsidising airlines in 2016, mostly for them to start direct services to far-flung places such as New York and Paris. These payments, to both Chinese and foreign carriers, equate to close to half the 19.49 billion yuan in profits earned by the top four mainland-based airlines last year. As a matter fact, Chinese main airlines are protesting to their Central government to stop the subsidy to the smaller airlines on flights abroad as it is affecting their business. Top Chinese airlines like Air China, China Eastern Airlines and China Southern Airlines have already used up their quota for popular destinations.

Interestingly, several national level carriers have expressed concern over the handouts. Air China's finance chief Xiao Feng has said heavily-subsidised direct flights from lower-tier Chinese cities are "unsustainable". Foreign airlines have also started to pull out of smaller cities, citing unsatisfactory performance. British Airways cancelled direct flights from London to Chengdu in western China after three years of service. United Continental Holdings abandoned Hangzhou and scrapped its seasonal flights between San Francisco and the western Chinese city of Xi'an. As a result, Chinese airlines are gaining an upper hand over the foreign airlines in traffic to and fro from China, entirely the opposite of what's happening in India.

"In addition to a growing need for international exchange resulting from China's economic development, local governments' increased subsidies are driving Chinese carriers' global route expansion," Shanghai-based Cadas said, in a report.

Local government subsidies surpassed Chinese airlines net income in 2016.[9] As economic growth and rising incomes led China to become the largest source of outbound travellers, major airports in Beijing and Shanghai have been stretched beyond their capacity. The battleground for long-haul flights has shifted to lower-tier cities, where state and private carriers like Hainan Airlines Holding Co. are offering international flights at low fares. Such flights would hardly make any money without government subsidies, according to Cadas. While domestic travel figures continue to rise, price wars among airlines and the spread of the country's high-speed rail network mean companies operate on thin profits to stay competitive.

"Airlines still face significant operational risks even if their long-haul international flights from second-tier Chinese cities are subsidised," Cadas said. "Rather than bringing in more foreigners to China, local governments are subsidising Chinese outbound travel, with little positive economic impact on local economies." However, this contention can be challenged. China is using this subsidy as a part of their foreign policy to award and discipline foreign countries as China can divert its outbound passengers to desired locations.

According to Andrew Herdman, Director General of the Association of Asia Pacific Airlines, the Chinese government has gradually eased regulations on the aviation industry, lifting a six-year ban on the establishment of independent air carriers. It has recently allowed two new privately owned airlines to commence operations, leading to increased competition. But even as they seek greener pastures, their relatively late entry into the international travel arena has made it an uphill battle for Chinese airlines, says, director-general of the Association of Asia-Pacific Airlines.

Chinese airlines are flooding the world with some of the lowest long-haul fares ever seen. From Delta Air Lines and American Airlines Group in the US, to Cathay Pacific Airways and Korean Air, many operators are feeling the squeeze from the extended reach of mainland Chinese carriers.

"They don't just offer cheap fares on routes long-dominated by national airlines like Korean Air. They're also adding hundreds of overseas flights from little-known Chinese cities to airports all over the world."

"Chinese airlines are still hardly scratching the surface of their potential, not just in China, but globally," said Will Horton, a Hong Kong-based analyst at the CAPA[10] Centre for Aviation. "If an airline today cannot compete with or grow alongside a Chinese airline, the future will be bleak."

According to CAPA, mainland Chinese airlines have opened 75 long-haul markets since 2006, led by Air China and Hainan Airlines. More than two-thirds of those routes opened only in 2016-2017. China's three biggest carriers—Air China, China Eastern Airlines Corp. and China Southern—are state-controlled and listed in Hong Kong and Shanghai.

"Chinese airlines do face competitive disadvantages when they go international—in terms of product, perception, brand awareness, distribution, capability and so on," he says. But the fact remains that Chinese Airlines are taking away traffic from US and other countries' passengers over Hong Kong or Singapore by offering lower fares. It is not clear how they manage to do so when it is reported that they pay their foreign pilots handsomely to attract them. Is there any hidden subsidy coming to Chinese Airlines? This issue has already been confirmed as the Chinese Big Four airlines have protested to the Central Government to stop the States/Provincial Governments subsidising State-level Airlines.

"But historically, long-haul flights to China were inbound-focused and the market source was the EU and America, so the Chinese airlines have had a disadvantage in terms of brand awareness and distribution presence in those source markets. With the growth of incomes in China and the fact that we now have a lot of outbound travel, that plays to the strength of the Chinese airlines because they are brands that are well known to Chinese travellers."

The increasingly refined tastes of travellers from the Chinese mainland also add to the potential success of new long-haul routes operated by China's airlines.

While global alliance partnerships have ensured that the airlines operate to international standards, most well-to-do Chinese vacationers still opt to go with international brands because they are perceived as more luxurious, says Herdman. "Sophisticated mainland customers are quite savvy about which brands they choose, as you can tell by the kind of cars they buy and the type of luxury goods they buy," he said.

According to a survey by PricewaterhouseCoopers, US airlines operated 53 per cent of the routes between the US and China during 2013-2014, a drop of nearly 7 per cent from the year before. Chinese airlines were responsible for the remaining 47 per cent.[11] A 43-year-old Boston resident and her friend saved hundreds of dollars last year choosing China Southern Airlines over a direct flight from Seoul with Korean Air Lines or Asiana Airlines. "We didn't mind the layover because it was so much cheaper," she said. "Like, almost half the price." The cheapest way to travel from London to Australia, for instance, is no longer via Dubai or Abu Dhabi but through Guangzhou, Shanghai or Wuhan. The Chinese have also loosened visa requirements to encourage this kind of transit traffic.[12]

Cathay Pacific has felt the tremor of this development as first-half profit sank 82 per cent as Chinese travellers bypassed its Hong Kong base. Delta President Glen Hauenstein told analysts that China "continues to be challenged" as capacity growth outpaces demand. American Airlines President Robert D. Isom said that there's "continued weakness in China" as excess capacity seeps into the airline's new services from Los Angeles to Hong Kong, Haneda, Sydney and Auckland.

A round trip with China Eastern between New York and Bangkok, via Shanghai, costs $ 570.06, according to Webjet.com. The same trip with United Airlines through Hong Kong costs $ 714.80. Flying from

Los Angeles to Hong Kong with China Airlines is one-third cheaper than with American Airlines. "While it might not work for foreign carriers to fly to second-tier cities like Chengdu and Xiamen, it will still work for the Chinese because the originating market is very big,"[13] said K. Ajith, an analyst at UOB Kay Hian Pte in Singapore. "There's an underlying desire to travel."

China has also started using Aviation as a tool of its foreign policy:[14] *There is no doubt that the Chinese government has realised the importance of outbound Chinese traveller as a tool of diplomatic policy with 135 million outbound travellers spending about US$ 260 billion.* As the Chinese becomes rich the desire to go abroad increases. China is able to kill two birds with one stone. Instead of restraining their people to stay within the country, they encourage them to travel abroad from their homes in metro as well as from Tier II and III cities following the policy of ADS in groups. As Chinese outbound travel grows, it becomes a good source of earning for many receiving countries. As a controlled society, it can stop their nationals from visiting a particular country thereby reducing substantially their tourism income as well as foreign exchange earnings. They have done so in the case of many countries. After South Korea installed the US Thaad Missile Shield to protect itself from North Korea's threat, China was annoyed. While Beijing did not officially sanction South Korea, it marshalled its public behind its economic offensive against that country. It did this by its controlled outbound travel using the mechanism of ADS. It stopped the Chinese from travelling to South Korea. Many other measures were adopted to run down South Korean business but the one that matters in aviation is that it banned stopovers in South Korea of Chinese tourists. As Chinese young (18-34 years of age) outbound tourists recorded 82 million trips (US citizens made only 75 million trips abroad) in 2016, constituting 60 per cent of their outbound travel and spending US$ 150 billion, it makes a difference.[15] Further, it has been recently reported in the press that as Malaysia under a new government found Chinese infrastructure projects worth $ 20 billion for East Coast Rail Link unsustainable and a white elephant and chose to cancel it, the Chinese annoyance was expressed by curbing import of palm oil from Malaysia and curbing the numbers of Chinese tourists bound for Malaysia.[16]

Here again we see how China is using its financial muscle to break into a market which was dominated by western airlines. Its outbound travellers number around 135 million. The estimated spend by Chinese outbound tourists was about to US$ 261 billion, according to UN World Travel Organisation.[17] As a centralised power it not only encourages them to go abroad but also channelises their direction through ADS and use of their airlines. If they want to punish a country they stop Chinese nationals from travelling to that country, thereby depriving it of tourism revenue.

The above proposition has been reinforced in an article dated February 5, 2017 in *Jing Daily,* a leading digital publication.[18] Daniel Meesak has described how Chinese tourists can serve as a cash injection into local economies of neighbouring countries, but this comes with strings attached. Often such cash injection could mean 50 per cent of their tourist arrivals. *As the Chinese have control over their tourists going abroad through ADS system, they can deny a country their tourists who travel in large numbers and are a good source of money for the host country.* Therefore, China's neighbours are increasingly cautious about letting the Chinese dominate their tourism industry. But this tool of sending and stopping their outbound tourists gives China substantial leverage over a country dependent upon their tourism. Even for a country as big as South Korea, the Chinese government's displeasure was conveyed effectively by diverting their tourists when they decided to install the US Thaad missile shield. Both Malaysia and the Philippines have felt this pressure. Malaysia felt it over their airline MH370 incident when China slammed their chaotic investigation. In the case of the Philippines, Chinese tourists went up after President Duterte made a visit to China after the International Arbitration decision over South China Seas issue. In the case of Vietnam, China issued to its citizens a travel warning after the Chinese Oil Platform issue. After it was resolved, the Chinese tourists bloomed in Vietnam. The Chinese government has realised the importance of their outbound tourism and treats its outbound travellers as a diplomatic tool to be used both as a carrot for good behaviour and a stick for bad behaviour Therefore, subsidies to their airlines can be considered as a part of their foreign policy investment.

A Proposal for Diverting Outbound Tourism from India

Linking Foreign Policy Objectives with India Outbound Air traffic

A Strategy for 50 Million Outbound Passengers from India

We see from the last chapter how, on the one hand, the Chinese government is using its civil aviation outbound power to dominate the existing international market by outpricing existing international carriers with subsidies to their airlines; and, on the other, using its controlled outbound passengers to reward or punish a country economically by sending or denying their huge outbound tourist traffic through use of ADS. It may be further added that aviation does not fall under WTO and, therefore, such subsidy is not violative of any rule. While India cannot control the direction of its outbound tourist traffic under its democratic freedoms, it can certainly incentivise the direction of tourists by various methods, including cash subsidy under the proposed International Connectivity Scheme (ICS).

While IATA has predicted 50 million outbound passengers from India by 2020 (which seems unlikely but may be possible in another few years), the Indian arrivals in Asia-Pacific region in 2017 and the growth trends. It may be noticed that apart from the expected ASEAN countries, Thailand, Singapore, Malaysia and Indonesia, the other six countries are missing. The graph below gives an idea of 'Outbound Travel Trends from India', major countrywise and Arrivals from India to selected countries during 2013-2017.

"Indian outbound is on the growth path and a lot of these markets are anticipating growth out of India and that this number will scale up as we go forward..."

—*Travel News*, "Outbound Travel Trends", at travelbizmonitor.com

UN World Tourism Organisation has predicted that India outbound will rise from the level of about 25 million in 2017 to 50 million by 2020 (which has not happened). While inbound is only about 10 million, the outbound is not only higher but also growing at a faster rate.[19]

Why can't we channelise this massive growth of India outbound tourists to help our foreign policy, that too in desired directions? China is using its current outbound tourists of around 135 million per year as an economic weapon to favour the favourites and to punish countries who digress from their favour. This is the crux of the issue. *How to incentivise Indian outbound tourists to countries important from our Foreign Policy angle?* Unfortunately, Indian Government has no control over the direction that their citizens take in their outbound tourism like the Chinese ADS described earlier. Further, India outbound tourists presently do not have similar inclinations for travel as our foreign policy needs. This book will, therefore, analyse the various types of outbound strategies which will influence the decision of the direction of Indian outbound tourists. We have also discussed above how China is using its large outbound tourist as a tactical weapon in its foreign policy. Being a totally controlled country, the channelisation, diversion and stopping its outbound tourists are well controlled by its regulatory authority. While we may not be in a position to have such a control, we still have some levers which can be used for such channelisation and these have been discussed.

More than half of the total passengers coming into India are accounted for by the countries in the Middle East (Gulf). The same pattern is observed for the number of India's outbound passengers, that is, more than half of the total outbound passengers are accounted for by the countries in the Middle East.

If we look at the specific countries within the region, it is found that the maximum passengers are carried to and from the United Arab Emirates (33.2 per cent) followed by Singapore (6.6 per cent) and Saudi Arabia (5.7 per cent). Among European Countries, United Kingdom is one of the hottest destinations as about 5 per cent international passengers travel to and from the UK.

Out of the 24 Indian cities from where international passengers Embark/Disembark, 5 Indian cities accounted for most (approximately 70 per cent) of the international passenger traffic. Delhi tops the position in this category with a share of 27.6 per cent followed by Mumbai 21.4 per cent share and Chennai 8.3 per cent share. Domestic and foreign carriers connect India to 58 countries through more than 300 routes. Out of these routes only 10 routes accounted for approximately 20 per cent of the total international passenger traffic during the first quarter of the year 2017. The maximum international passengers were carried on the Dubai-Mumbai route. Jet Airways and Air India are among the top five scheduled freight carriers with market shares of 10.6 per cent and 8.1 per cent respectively during the first quarter of the year 2017. Other Indian carriers carry approximately 2 per cent of the total international freight.

The Outbound Indian Tourist: Behaviour Pattern

There is a need to introspect on how to incentivise and channelise our outbound traffic to meet our foreign policy requirements within our own conditions and rules. Therefore, there is a need to examine the behaviour pattern of Indian outbound travellers and provide a mechanism to motivate and incentivise them to visit certain countries which would be favourable to our foreign policy. Further, it may be kept in mind that foreign exchange reserves in India are plenty and the spend by Indians in travels abroad is not of any consequence from the foreign exchange angle.

India has another significant advantage that the demographic factor is on its side. Unlike China, whose population is ageing, India is about to reap a demographic harvest. India has a large young population that will ensure its workforce can support both young and old for some years to come. This will also ensure that our strong outbound traffic will continue to grow as young people start earning more and have a greater propensity to travel on holidays, especially abroad. Further, many locations abroad may turn out to be cheaper than holidaying in India. Many of these locations will also coincide with our foreign policy needs.

There is a need to analyse growth and diversity of the Indian outbound traveller. Whilst much of the focus of the travel industry has been on the staggering growth of the Chinese market, India is emerging as a strong contender and has an advantage in that its growth is more likely to keep pace over time with aviation capacity. Travel is an 'ageless' occupation in India with a good spread of travellers across key age groups—although it varies by destination. But there is growth in travelling by the older age groups, according to Visit Britain. Family groups from India form a larger part of the international market and it is important both to showcase and deliver itineraries that satisfy a different range of family needs.

The Visiting Friends and Relatives (VFR) Opportunity

VFR is sometimes dismissed as a less attractive segment for the tourism industry. This ignores the opportunity of high repeat visitation, longer stays and a greater share of wallet for experiences, if staying with family is important. This is particularly true of India. The Indian diaspora contains a high proportion of affluent, educated and entrepreneurial individuals. This is further enhanced by the education tourism sector—affluent Indians travel to countries such as the US, Canada, Australia and the UK, initially to study and then to settle down. Besides their propensity to visit with greater frequency and stay for longer periods, affluent VFR travellers can also be extremely cost effective to target as they can be reached via VFR hosts in a destination's home market. Local business and community associations, community press and geographic targeting have proved to be effective means of targeting these groups. However, VFR do not provide any relief for our objective as VFR countries (largely with the Gulf, Europe and the USA) do not necessarily coincide with our objectives and will take place anyhow as these locations cannot be changed.

Travelling Abroad Outbound from Tier II and Tier III cities

Currently, most travel out is from the major airports with good international air connectivity, such as Mumbai, Delhi, Bengaluru and Hyderabad. Air access has also proved critical to driving traffic to specific destinations. In its review of the Indian market, OAG (Official Aviation Guide)[20] notes how much of the traffic now flows to and through the UAE with almost half of all seat capacity (47 per cent) out of India flowing to the country. However, a strong wave of growth in travel outbound is coming from 'Middle India'—the 400 towns with populations between one hundred thousand to one million. Therefore, direct non-stop flights from smaller Tier II and Tier III towns to certain destinations abroad under the proposed International Connectivity Scheme (ICS) may provide a partial solution to our problem.

This may be an attractive source market to tap. Given that short lead time it's clear that travellers need to be primed and ready when they do start planning. Direct air connectivity to destinations is important to both inbound and outbound travellers. For example, Angkor Wat in Cambodia is of great importance for those interested in history, archaeology, and Hinduism. If a direct flight from Indian cities was available to the UNESCO World Heritage, there would be a great response. Today, this place has no direct connectivity with India. All Indians, wherever in India they may be, have to connect through Bangkok or Singapore.

(c) Word of mouth is very important in all markets and this is particularly true of India. This is very often in the form of personal (i.e., face-to-face) sharing of ideas and opinions.

(d) The role of social media is growing. Indeed, India is one of the markets where social media is more important than email in inspiring travel. It is therefore critical for destinations and tourism businesses to ensure they deliver on the experience and that they facilitate social sharing for Indians.

Indians are also likely to share information whilst travelling or to post reviews after their visits. These sources are increasingly influential. In using content marketing, it is important to note that India is a highly mobile-dependent market. Three-quarters of Indians have access to a mobile phone, so providing content in mobile friendly formats is vital. Although internet penetration is low, it is highly correlated with travel incidence.

(e) The Online Travel Agent (OTA) sector is growing fast in India, but is more strongly used for domestic travel, or shorter trips. Its use is still more in the domestic tourism space (as the presence of many local rail sites also indicates).

What Motivates Indians to Travel?

Normally, Family is central to Indian life and spending time with loved ones is a key motivation to travel for Indians. They often travel in family groups and there is a pressure to make the trip enjoyable for everyone. Helping multi-generational trips to be stress free and enjoyable is a major opportunity for the industry to stand out. Mental well-being is also important. Needing a break is a common reason but travelling abroad for tourism is a new and growing phenomenon. The traditional spots to visit were Singapore or Dubai for shopping and London for legacy purpose. But shopping is no more a desire as Indian markets offer all goods and, perhaps, cheaper too. Now it is the desire for relaxation and a new destination. Also, there are an increasing number from rural areas, Tier II and Tier III towns, who are travelling abroad. According to *TravTalk*, a trade magazine of the tourism sector, farmers of Gujarat have taken to holidaying abroad as it is not only enjoyable to see new areas but also sometimes cheaper to go to nearby countries than travel within India.

Most of all, Indian outbound travellers are hungry to engage with the world—no matter how far they travel. Wanting to visit other countries to broaden knowledge was the highest-ranking motivator for travel among Indians, according to Visit Britain. Discovery and sense of achievement are among the other two motivations for Indians. This is important because Indian visitors are looking towards gaining self-confidence and self-pride, both of which are a product of foreign travel.

What Drives Destination Choice?

The vast majority of travellers in the world, including Indians, say that it is important to them to visit a safe destination. Indians are also risk averse and, therefore, a safe destination is high on the priority list.

According to Dubai Tourism, 2.1 million Indian Tourists visited Dubai in 2017, which was the highest for a country score. India is their key market as they are able to use it as a hub for westbound flights. They also offer good reasons for stay in Dubai by offering leisure and MICE arrangements. They also enrol the top Bollywood stars for their campaign. Use of Bollywood Stars to promote a destination can be an important factor in decision making.

What Constitutes a Safe and Secure Destination?

For longer trips (either in terms of distance or time) or more especially for multi-destination trips, a known and reliable travel agent is important. Unlike many other source markets, there has been limited consolidation within the bricks and mortar travel agents' market in India. Tourism Australia, on the other hand, estimates that 80 per cent of its bookings are from this source.

(i) Value is also important to Indian travellers, and ranked 3rd in driving choice, according to Tourism Australia. Although Indians will seek to bargain for prices, this is not just about cost. High net worth individuals in particular are prepared to pay for experiences or to visit destinations that deliver unique experiences about which they can brag. Access to the best experiences within budget (30 per cent) or the most unique experiences (23 per cent) were the leading constituents of value according to Tourism Australia—far outweighing the cost of accommodation.

Perception: Important Role Played by Bollywood Movies for India Outbound: The Case of Switzerland

Tourism industry is replete with studies that identify specific movies and then examine how they have induced tourism to destinations worldwide. Some of the biggest blockbusters of Bollywood, shot in Western Europe, have led to growth in Indian outbound tourism to these countries. In this context, many foreign countries offer incentives to Bollywood film industry to come to their country to shoot their films. Therefore, less directly, the role of Bollywood is important in influencing destination of choice. Switzerland has been among the leaders in promoting itself using Bollywood films. As a result, Switzerland figures high as an aspirational destination for Indian travellers—despite its reputation for being very expensive. Other countries are following the example of Switzerland. As already stated, Dubai has also used Bollywood stars to promote its destination. Some Indian companies specialise in offering/arranging location management services in countries abroad. Russia and CIS countries too have joined in. It should be the endeavour of our government to induce Bollywood to shoot films in certain countries where we feel our foreign policy ends will also be served. This could be done through bilateral discussions with these countries to offer incentives, or India can offer tax incentives to the film industry to shoot in these countries. Many innovative schemes on these lines could be thought out.

New Trends in India Outbound

It has been reported that travellers across age groups from smaller towns of India are increasingly travelling to international destinations, such as Dubai, Europe and South East Asia. It is said that about 30 per cent-40 per cent of the outbound business, both online and offline, comes from Tier II and Tier III towns. The growth in Tier II & III is reportedly higher than in large cities on year-on-year basis.[21] Further, about 30 per cent of total departures from India is on account of leisure travel, compared to the global average of 53 per cent. Popular destinations are, Dubai, Saudi Arabia, Bahrain, France, Malaysia, Singapore, Thailand, Sri Lanka, Hong Kong, Indonesia (primarily Bali), the US and Switzerland. One of the factors determining the growth of Tier II & III cities outbound traffic is the availability of direct international flights which facilitates families and groups to go straight to their destinations without wasting time in a major Indian airport and save time and money. Travel Agents in India have found it attractive to concentrate on Tier II & III towns for outbound traffic as the growth lies in those areas. However, outbound destinations are largely Australia, Singapore, Malaysia, Hong Kong, Dubai, Sri Lanka, South Africa, Europe and the USA.[22]

Besides the ease of direct connectivity from Tier II & III towns, the destination of travel holiday is also influenced by social media. While metro city travellers are more independent in their decisions it is not so with others. Tourism Boards of foreign countries have already shifted their focus to potential travellers from Tier II & III towns. Tourism Boards of Dubai, Singapore, Indonesia, the US, Czech Republic, etc., are actively leveraging potential passengers of Tier II & III towns with branded content and social media influencer marketing campaigns across Instagram, Facebook and YouTube. Specialised language products have also been made.

Changing Profile of the Traveller

International travel is no longer confined to the rich—the middle class is taking the plunge more often. According to some rough estimates around 27 per cent of the tourists going overseas from Gujarat are farmers or others associated with agriculture. Teachers and government officers (banking, etc.) from small towns of the state comprise another 9 per cent or so, while shopkeepers and small businessmen make up 20 per cent of outbound travellers from the state, apart from senior citizens who constitute around 12 per cent of outbound tourists.

While the break-up might vary with states, the fact remains that more people from the middle classes are opting to travel internationally. Mahendra Vakharia, former president of the *Outbound Tour Operators Association of India (OTOAI)* said that with domestic travel becoming more expensive (a Dubai trip from Mumbai or Ahmedabad can work out cheaper than a trip to Kerala, for example), the middle class is travelling more often.

Better Connectivity from Tier II Towns

International budget carriers are offering cheaper fares and direct connectivity to overseas locations from tier II towns—for example, Thai Smile to Varanasi, Jaipur, Ahmedabad, Lucknow, and Gaya; Thai AirAsia to Trichy; Scoot (low-cost airline of Singapore Airlines) connecting Jaipur and Singapore; AirAsia from Bhubaneshwar to Kuala Lumpur.

Vakharia said, "Not only better connectivity, but competition has ensured that international fares are affordable. Travelling within India is at times more expensive." Most outbound travel happens from Western India followed by North. "Marwaris and Gujarati communities are the most avid outbound travellers," he added.[23]

Recognising this immense potential in outbound travel from India, more than 70 National Tourist Organisations (NTOs) from around the world have set up local offices in India and are aggressively marketing their destinations. For volume growth, the top five destinations are Saudi Arabia, Thailand, Kuwait, United States and Singapore. Australia and France are good examples of destinations that are succeeding in their promotional efforts. For France, a key strategy has been the launch of the campaign "France Celebrates India", which offers Indian travellers an array of travel services. It is not surprising that even destinations like South Africa and Dubai have stepped up their efforts to boost Indian outbound numbers to their respective countries.

How to channelise India Outbound to meet India's Foreign Policy Objectives?

The Proposed International Connectivity Scheme (ICS)

This is an important issue as it involves incentives and persuasion with changing preferences. Since the Indian political system will not allow a Chinese type Approved Destination Scheme (ADS) described in chapter 4, a number of alternative suggestions have been made. Ministry of External Affairs should draw up a list of preferred destinations like UDAN does by making a list of unserved and under-served airports. While UDAN goes for reverse auctions to give these routes to an air operator with exclusive rights for three years, in our proposed international connectivity scheme or ICS, airlines can be given these routes with exclusive rights for 3 years under similar conditions. However, three more incentives can be added. Relaxation of 0/20 rule could apply to these rules so that new airlines can take up the challenge, government Leave Travel Concession (LTC) provision of once in four years can be extended to some of these ICS routes and further encourage direct outbound flights from smallest tier II & III towns by cash subsidy to airlines and other incentives to desired locations under ICS. For example, the airport at Port Blair has announced no landing charges for foreign airlines for three years if they fly in directly from abroad. Similar non-cash and cash incentives can be kept under an ICS Fund, similar to what has been proposed as a draft by the Ministry of Civil Aviation for external flights by State Governments. This scheme will, however, will be managed by the Ministry of External Affairs or its affiliates like Indian Council for Cultural Affairs. The Indian Council for Cultural Relations (ICCR), was founded in 1950 as an autonomous organisation under the Ministry of External Affairs to actively participate in the formulation and implementation of policies and programmes pertaining to India's external cultural relations; to foster and strengthen cultural relations and mutual understanding between India and other countries; to promote cultural exchanges with other countries and people; and to develop relations with nations. ICCR would be the ideal candidate to manage the ICS scheme on behalf of Ministry of External Affairs in collaboration with Ministry of Civil Aviation. A similar activity of Ministry of External Affairs was the sponsorship of Haj Pilgrimage in collaboration with the Haj Committee and Ministry of Civil Aviation. A similar type of mechanism could be evolved for ICS.

The Need for Government Intervention in India Outbound Policy for Both Foreign Policy and Aviation Policy Objectives

As we have already elaborated earlier there have been policy lapses in the Civil Aviation sector which allowed airports abroad in our neighbourhood to become hubs for Indian travellers as our airports till 2010 were not good enough for it. Subsequent to 2010, we continued through our bilateral ASAs to promote these hubs by giving liberal seat rights and opening many more points of landing within

India to enable them to take Indian outbound passengers direct to their hubs.

On the Foreign Policy angle, we made attempts since 2003 to opening our country's metro and smaller airports in 18 locations to SAARC and ASEAN countries but without any well-thought-out plan of action, resulting in only those countries like Singapore, Thailand and Malaysia, that had well developed flights into India, to develop their airports as hubs further with Indian outbound traffic. The rest of the countries in our Act East Policy as well as Look West policy remained as before. The need now is to correct the aviation policy lapses and also merge our foreign policy requirements to induce our airlines to go to destinations—where they feel hesitant on commercial grounds—by incentives to them, as well as to the Indian outbound travellers to these destinations. Luckily both these tend to coincide and, therefore, should support each other.

Indian Council for Cultural Relations (ICCR) could well be tasked with channelising Indians going abroad. They could take advantage of the existing Outbound Tour Operators Association of India (OTOAI) as well as Bollywood film producers to direct the outbound traffic to desired destinations like it was done by Switzerland and some other countries to promote their country to Indians outbound. In a similar manner, India Tourism Development Corporation (ITDC), whose main job is to encourage inward tourism, should also be tasked to divert Indians going abroad to destinations desired under our foreign policy in collaboration with ICCR. Between ICCR and ITDC offices abroad, there could be greater collaboration and avoidance of duplication. At the same time ITDC and ICCR could mount a special programme from selected countries to promote visit India projects. If a proactive policy is followed to divert our outbound tourists, then we can get the foreign policy dividends out of our future projected 50 million tourists travelling abroad. Further, once regular flights start, trade will follow. Therefore, if incentives are to be offered, there should be no qualms about it. Such flights would also bring into India tourism from these new destinations if proper publicity is given. Lastly, Ministry of External Affairs has been subsidising annually Haj Pilgrimage flights to Saudi Arabia since early

2000 to the tune of upto Rs. 700 crores which has been stopped under orders of the Hon'ble Supreme Court since 2018. If a similar amount was kept for subsidising flights to ASEAN and CIS countries, we could achieve a lot more.

Correcting Former Mistakes in Civil Aviation

Did the bureaucratic inertia of the Ministry of Civil Aviation in not allowing airlines and airports to grow till about 2010 stifle the industry and the economy? Yes, all evidence points towards it. This wrong needs to be corrected. In his term as Prime Minister during 1999-2004, PM Atal Bihari Vajpayee had sent instructions to the Ministry of Civil Aviation that we need to have 'world class' airports in India. Then started the long-drawn effort to privatise the Delhi airport which took about 10 years to materialise and evolve into the present Delhi International Airport Limited (DIAL) in 2010 with 26 per cent only equity with Airports Authority and the balance in the hands of private parties. This model led to further development of Bengaluru, Hyderabad airports as greenfield and Mumbai as brownfield.

Till 2004 no private airline of India was allowed to go abroad as it remained the monopoly of Air India. Even when allowed in 2004, Air India retained 'the right of First Refusal' and the rule 5/20 was imposed. This harmed the cause of Indian airlines from setting up robust routes abroad.

It is, therefore, desirable that we encourage more direct flights by Indian carriers from our international airports and even domestic airports to destinations abroad even if they are not viable under ICS. We should discourage fresh allotment of rights to countries that are using their airports as hubs for 5th and 6th freedom traffic so that our own metro airports are able to come up as hubs. It is also desirable not to allow any new airport in India to foreign airlines for direct landing till we reach overall parity between Indian airlines and foreign airlines in utilisation of bilateral air traffic rights.

Selective use of Leave Travel Concession (LTC) to a few selected countries abroad in sync with our foreign policy, i.e., Cambodia, Vietnam,

Indonesia, the Philippines, Uzbekistan and other central Asian countries, Mauritius Seychelles, Maldives, etc., should be done.

Proposal: Introduce formally an International Connectivity Scheme (ICS) to channelise our outbound tourist to desired destinations as opposed to International Air Connectivity (IAC) scheme

While International Air Connectivity (IAC) proposed by Ministry of Civil Aviation is for state governments who want a direct international flight from their state to a desired destination abroad due to their political requirements, the International Connectivity Scheme (ICS) would be a parallel Scheme proposed for Ministry of External Affairs. While many of the features in each of these Schemes could be common, there will be some variation. The State Governments would suggest a direct flight to the country from their state largely because the Indian diaspora from that state is large. In the case of ICS, the suggestion to have a direct flight will be based on foreign policy considerations. For example, connecting cities that fall on our routes of India-Iran-Afghanistan Agreement or Ashgabat Agreement or INSAT Agreement or direct connectivity to ASEAN/SAARC countries from various cities of India may be a political requirement.

Having described the motives behind location of travel there is a need to involve ICCR and ITDC/State Tourism Corporations/Outbound Tour Operators Associations of India in inducing Indian outbound traffic to desired countries. This will require a proper coordination with these three Institutions who could arrange FAM tours of Indian travel agents to desired locations or exhibitions for travel to desired locations. Companies that arrange shooting abroad of Bollywood films could be asked to get involved. Golf tourism is also on the upswing in India. Indian golfers take part in golf tours abroad. Some countries, like Vietnam, offer excellent and very competitive golf facilities. Indians are also taking to Scuba Diving and are interested to go to new Scuba dive spots in ASEAN countries as South East Asia offers excellent locations.

The Position with Regard to Subsidies Provided to Aviation

Aviation in India has never been a sector which gets direct budgetary subsidies (except to Air India after 2014); on the other hand, it is highly loaded with taxes and fees, especially the domestic sector. At the same time there are some hidden subsidies which are/were provided in some sub-sectors of aviation. For example:

- Air India was able to negotiate royalties/favourable code shares or allotted cheap tickets of the other airline during the course of bilateral government-to-government air service negotiations. This has since been stopped.
- Vayudoot Airline, a 100 per cent jointly owned by Air India and Indian Airlines, provided regional connectivity and its losses were met jointly by Air India and Indian Airlines. This Airline ran for about 10 years from 1981 to 1991.
- The Route Dispersal Guidelines (RGD) were introduced after liberalisation in the early 1990s after Vayudoot shut down, and still continues. It is an internal cross-subsidy by each airline.
- Regional Connectivity Scheme (RCS), introduced in the NCAP 2016, is again a subsidised scheme in which each commercial airline pays Rs. 5,000 per air trip (with some exceptions) into a fund called RCF. AAI also puts in money into this fund to meet the shortfall. State Governments also contribute in cash and kind. So far no budgetary support has been given to this scheme.
- Some state governments do subsidise helicopter services to difficult terrains in their state.
- Non-direct subsidies impacting Aviation: There are, however, subsidies offered to passengers in some cases. For example:
- Haj Pilgrimage was a subsidised trip to Mecca by Indian nationals existing since pre-independence era and has since been stopped by a Supreme Court order. It was initially by ship but later changed to Air. The last subsidy in 2018 was between about Rs. 600-700 crores with about 150,000 persons availing of it in that year. This has since been stopped under orders of the Hon'ble Supreme Court.

- Government of India subsidised pilgrimage to Mansarovar Lake/ Mount Kailash in Tibet but it is not by air. In addition, Governments of UP and Gujarat also give subsidy for it. But not by air.
- The State Governments of Madhya Pradesh, Gujarat, etc., subsidise pilgrim tours within India. Again, not by air.
- The Central Government after 2014 has announced a subsidised pilgrimage scheme called Punyadham Yatra to Puri, Vrindavan, Ajmer Sharif, Mathura and Vaishneo Devi. Again, not by air.
- Andaman and Nicobar Administration gives subsidy for Mainland-Island and Inter-Island passenger shipping. However, no subsidy is given on air travel expect on a chartered flight once a week from the mainland and internal helicopter flights.
- At the same time, as described in Chapter 2, there are already two subsidised domestic Schemes at work, i.e., Route Dispersal Guidelines and Regional Connectivity Scheme.

Subsidy in the aviation sector for remote connectivity is given also in developed countries like the USA, Canada, Australia through budgetary allocation. Soviet Russia used to provide subsidised air services.

State Government of Assam has announced that it will subsidise outbound flights from Guwahati Airport to neighbouring countries of SAARC and ASEAN with an allotment of Rs. 100 crores per year for three years. The Chief Minister of Assam has further stated that he would like to make Guwahati airport as a hub in Northeast India for both RCS and ICS. If this works out, perhaps other state governments will also do the same. This is an interesting beginning. The Ministry of Civil Aviation has also put up in its website the draft rules for International Air Connectivity Scheme (IAC). In case of China, the subsidy that is being provided to some of their airlines is by their State Governments to encourage them to fly directly abroad from the state airport, and it is in direct competition with their Big Four national airlines (who may also be getting subsidies), thereby giving their national airlines a commercial disadvantage. In the case of Assam while no foreign or domestic airline has come forward for a direct service between Guwahati and abroad, Air

India which started a direct service from Guwahati to Bangkok had to close it down due to lack of viability.

Therefore, to connect our foreign policy requirements with growth of outbound Indian tourists to destinations desirable from a policy point of view, but not popular with our public, incentivising such destinations needs to be done through various methods described above, including subsidy, when necessary. The International Connectivity Scheme (ICS) will include of all these.

Notes

1. Elizabeth Roche, "India seeks better flight connectivity with Central Asia", *Mint*, January 14, 2019.
2. "India opens its skies to ASEAN", m.Rediff.com, December 11, 2003.
3. For a study of growth of Chinese Outbound tourism see, Yinzhi Gua, Samuel Seonseop Kim and Dallen J. Murphy, "Development Characteristics and Implications of Mainland Chinese Outbound Tourism", in *Asia-Pacific Journal of Tourism*, vol. 12, no. 4, December 2007, at researchgate.net
4. "Huānyíng to the new Chinese traveller", McKinsey & Company, 2017, *China Outbound Travelers Survey.*
5. In what ways does China use tourism to influence international politics? See, "Is China Attracting Foreign Visitors?, *China Power*, at www.chinapower.csis.org
6. 2017 Outbound Chinese Tourism and Consumption Trends: 2017 Survey, Nielsen, at www.nielsen.com>dam>docs
7. Oliver Smith, "The unstoppable rise of the Chinese traveller—where are they going and what does it mean for overtourism?", *The Telegraph*, UK, April 11, 2018.
8. Bloomberg News of December 21, 2017.
9. Sources: Cadas, Airlines' 2016 financial reports.
10. The Centre for Aviation provides independent market intelligençe, research and data solutions.
11. Asia News Network, Hamburg, Germany. Distributed by MCT Information Services. See Todd Balazovik, "Chinese Airlines fight for greater share of International Travel Market", in *China Daily*, January 19, 2014.
12. *The Economist*, taken from *Indian Express*, April 9, 2018.
13. K. Ajith, an analyst at UOB Kay Hian Pte Ltd. in Singapore.
14. *Mint*, November 25, 2017, article by Abhijnan Rej, Fellow, Observer Research Foundation.
15. *Bloomberg Businessweek*, November 6 to January 8.
16. "Belt and Road", *Indian Express*, February 8, 2019.
17. UNWTO Workshop on Chinese Outbound Tourist Market, January 17, 2018, at www2.unwto.org
18. Daniel Meesak, "Travel trends", in *Jing Daily*, February 5, 2017, at www.jingdaily.com

19. "The Indian Outbound Travel Market", at https://publications.unwto.org/sites/all/files/pdf/090616_indian_outbound_travel_excerpt.pdf
20. "India Outbound Travel", September 2015, pata.org report by OAG.
21. Saumya Tewari, "Small-town Indians are new globetrotters", in *Mint*, November 16, 2018.
22. "STHI eyes smaller cities", in *TravTalk*, April 18, 2018, 2nd fortnight issue.
23. Sohini Das, "India will account for 50 million outbound tourists by 2020. 3.7 times increase in spend by Indian travellers taking trips to international destinations this winter". *Business Standard* report, Ahmedabad. Last updated January 8, 2018, 02:12 IST.

5

The Missing Link in the Act East Policy

Andaman and Nicobar Islands: India's Untapped Strategic Assets in the Bay of Bengal[1]

Soft Power to Compliment Hard Power

An enigma in our Act East Policy is overlooking of the Andaman and Nicobar Island (ANI) chain of islands in the Bay of Bengal. This chapter presents a new perspective to fulfilment of the Act East Policy. Use of Andaman and Nicobar Islands (ANI) as a Strategic Asset both as a soft and hard power and how direct air connectivity between these islands and ASEAN/BIMSTEC countries can change the narrative.

As Robert D. Kaplan in his book *The Monsoon*[2] has stated, "Hemmed in on land by a combination of Himalayan Mountains and failing states of Pakistan, Nepal, Bangladesh and Myanmar, India can best project power at sea. India stands sentinel astride the major sea lanes from the Strait of Hormuz to Strait of Malacca, where the threat of naval containerised terrorism is very real.... India can play the role of chief balancer vis-à-vis China."

He has also mentioned the advantage India possesses in having the Great Nicobar Island as it is only 90 km from the western tip of Straits of Malacca. India's land border issues with China—including the unfortunate acceptance of Tibet as a region of China in 1954 without a quid pro quo, the Chinese meddling in the disputed Kashmir issue with Pakistan, and the CPEC passing through Indian territory, the string of pearls policy adopted by China—can only be countered by using the

Map 4: India-South East Asia-Andaman and Nicobar Islands

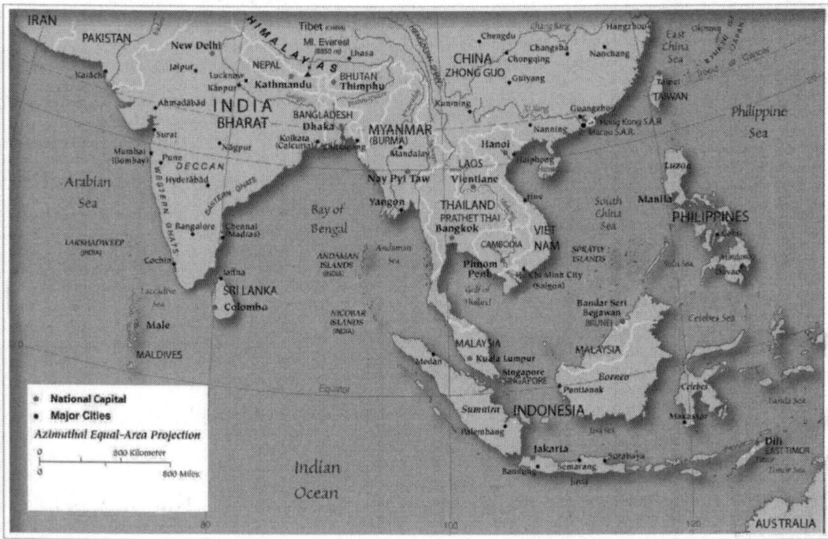

strategic advantage that India has in the Bay of Bengal. As strategic depth of world powers shifts to the Indian Ocean and growth in international trade, the importance of Straits of Malacca increases, especially for China. India's most strategic asset in Andaman and Nicobar Islands is the Great Nicobar Island (GNI). The fact that the ASEAN members are wary of Chinese designs is an advantage to India to be leveraged. China, being a much bigger economy and a more powerful military nation, always seeks an advantage over other countries not so wealthy or powerful. The Chinese Tibetan and South China Sea claims are an example of how China is bullying its neighbours to settle its claims, however irrational they may be. China always looks for a tactical advantage. The Chinese attack on India in October 1962 was during the period of Cuban missile crisis when the attention of the then two Superpowers, the USSR and USA was diverted. It withdrew unilaterally once the Cuban crisis got resolved. China, therefore, waits for an opportunity to happen. Already it is sending its submarines around the Andaman and Nicobar islands and through the Ten Degree Channel which separates the two archipelagos. Unfortunately, India is helpless as these islands did not got the archipelagic status which India was seeking from the United Nations Convention on the Law of the Sea (UNCLOS), a claim Indonesia got from UNCLOS.[3]

As stated in chapter 3, the Bay of Bengal is not only a zone of peace but full of promise. The hydrocarbons potential cannot be denied. Yadana and Yetagun in Myanmar and Arun in Indonesia have oil. The exploration activities in the Andaman Basin commenced in 1959 by the Oil and Natural Gas Commission (ONGC) Ltd. of India with about 4,533 sq km of the islands covered by reconnaissance survey. The Andaman Basin should be considered as the frontier area for hydrocarbon exploration. So far 21 wells have been drilled and some gas has been discovered which was considered sub-commercial. Geological formations of Thermogenic and Biogenic nature were found, similar to Yadana and Yetagun gas fields in Myanmar and Arun gas field in Sumatra. It is generally felt that continued exploration activities will definitely prove availability of commercial hydrocarbon in the Andamans. It is all the more necessary that we should show greater occupancy of these islands. Showing India's physical presence is very important as only 38 islands out of 571 islands/islets are inhabited. The experience of the Chinese land grab over India's un-administered territory like Ladakh (Aksai Chin region) in the Western Himalayas of India—which they occupied in 1962 and continue to occupy still—should have taught us a lesson. The recent Chinese military occupation of Paracel Islands in South City of Sansha, with their flag and supported by their navy, is another case in point of the need to have actual jurisdiction over one's own territory. These 572 islands, islets and rocks can leverage a lot of goodwill and soft power, besides the strategic location, in enhancing our presence in the Bay of Bengal. While Chinese have not claimed directly any of these islands as yet, it is reported that they have set up a listening post and an airfield in the Coco island of Myanmar right on the northern tip of the Andamans.

It is, therefore, all the more necessary to carry out a full revamp of our outdated policies towards these islands. A policy of proactive presence, taking into account the environmental factor, needs to be adopted. We should also consider our huge EEZ and its potential wealth.

This is the missing link of the Act East Policy. The existing unwritten policy towards the Andaman and Nicobar Islands has been described as that of "Masterly Inactivity and Benign Neglect".[4] But now is time to leverage these strategic assets. This chapter also looks into the failure of the present administrative set-up to leverage the huge potential of this island territory and its EEZ both from soft and hard power angle from the prism of Act East Policy. As part of leveraging our potential we should provide high value- low volume tourism by directly connecting theses islands with flights from some Asian countries to show our soft power in the Bay of Bengal.

Although available land mass for development is limited on these islands, India has a huge Exclusive Economic Zone (EEZ), nearly one-third coming as a result of these islands. With a huge EEZ, the canvas of India's strategic region of planning becomes stretched. Indian Navy and Air Force have a much wider area to cover after United Nations Conference on the Law of the Seas (UNCLOS) III gave an additional 0.66 million sq km of EEZ in Andaman and Nicobar Islands. Consequently, the defence forces formed its first joint Tri-Command in 2001 in Andaman and Nicobar Islands. This is a positive step, as was necessary at this stage to complement the vast responsibility of surveillance over the EEZ. The Andaman and Nicobar Islands stretch from south of Myanmar to north Sumatra. As a result, India's maritime border also gets stretched. India has five countries with which it has a maritime border on the eastern side in the Bay of Bengal, namely, Myanmar, Thailand, Malaysia, Indonesia and Bangladesh. As under-sea surface wealth becomes extractable the value of the Economic Zone gains importance. Then there is also the issue of Continental Shelf. The limits of the continental shelf as required by the UNCLOS are still to be determined.

Chinese ships and submarines have been going past these islands for some time. As pointed out by Bertil Lintner, "In August 2017, 14 People's Liberation Army Navy (PLAN) ships were spotted by Indians near Andamans. They were said to be tasked for 'anti-piracy duties'—one of the reasons also given for acquiring a base in Djibouti—but ships were accompanied by Chinese submarines. Admiral Sunil Lanba, the chief of

Indian Navy, said in a press conference in New Delhi on 1 December 2017 that PLAN deployments in the Indian Ocean comprise on average six to seven ships on two deployments annually."[5]

Andaman and Nicobar Islands (ANI): Soft Power Complementing Hard Power

While an attempt has been made to build up the Andaman and Nicobar Islands in military terms, if India can attract tourists from ASEAN countries to these islands directly by air by creating world-class ecotourism resorts with top-class amenities, keeping in mind all environmental constraints, India would dramatically change the perception of both Indians and foreigners with regard to India's reach in the Indian Ocean. India needs to leverage this soft power. "Soft Power" as a concept was developed by Joseph Samuel Nye[6] of Harvard University who described it as the ability to extract and cooperate, rather than coerce, use force or give money as a means of persuasion. In his book, *Soft Power: The Means to Success in World Politics*, 2004, Nye says that "Seduction is always more attractive then coercion and many values like Democracy, Human Rights and Individual Opportunities are deeply seductive." Therefore, it is better to co-opt people than coerce them. Soft Power is not merely the same as influence. Soft power is also more than just persuasion. It is the ability to attract and attraction often leads to acquiescence.

The location of the Great Nicobar Island (GNI), a 921 sq km island (Singapore is 721 sq km) and southernmost tip of India, near the western entrance of Straits of Malacca and about 80 km from Sumatra, gives it great strategic potential. With the opening of Naval Air Station (NAS) Baaz at Campbell Bay in Great Nicobar Islands, opportunities to fully exploit the geographic location of Great Nicobar Islands in commercial terms in coordination with defence requirements should be carried out without any delay. This will complement the soft power that India needs to display at the western entrance of Straits of Malacca. About one-third of the world's seaborne trade passes by GNI. This activity will not disturb the forest and biosphere reserves in the GNI but will enhance India's status in the Malacca region. The Nancowry-Kamorta harbour in the Nicobars is yet another fantastic feature of the Nicobar. This harbour is excellent for ships and submarines and is quite close to Great Nicobar Island. In a major development, India is developing its maiden deep-sea port of Sabang island in Sumatra of Indonesia opposite the Great Nicobar Island, barely 100 km across the seas on the western entrance of the Malacca Strait. During the visit of Prime Minister Modi to Indonesia in May 2018, it was decided to set up a special task force to enhance the connectivity between the strategic Andaman and Nicobar Island and provinces of Sumatra island to promote trade, tourism and people-to-people contact. A joint statement was also issued in this context. While no mention was made of Naval ships being permitted to visit this port, the Indonesian side did say, "I think it's important to build balance of power to be built here, so that no superpower can create instability."[7] Bert Lintner has stated in his book,

> That is still being discussed, but, in May 2018, India secured access to the strategic island of Sabang on the norther tip of Sumatra. India will invest in the port and an economic zone of Sabang, which is located less than 500 kilometers to the entrance of Malacca Strait. Besides development of its 40-metre deep port, good for all types of vessels, including submarines, Indian Naval ships will also be permitted to use those facilities. Luhut Pandjsitan, Indonesia's minister for Maritime affairs and a former military officer, said at the time that he was critical of China's Belt and Road Initiative: "We do not want to be controlled by BRI". He also questioned China's unilateral claims including parts of Indonesia's maritime exclusive maritime zone.[8]

Leveraging Soft Power

That Bay of Bengal is truly Indian is correct as we have the Andaman and Nicobar Archipelagos going right across it. Opening these islands for foreign tourism for display of soft power will have a great impact and will be a showcase of our Act East Policy. However, it will have to be conditional to environmental considerations of a fragile ecosystem and the Indian Supreme Court's order on it. It is ironic that while the defence forces in the 1970s and 1980s did not allow tourism to come up in these islands for fear of 'foreign power', in the 1990s they reversed this hypothesis as they felt that tourism can be a good source of intelligence. With 572 islands and islets and a large Exclusive Economic Zone (EEZ), which is one-third of India's total, to guard against poachers, pirates, non-state actors, it is a near impossible and expensive task as only about three dozen of these islands are inhabited. New settlements in these islands are ruled out as most of the islands are declared as forest reserve. About 96 per cent of the land in these Islands is under forest cover. Therefore, a strategy of tourism development with security and environmental sustainability in mind needs to be evolved. This is possible when tourism resorts are developed with specific locations which command a position for surveillance and are not put together at one or two islands, as is being done now. Similarly, tourism requires highly skilled and trained staff coming out of hotel management institutes. Some such locals or others can be picked and trained by security agencies for providing accurate intelligence while they work. Therefore, tourism and security should be intertwined with Foreign Policy to achieve the best results. There is a need to abandon the unwritten policy followed so far of "Masterly Inactivity and Benign Neglect" for these islands, and go for proactive development.

Therefore, for any Act East Policy, India's 572 islands, islets and rocks running as two archipelagos for 750 km connecting Myanmar to western entrance of Malacca Straits, is a great asset waiting to be put to use.

Chinese Views on Andaman and Nicobar Islands

Chinese commentators readily acknowledge India's superior geographical position in the Andaman and Nicobar Islands just like the Chinese have in Tibet which they occupied by military force in 1950. Further, a Chinese commentator sees the establishment of Andaman and Nicobar Integrated Command in 2001 as a potential challenge to them. As Liu Jianzhong writes, "By virtue of its geographical advantage,

India has taken a lead in enhancing its control over the western exit of Straits of Malacca between Malaya peninsula and the Sumatra Island."[9] Ma Ying[10] from the Shanghai Institute of International Studies (SIIS) states that the geopolitical-political position of Andaman and Nicobar Islands is such that being only 80 miles from Straits of Malacca it is like an unsinkable super carrier. As a matter of fact, with four airfields in these Islands there may be no need to keep an aircraft carrier in the Bay of Bengal. It is also like a protective screen and guards India's SLOC. *The Military Command at the Andaman and Nicobar Islands is seen to be part of an exclusionary policy of India designed to keep extra-regional powers out.* It could provide a check on China's westward expansion into the Indian Ocean.[11] Further, as Shi Chunlin of Dalian Maritime University (DMU) states, while India's increased military deployment plays a role of guardian over Straits of Malacca and can monitor in peacetime the transit of Chinese warships and merchant vessels, in wartime the Indian Navy could quickly seal off the Straits of Malacca and other passages entering the Indian Ocean from the east. Liu Quing[12] of the National Defence University (NDU) goes further and states that "based on the 2009 Indian Maritime Doctrine Andaman & Nicobar Command could not only direct a distant blockade against China on the western side of the Straits of Malacca, it could also launch a naval offensive ashore against the Chinese mainland." The Indian interest in the Straits of Malacca is further enforced by India's Look East Policy (LEP) of 1991.

India's oil interests with Vietnam in South China Sea and the offshore blocks that Indian companies have acquired in areas like the Sakhalin Islands off Vladivostok in Eastern Russia and even the oil blocks off the Venezuela coast require that the Straits of Malacca remain open, peaceful and within India's capacity to ensure that no unwanted power tries to block it. Protecting the western entrance of the Straits of Malacca is not only in India's interest but falls into its blue-water capabilities as the Great Nicobar Island (GNI) tip is only 80 miles from it. While it is true that in 2006 the Indian Fleet Review showcased its blue-water capability with over 50 naval vessels including an aircraft carrier, submarine and advanced stealth frigates, India is yet to consolidate its naval presence in Andaman and Nicobar Islands. Setting up of a new Naval Air Base Baaz in Campbell Bay in the Great Nicobar Island in 2012 is a step in this direction.

It may be noted that South China Sea, claimed by China, has had presence of Indian naval ships. In 2000, a naval flotilla of five ships, including a submarine, was sent to South China Sea with port calls at Singapore, Vietnam, South Korea, Japan and Indonesia. This was seen as a challenge to China by the Chinese authorities. In three separate steps Indian naval ships were sent to South China Seas to familiarise them with a potential theatre of operation. *The Economist* magazine has stated that the US Navy finds the Indian Navy up to North Atlantic Treaty Organisation (NATO) standards.

The Indo-Pacific and The Nicobar Islands—Strategic Angle

The Great Nicobar Island

There is a special need to concentrate on the Nicobar Islands in order to implement the Act East Policy in full. Despite the rising stakes in the newly defined Asia-Pacific, with US and Quad group confronting China for its hegemonic role, India has yet to define its role and leverage the game changer in its Andaman and Nicobar group of islands.[13] The report of the Trade Development Authority on the Great Nicobar Island, the largest of the Nicobar group, produced in the early 1970s needs to be reviewed and revised. This report had proposed that after the British leave Hong Kong and Hong Kong merges with mainland China, a number of rich Indian business groups would look for a location to relocate themselves. It was envisaged that Great Nicobar Island as a free port had great potential in attracting such people. Unfortunately, no decision was taken by the Government of India and Hong Kong is now a Special Administered Region (SAR) of China but the option is still open. However, with the latest developments in Hong Kong and the Chinese Government not honouring their treaty obligations with the United Kingdom, the future of Hong Kong is in a balance. The Great Nicobar still retains its potential due to its strategic location on the mouth of Straits of Malacca. This island has nearly 1,000 sq km of land mass (larger than Singapore) with sufficient fresh water. However, about two-thirds of the Great Nicobar Islands have since been declared as a Biosphere Reserve, consisting of 885 sq km. Within it is the Campbell Bay National Park of 426 sq km. Therefore, only one-third of the landmass is available. Of this, some land at the southern tip facing Straits of Malacca has gone under water, including the lighthouse, due to the Tsunami of 2004. In effect, about 130 sq km will be available for development, including defence requirements and land for local settlers. Even with 130 sq km of land and more by land reclamation, the potential for declaring the Great Nicobar Islands as a free port is still a viable option. Already a container terminal at Campbell Bay of the Great Nicobar Island is coming up, and will provide transhipment, water and bunker facilities. The Indian Navy has an air base called 'Baaz' located at Campbell Bay with a short airstrip which is under expansion and hopefully will be a full-fledged airstrip soon. The strategic decision to be taken by India is to announce the creation of a free port at the Great Nicobar Island to come up over the next ten years or so.[14]

The only strategic decision taken by the Government for Great Nicobar Island so far was to settle 330 odd ex-servicemen families in the Great Nicobar Island in 1969 as part of government sponsored ex-serviceman rehabilitation scheme. It was considered that they will be the eyes of the government and will report any suspicious activity. These ex-servicemen families can now be used for tourism and other purposes as it has a small population of educated farming community there and have land with them.

Declaring Great Nicobar Island as a Free Port

Hong Kong was handed back to China on July 1, 1997 by the UK, peacefully, after more than 150 years of British rule imposed after Britain defeated China in the First Opium War. China had never recognised the "unequal treaties" allowing Britain's rule of Hong Kong island, the Kowloon peninsula and later its lease of the rural New Territories. However, under the Joint Declaration of 1984 on handing over of Hong Kong by the British to the People's Republic of China, it was agreed by China that Hong Kong's autonomy was guaranteed under the "one country, two systems" agreement enshrined in the Sino-British Joint Declaration signed by then Chinese Premier Zhao Ziyang and British Prime Minister Margaret Thatcher in 1984. The imposition of a security law on Hong Kong in July 2020, after a major protest by students and others of Hong Kong, was seen as a "clear and serious" violation of the 1984 Joint Declaration, and consequently the UK offered around 3 million residents of the former colony a path to British citizenship. The student movement in Hong Kong, which continued for many months, was ruthlessly suppressed after passing of the laws. Also known as the Anti-Extradition Law Amendment Bill Movement and the Fugitive Offenders amendment bill by the Hong Kong government in 2019-2020, the bill would allow extradition to jurisdictions with which Hong Kong did not have extradition agreements, including mainland China and Taiwan.

This led to concerns in the West that Hong Kong residents and visitors would be exposed to the legal system of mainland China, thereby undermining Hong Kong's autonomy and infringing civil liberties.

The US House of Representatives passed a bill on October 15 sought by pro-democracy protesters in Hong Kong that aims to defend civil rights in the semi-autonomous territory, prompting an angry response from China. The Hong Kong Human Rights and Democracy Act[15] has drawn rare bipartisan support in the US Congress. The law would end the Hong Kong-US special trading status unless the State Department certifies annually that city authorities are respecting human rights and the rule of law.

Considering the brewing issues described above, the future of Hong Kong as an international financial centre is possibly in jeopardy. In a recent development the Hong Kong government plans to raise the stamp duty on equity transactions by 30 per cent to boost its revenue as the city is set to rack up a record fiscal deficit, and Financial Secretary Paul

Chan warned that the shortfall would persist for several years. This is the first time since 1933 and has already sent shock waves in the local stock market.[16] It is, therefore, the right time to fill the vacuum created by happenings in Hong Kong to declare and create a Free Port in the Great Nicobar Island.

In a recent article by the author,[17] it was proposed that the time is ripe to revisit the old proposal of declaring the Great Nicobar Island as a Free Port:

> China's peaceful takeover of Hong Kong on 1 July 1997 was based on a properly signed agreement between the Government of UK and People's Republic of China and was registered with the United Nations, in which the Chinese guaranteed a 50-year extension of its capitalist system. It, therefore, provided for the continuation of the existing British legal system until 2047. However, China's move to change the same, in violation of the agreement, the imposition of its harsh national security law and the rise in tension with the West in general and the United States in particular, have jeopardized the future of Hong Kong as a global financial centre and a free port. As flight of capital takes place from Hong Kong, there will be a search for an alternate venue. On the south-west of Hong Kong is Singapore, an island and another leading global financial centre, located at the confluence of the South China Sea and the eastern entrance of the Malacca Strait. While at the western entrance of the Malacca Strait is India's Great Nicobar Island—the entry point to the Bay of Bengal and Indian Ocean.[18]

With the UK and US reacting to these developments in Hong Kong it is expected that this will be followed by other countries as repressive rules start to choke the spirit of Hong Kong. This is a great moment for India to cash in. In Bay of Bengal the location of the Great Nicobar Island is such that it is on the international shipping route near the western entrance of Malacca Strait with about 100,000 ships passing by. Already a Container Terminal is coming up at Campbell Bay of

Great Nicobar island.[19] Over time a Free Port should come up provided the Government makes an announcement now so that it gets the first-mover advantage. The great advantage of the Great Nicobar Island, besides its location, is the availability of land and fresh water by perennial rivers. While the Great Nicobar Island consists of 1,044 sq km in area (bigger than Singapore at 720 sq km and smaller than Hong Kong at 1,106 sq km, over time about two-thirds of the island has been put under forest reserve or biosphere reserve. Still, a third of the island is available for development. Further, either the forest can be denotified, which is not recommended, or new land reclamation from the sea can be done. With 330 ex-servicemen families settled in 1969 under a rehabilitation scheme with allotted land and dairy animals, the island has a great potential.

By declaring the Great Nicobar Island as a Free Port, India's case to join the Malacca Strait Patrol (MSP), consisting of Singapore, Indonesia, Malaysia and Thailand, becomes stronger.

For any Act East Policy India's 572 islands, islets and rocks running as two archipelagos for 750 km connecting Myanmar to the western entrance of Malacca Straits, is a great asset waiting to be put to use.

The Indian interest in the Straits of Malacca is further enforced by India's Look East Policy (LEP) of 1991 and Act East Policy of 2014. India's oil interests with Vietnam in South China Sea and the offshore blocks that Indian companies have acquired in areas like the Sakhalin Islands off Vladivostok in Eastern Russia, and even the oil blocks off the Venezuela coast, require that the Straits of Malacca remain open, peaceful and within India's capacity to ensure that no unwanted power tries to block it. Protecting the western entrance of the Straits of Malacca is not only in India's interest but falls within its blue-water capabilities as the Great Nicobar Island (GNI) tip is only 80 miles from it. While it is true that in 2006 the Indian Fleet Review showcased its blue-water capability with over 50 naval vessels including an aircraft carrier, submarine and advanced stealth frigates, India is yet to consolidate its naval presence in Andaman and Nicobar Islands, especially the Nicobar group of islands.

The Nicobar group of islands are ideally located for tourism as well as strategic surveillance of the Bay of Bengal. The Indian Navy under the Joint Command conducts biennial exercise called MILAN along with a large number of Navies from Indo-Pacific since 1995. Now over 17 friendly countries participate with their ships. The 2020 Milan exercise which was to have 30 foreign navies, had to be postponed due to the Corona virus. Therefore, from a strategic point of view, these archipelagos are getting their importance but their awareness from a civilian point of view leaves much to be desired. Opening these islands to international tourism will give India the much desired leverage in the Indo-Pacific.

Access by Air: Direct International Connectivity

Although these islands are over 750 km long they are connected by commercial air flights only to Port Blair, the capital city, while there are three other airports available with the defence forces. In the Nicobar group of islands there are two airports, the big one at the Air Force base in Car Nicobar, which has an airstrip long enough to take all types of aircraft, and another smaller one in the Great Nicobar Island at Campbell Bay. So far Port Blair is connected by civil flights only from Chennai, Kolkata and Delhi (via Bhubaneshwar) in India, though there has been much improvement over the years. There are, however, no direct flights from abroad. Foreign tourist charter flights are also permitted to land at Port Blair subject to the fulfilment of guidelines of the Director General of Civil Aviation (DGCA). But there are hardly any. Two more short airstrips are available with the defence forces in Dilglipur (Shivpur) in the north Andamans and at Campbell Bay in the south in the Great Nicobar Island. Both these are getting extended and have been declared Naval airbases. A few islands are also interconnected by helicopters operated by Pawan Hans. However, not many seats are available in these small helicopters and are largely used by officials travelling up and down. There is a differential tariff structure, one for islanders which is subsidised, and the other for the rest. Recently a sea plane service has been introduced to a limited number of destinations. Port Blair is 1,200 km from mainland India (Chennai or Kolkata). Air connectivity is limited and expensive and is two hours by jet aircraft from either place. There is very little connectivity within the islands in spite of four airstrips available from Diglipur in the north Andamans to Campbell Bay in the Great Nicobar Islands in the south. Only recently a passenger helicopter service has started with very limited capacity. While Andaman is within the Directorate General of Civil Aviation's (DGCA) Group Disbursal Guidelines which forces airlines to connect to North-East, J&K and Andamans, the services are inadequate, and only Port Blair is being touched in spite of the fact that island of Car Nicobar offers an excellent airport with a growing traffic. Earlier Indian Airlines used to have a weekly service from Kolkata, Port Blair, Car Nicobar, Chennai. This exists no more. Further, due to free pricing, air tickets can be prohibitive during seasons. There are no international flights connecting Port Blair or any other island in spite of the fact that this airport was declared international over a decade back.

Complementarity between Tourism and Security

Tourism can be a means to display India's soft power and physical presence. Similar to what Bollywood films have done to India's image abroad, by encouraging high-end tourism into Andaman and Nicobar Islands from foreign nations with direct flights from South East Asia, India will display its soft power. This is what China is doing in Hainan Island where both tourism and an underground submarine base exist. It will make other countries, non-state actors and poachers realise and appreciate that India has effective civil jurisdiction right up to Straits of Malacca. Mere show of military strength is not the best manner of befriending other nations. Opening these islands with a welcome greeting will make them feel welcome.

Traditional Poaching and Its Consequences

Over time India's EEZ around these islands (constituting nearly one-third of India's total), have been misused by fishermen coming from countries like Thailand, Myanmar and beyond, violating its marine environment and wealth. These encroachments upon Indian territories were minor in nature as these fishermen normally came in small boats and would set up a temporary camp in a remote island and go away when their boat could not hold any more fish, sea cucumbers, corals, etc. However, over time poaching got more organised with 'mother ships' waiting on the High Seas within India's EEZ to collect the fish and other marine products from their smaller ships. Increasingly there were cases where these islands started getting used by terrorists and other organisations for purposes of arms, drug transhipments or any such similar activity.

Leaving these islands alone with poor surveillance is more dangerous than using them. It is, therefore, necessary to have a policy of proper surveillance through tourism which could also be cost effective. This theft of marine products and environmental damage could be worth US$ 100-200 million. New settlements in these islands is not possible for many reasons. Largely because, over time, 96 per cent of the surface of the islands has been declared as Forest and therefore allotment of land for settlement is not possible. Second, there may be issues of availability of potable water. Prevention of these activities could, perhaps, be achieved by having a tourism policy which at one end would support and complement the security issues and on the other end take care of environmental issues as well as be remunerative and employment creating.

Policy of Masterly Inactivity and Benign Neglect

Government of India has been taking a line of least resistance, maintained an undeclared policy described as 'Masterly Inactivity and Begin Neglect' towards these islands and continued to keep them isolated and undeveloped. The Ministry of Home Affairs (MHA) which was directly responsible for these islands did not encourage any major improvement. The undeclared policy of Masterly Inactivity and Benign Neglect continues even now, but is slowly changing. The Government is now keen to open up more islands for tourism. With subsidised shipping for the islanders to keep a link with the mainland, a bit of subsidised inter-island shipping, resettlement of a few ex-military soldier families in the Great Nicobar Island to keep vigil, an attempt to grow rubber in Katchal Island of Nicobar, and resettlement of east Bengali refugees in the Andaman Islands some steps were taken but no major change was permitted. All other proposals to develop these islands like a free port in Great Nicobar Islands or opening a medical college in Port Blair was discouraged by the Home Ministry which was administratively in charge of these islands. The tribal policy to keep the tribals away from exploitation by non-tribals followed by the British in these islands was retained.

These islands have extremely dense forests and are an environmentally sensitive region. Based on a public interest litigation filed by an NGO on misuse of the islands environmentally, Prof. Shekhar Singh of Indian Institute of Public Administration was asked by the Supreme Court to prepare a report on Environmental Issues of Andaman and Nicobar Islands which he submitted and was accepted by the Supreme Court. While the report is long and needs changes in the present scenario, in so far as tourism is concerned it states:

> Eco-tourism: The landscape of Andaman & Nicobar Islands has good potential for eco-tourism. Interpretation Centres, camping facilities, bird watching, cruise in the creeks and trekking programmes should be provided under eco-tourism development. Rich flora and fauna sites could be added attractions for tourism in the islands. Potential for low volume, high value eco-tourism aimed at promoting education and appreciation of nature should be exploited. It is important to check growing commercialisation of eco-tourism through introduction of environment audit system.

It would, therefore be correct to say that the Supreme Court judgment gives a direction to tourism which is ecotourism and in that it qualifies that it should be "low volume-high value". However, the present tourism policy followed by Andaman and Nicobar Islands has not taken into account the "low volume-high value" tourism concept. Tourism has an outstanding potential in these islands as there are very few archipelagos left undisturbed in the world. In addition, it also has four airfields; two long airfields and two smaller ones (which are being upgraded) and are close to South East Asia.

Security, Environment and Act East Policy: A Synthesis Needed

Now Security, Environment and Act East Policy have to come together to maximise the potential of these islands. Ecotourism sites with built-in environmental safeguards are a major attraction and are found in all parts of the world. The business of ecotourism is to sell environment in its full beauty and not allow it to be degraded. In the US, the National Park Services (NPS) are known to provide excellent facilities for ecotourism which are very popular but at the same time take into account environmental safeguards. Over 6.2 million tourists visited the national parks of the US in 2007. Of late, even leading and respectable Indian magazines like *India Today*[20] have condemned some acts of over enthusiasm by MoEF and described self-proclaimed over-enthusiastic environmentalists as green terrorists. There is also a need to review the various rulings/court orders pertaining to the Islands to ensure that strategic and development issues are not sacrificed in the garb of environmental protection or unnecessary security precautions.

Ecotourism is also a protector of environment. This is so because the ecotourism industry thrives on a good environment and its preservation is most important to them. The real ecotourism of these islands lies in its fabulous coral wealth and the big fish which will attract scuba divers and deep-sea anglers from all over the world. It also lies in its dense rain forests and bird life. Of course, the ecosystem of these islands is fragile and needs careful management. This means that limited tourism can flourish in these islands without necessarily opening the hinterland. The sport of scuba diving is a major specialised tourist attraction. In only a few places in the world are coral reefs with clear water available as they have to be within a specific water temperature zone.

Nils Finn Munch-Petersen,[21] who had submitted the preliminary project formulation framework for UNDP in 1992, had stated that "Present Trends in International Tourism Market indicates that travellers comprising of upper sections of the market are becoming more sophisticated and search for destinations that not only offer sun, sand and entertainment. ... Diving, sports, fishing and nature oriented tourism (Eco Tourism) comprise significant special interest in the market." He further stated: "In Tourism Industry, down market drives out the upmarket." He gives the example of Bhutan and Galapagos as upmarket, Maldives as midmarket and a planned tourism area, while Nepal was an example of unplanned tourism. He emphasised the need and importance for planned tourism development as "well planned tourism may be a vehicle for growth". In this context, he further states that "Andaman & Nicobar Islands are dangerously close to defining themselves as a down market destination in the future." The report has gone into details of tourism sites like grading of beaches with sand quality, water, gradient and character, marine parks, national parks and sanctuaries with area plant and wildlife available. It has also identified potential markets.

The six-volume UNDP report on Environmentally Sustainable Tourism Policy for the Andaman and Nicobar Islands carried out under supervision of the World Tourism Organisation[22] in the 1990s has been ignored by the Andaman and Nicobar Administration. However, Andaman Islands as also Nicobar Islands have the potential to become international high-end tourist destinations if full environment safeguards are introduced and implemented. What is happening at present is that neither a policy towards environmentally sustainable tourism nor any policy to integrate tourism with strategic vision is being followed.

There is a serious need to examine the policy towards connecting these islands to the mainland and to foreign destinations at a reasonable cost to attract tourists. Amitabh Kant, a well-known tourism expert and policymaker in India, in his book *Branding India* states that Andaman and Nicobar Islands attract backpackers who come by boat to these islands: "a single backpacker consumes a total subsidy of Rs. 12,000 whereas he spends only Rs. 9,000 during his stay in the islands.... The upscale tourist spends US$ 1,500 or more during one week's stay as compared to US$ 200 spent by a backpacker".

Leveraging Soft Power

Based on an assessment of the Intelligence Bureau no uninhabited island was allowed to be developed for tourism. A diametrically opposite view was taken by Maldives who opened their uninhabited islands but did not allow foreign tourists in their islands where there was a settled population in order to avoid conflict of cultures. Instead, they allotted full islands to well-known Resort Hotels who have established credentials as eco-friendly hotels on payment of royalty.

Professor Aprajit Biswas of Centre of African Studies, University of Mumbai in an article on Small Arms and Drug Trafficking in the IOR has shown how Andaman and Nicobar Islands have been used by drug traffickers, ISI of Pakistan and LTTE of Sri Lanka. The potential complementarity between security, environment and tourism needs to be studied in a holistic manner for Andaman and Nicobar Islands. While security is paramount, environmental protection is equally important. There is a need to fine tune the meeting ground of security and environment and show how controlled ecotourism can complement the needs of security and environment of these islands.

Once security becomes lax, as it is today, with insufficient surveillance over the 572 islands and islets, the encroachment that starts to take place with/without the knowledge of the authorities by illegal immigrants leads to degradation of forests and environment. Since many of these islands and islets are not visited by even the lower government authorities for years, there is no way of finding out the encroachment. The lower functionaries of government—be it tehsildar of revenue department or forest inspectors—do not have any independent means of transport between islands, and activities on some uninhabited islands go unreported. The example of Myanmarese fishermen collecting sea cucumbers illegally in these islands even these days and having permanent hideouts for spares and equipment in uninhabited islands has been found. Such hideouts are serious security threats.

While the MHA remains conservative, the military has now realised that opening the islands to tourism is advantageous from a security point of view. There is a need to reconcile these two views. The degradation done by illegal immigrants and low-end tourists is far more damaging than that done by high-end tourists. This is so because high-value tourists are far more eco-conscious than low-value tourists or illegal immigrants, and can be better regulated. Further, low-end hostels, one or two-star hotels do not have the facilities, funds or even the desire to manage sewage and waste, which is necessary. Further, locating resorts in habited islands can easily lead to conflict of cultures and its consequences. Creating high-end resorts in uninhabited islands will have its virtues and potential intelligence gathering to ensure that nothing anti-national or illegal takes place.

Environment conundrum became a deterrent to security and tourism. Two recent issues show how powers provided under Environment Protection Acts have become a deterrent to security and tourism. First is the case of Narcondam Island, where the Navy was refused permission from setting up a radar due to a population of about 300 Hornbill birds which are, perhaps, endemic to the island as it was felt by some environmentalists that the birds may get disturbed. There is, however, no basis to the argument as hornbills are found in urban areas and setting up a radar should not cause disturbance. This issue was subsequently resolved and permission granted. The second is the case of land allotment to a leading Five-Star group for a resort in Havelock Island under a duly approved scheme and with proper process. Having got the land for the resort they are unable to do anything with it as the rules regarding coastal regulation changed which made it difficult for them to construct. When the tender was issued rules provided for no construction up to 250 metres of high tide line. After the award of the tender, the rules changed and disallowed any construction up to 500 metres of high tide line. This makes respectable hoteliers with a good and environment friendly record shy away, and unscrupulous entrepreneurs take over. Inconsistency of government policy and frequent changes in it is of course the bane of India's economic model and applies to Andaman and Nicobar Islands also.

There are National Parks, Sanctuaries and Reserve Forests each having different levels of regulation. These three categories take away 7,000 sq km of land surface out of 8,249 sq km. While it may be difficult to go in for tourism activities in national parks and sanctuaries, reserve forests do allow limited use for ecotourism. However, the Forest Department of Andaman and Nicobar Islands has as yet no plans for development of tourism inside reserve forests which is a done practice worldwide. Once this issue is sorted out there is possibility of limited high end eco-friendly tourism in remote locations. Worldwide reserve forests have been developed for ecotourism under certain rules and guidelines which are strictly followed. Wildlife sanctuaries like Kruger National Park in South Africa also have enclaves for tourists where they can stay under strict rules of not making noise or throwing garbage, etc.

The Andamans also represent India's cultural Heritage. The British made these islands into a Penal Settlement from 1789. Consequently, the Cellular Jail and Ross Island and other buildings are part of the Penal Settlement days when Indian political prisoners, also called freedom fighters, were incarcerated in these islands. The old Cellular Jail is now declared as a National Monument and Ross Island, the seat of the British Chief Commissioner, is being preserved by the Navy and is a tourist site. These islands were the only part of India under Japanese occupation for three and a half years during World War II. Their cement bunkers and canons guarding many of the islands are still available for viewing.

Mother Nature has been extra generous to Andaman and Nicobar Islands in endowing them with a phenomenally rich biodiversity which is displayed in its varied assemblage of flora and fauna on land and in water surrounding the islands. Their uniqueness lies in high degree of endemism, particularly in fauna. Andaman and Nicobar Islands are also a great attraction for bird watchers as much as for their rich, unique and endemic biodiversity. As many as 270 species and sub-species are reported by ornithologists. These islands are part of the 218 Endemic Bird Areas (EBA) of the world. Its mangrove vegetation protects these islands from soil erosion. Its wildlife consists of wild pigs, dugongs, elephants, turtles, snakes. Coral reefs, sea cucumbers, and shells of various types form part of marine wild life. It has 96 wildlife sanctuaries, nine national parks and one biosphere reserve. This can be a great attraction for nature loving tourists if facilities for stay are provided and tours under controlled conditions are made mandatory.

The potential for deep sea fishing is immense. However, on ground there does not appear to be any actual improvement. The coastline of all the islands adds up to 1,962 km in length. It is bordered with luxuriant mangroves and magnificent coral reefs on the fringes. A clean and pollution-free environment and lush green forests of the islands surrounded by blue sea water should make Andaman and Nicobar Islands one of the most favoured destinations for ecotourism in the world. However, this is not so. The poor quality of infrastructure and, in addition, the increasing population of crocodiles in the beaches and creeks is a cause of concern. Crocodiles breed very fast and the ban on their killing is making it more difficult to encourage beach tourism. There is need to review the ban on killing of crocodiles as it is leading to attacks by them on human beings and many people have died and lost limbs while swimming. Notices at beaches to beware of crocodiles is driving away tourists from the beaches. There is need to take the crocodile out of the endangered list for Andamans as it is no more endangered.

It may be seen from the Table 1 that Andaman and Nicobar Islands has the highest percentage of forests at over 90 per cent of land surface when compared to other islands elsewhere in the world and lowest percentage of agriculture. This should be seen as an advantage as ecotourism with dense forests and beaches is a preferred option with ecotourists. In fact, the high level of forest reserves gives Andaman and Nicobar Islands a special place for nature related activities and reduces the pull of social resort tourism. Forest area has a number of restrictions which have to be honoured and generally allow only upmarket tourism because of these restrictions. Worldwide forest tourism in reserves is becoming popular. However, as already stated Andaman and Nicobar Islands have no forest related tourism as yet, especially when the forests of Andaman and Nicobar Islands are extremely dense rain forests rarely found in the world today. Andaman and Nicobar Islands do not have any major animals in the forest which are likely to be hunted. There are iguanas, other reptiles and birds. The protected species have already been listed by the Forest and Environment Department. Unlike forest departments in countries like the US, Australia and New Zealand and even some forest departments of Indian States, there has been very little work done by the Forest Department to promote ecotourism in the forest areas. There is a need to plan out the high quality of the limited number of tourist resorts inside these forests. There is a growing breed of nature lovers who travel to all corners of the world to such locations. It will not only be a revenue earner but also bring awareness of the environmental degradation happening inside, if any.

The Tourism Policy document issued by the Andaman and Nicobar Islands clearly states in its strategy to go in for Strategic Partnerships. It states, "Formulate strategic tourism partnerships with neighbouring international destinations like Phuket for leveraging increased visits to these islands." So far, no such partnership has been signed or even negotiated. The only document is the MoU signed between the Lt. Governor of Andaman and Nicobar Islands and Governor of Phuket signed in 2005 but this remains unimplemented. This is unfortunate as this agreement talked of tourism promotion, solid waste management and cultural exchanges, amongst other things. In order to compare tourism policies of other countries, given below is a comparison with Bhutan, South Pacific Islands based on a UN Report, the Maldives Model and Report of Ecotourism Association of Australia (EAA).

Comparative Tourism Policies of Selected Countries

Tourism Development in Bhutan: High Value-Low Volume Tourism Policy

It goes to the credit of the Royal Government of Bhutan that they were aware that unrestricted flow of tourists can have negative impacts on Bhutan's pristine environment and its rich and unique culture. The government, therefore, adopted a policy of "High value-low volume" tourism, controlling the type and quantity of Tourism right from the start. Until 1991 the Bhutan Tourism Corporation (BTC), a quasi-autonomous and self-financing body, implemented the government's tourism policy. All tourists, up to that time, came as guests of BTC,

Table 1: Comparative Statistics of Andaman and Nicobar Islands with Large Tropical Islands

Name of Island Nation	Land Area (km)	Population in Lakhs 2001-2005	Density of Population (net density of Population)	Per Capital Income in 2005 in US$	Area Under Forest (per cent)	Area Under Agri-culture (per cent)	Tourists arrival in Lakhs 2005
Andaman and Nicobar Islands	8,249	3.56	43 **(431)**	67	90	2.3	0.56
Solomon Islands	28,896	5.81	20 **(180)**	1,900	88.8	0.03	0.09
Trinidad & Tobago	5,128	10.56	206 **(416)**	21,700	50.5	26	4.63
Fiji	18,274	9.18	50 **(91)**	4,100	44.6	35	5.5
Samoa	2831	2.17	77 **(122)**	5,400	37.2	33	1.01
Vanuatu	12,189	2.11	17 **(27)**	2,900	36.7	12	0.62
Jamaica	10830	27.8	257 **(367)**	4,800	30	47	14.78
Cape Verde	4,033	4.99	124 **(157)**	7,000	21.1	18	1.97
Barbados	430	3.56	656 **(688)**	18,900	4.7	-	5.47
Maldives	300	3.86	1287 **(1331)**	4,600	3.3	-	3.95
Seychelles	451	0.82	182 **(546)**	16,600	66.7	-	1.29
Singapore	707.1	46.08	6,517 **(679)**	49,990	3.3	-	89.43

Source: Tourism Policy issued by Andaman and Nicobar Island Administration.

which in turn operated the tour, transport services and nearly all the hotels and accommodation facilities. The government privatised tourism in October 1991 to encourage increased private sector participation in the tourism sector. What Bhutan insists on is a minimum payment/ spend by a tourist per day which is about US$ 200 per day. This might vary from high to low season but it acts as a filter to discourage low-value tourists who add to volumes but not revenues and may cause environmental damage. This strategy adopted by Bhutan is working well as it keeps this sensitive area free of the ill effects of pollution and degradation which comes with low-end tourism.

Tourism Development in South Pacific Islands is based on the concept of ecotourism that respects tradition and culture; protects and preserves the environment; and educates and welcomes visitors. In addition, ecotourism should be sustainable economically over the long term. In American Samoa, this definition is intended to define ecotourism at the national and local level. A UN Report on tourism in South Pacific has come out with policy recommendations for ecotourism. The government adopted a definition of ecotourism that was further developed by the Pacific Business Centre at the University of Hawaii. The American Samoa National Park was established by the United States Congress in 1988. This makes the park part of the US National Park System (NPS).

Mass tourism is considered the main threat to the sustainability of ecotourism, especially since the environment in the national park is so fragile. There is a national park staff trained to counteract some aspects of this threat. For example, they monitor tourist activities and educate villagers about using the park site for low-impact tourism development. Home stay programmes are encouraged and initiated instead of hotel development. Villagers are able to coordinate tours rather than face the risks presented by group tours. Educational ecotours are also promoted.

The Maldives Model

The Maldives is an archipelago in the Arabian Sea/Indian Ocean which has evolved into a high-end eco-friendly tourism destination. In its environmental regulations and standards for the tourism sector, it has adopted certain principles like maximum built-up area to be restricted to 20 per cent of land mass. Reservation of aesthetics, integrity of the resorts, with height restricted to the height of vegetation, with as much use of local material as possible. While construction on reefs and lagoons was discouraged, as water-side bungalows are very popular amongst tourists, their construction is permitted if equal size open space is left on the land for each bungalow being developed on the lagoon.

Australian Model

Formed in 1991, the Ecotourism Australia (EAA) serves as the apex national body for Australia's ecotourism industry. Currently, EAA has approximately 500 members, publishes an annual Australian Ecotourism Guide, and hosts an annual conference. In addition to strengthening the industry network of ecotourism operators, the EAA actively promotes "best tourism practices" through self-regulation and accreditation. Attracting high-value visitors in order to develop a more profitable tourism industry rather than just pursuing growth in visitor numbers should be the goal, according to Ecotourism Australia. To provide tourists and the travel trade with a recognisable and authentic ecotourism product, Ecotourism Australia initiated the National Ecotourism Accreditation Programme (NEAP) in 1996 in cooperation with the Australia Tourism Operators Network (ATON) and the Tourism Council of Australia, with funding support from the Office of National Tourism.

Creating a favourable impact in ASEAN countries is most important. While Thailand has already taken a lead, other countries of South East Asia are catching up fast. Vietnam is developing the island of Kien Giang and is looking for investors in a big way. It already has an Investment, Trade and Tourism Promotion Centre which is in touch with investors. Same is true of Hainan island of China. So, any development of ANI must keep in mind the exclusiveness of the destination to make a mark on its Act East Policy.

As already pointed out in the case of Bhutan, the Maldives, South Pacific Islands and Australian tourism, mass tourism can lead to the destruction of the environment, especially if enforcement is weak. India has already seen degradation of the environment in tourism areas in the Himalayas due to mass tourism and slack implementation of rules and its strict enforcement.

The Bhutan model is perhaps one option. Having kept a minimum expenditure per tourist at about US$ 200 per tourist per day it provides a good filter. Further, there is a need to put minimum requirements on hotels and guest houses for cleanliness and garbage disposal, both wet and dry. As a matter of fact, a minimum ceiling on quality should be kept. The existing accommodations should be asked to upgrade so that in the course of a couple of years this destination becomes a high-end destination. Further, in remote locations issues of water availability need to be sorted out. With heavy rainfall concentrated over nine months, water harvesting methods can be employed. The issue of electricity remains a problem as Andaman and Nicobar Islands are dependent upon diesel generation and so far no major breakthrough has been achieved in this area. Diesel generation, with the new type of silent generators, is still polluting.

Ecotourism is the fastest growing segment of the tourism industry. Why is it so? This is so because tourists have shifted away from casino-based tourism to environmental-based tourism. Such tourists are not looking for music, television or evening entertainment but are looking for a quiet peaceful time. As a result, many countries, especially forested countries and island countries, have issued guidelines for this specialised tourism. So far, no such guidelines have been issued by ANI administration.

Tribal Policy and Tourism

Opening of Nicobar Islands for Tourism: Andaman and Nicobar Islands Protection of Aboriginal Tribes Regulation, 1956 and the Rules framed thereunder provide the framework of the Tribal Policy. There are four tribes in Andaman Group and two in Nicobar. Tribes of Andaman are Jarawas, Andamanese, Sentinelese and Onges, each residing in a separate region. The Sentinelese reside in Sentinal Islands which are isolated and they are hostile to other human beings. They are still in hunting and gathering stage and do not want to be disturbed. There is, therefore, no problem with them as long as they are left alone. The Andamanese were the residents of Port Blair region about half a century back but are now relocated in Strait Island, shifted by the British Government. They are about to get extinct with less than 20 members left. The Onges are in Little Andamans living under the Tribal Department's Welfare Scheme and there is no issue with them. The only conflict of the people is with the Jarawas Tribe which is primitive and lives north of Port Blair.

The Nicobar Group of Islands

The Nicobars, however, is another story. The Nicobar Group of Islands consisting of about a dozen inhabited islands and another half a dozen uninhabited islands, has Nicobarese tribals in practically all inhabited. These are very progressive tribals who have joined the mainstream. Nicobarese boys have been winners of All India Subroto Mukerjee Trophy in Football many times. They excel in many other sports also. The Nicobarese children are all literate and attend schools. Older ones are working in various government departments, including defence forces, and are doing well. In fact, according to a senior Nicobarese officer, Nicobarese are now facing issues of educated unemployment as the children passing out of schools and colleges do not get absorbed in the Nicobars and have to seek a living outside their homes. Another very small group of tribals called Shompens is found in Great Nicobar Islands. They are still hunters and gatherers and can be called primitive. These tribals are shy and live in the forest areas. Yet they are friendly and come into Campbell Bay to barter their products for food, etc.

The Nicobarese have now reached the stage of development and integration where they need to be more actively involved with the rest of the country. Further, their main activity in the Nicobar Islands is around coconut trade which has suffered due to the tsunami and reached a saturation point. They need a new economic venue to absorb the youth, especially the educated youth, and a policy of controlled tourism after taking into confidence their Tribal Council. Leading Nicobarese have stated that their coconut trade has reached a saturation point and they need to start a new economic activity. The obvious choice would be to allow growth of tourism in Nicobars. As part of India's enlightenment policy adopted towards the Nicobarese, there is a need to enter into a dialogue with them regarding regulated tourism in these islands. It is necessary that all decisions are taken after due consultation with their Tribal Council, which they respect. As the younger generation looks for jobs after getting educated, there is a need to allow tourism so that more jobs are created in the island rather than these people going out to look for jobs. Nicobarese have enough expertise to run their own company as they had run their own coconut trade in a village based cooperative venture.

Of late the Government has shown some awakening towards opening of these islands. The Island Development Authority (IDA) which has been non-performing since its constitution in 1985 has been revamped and named Island Development Agency (IDA). In June 2017, the government constituted the Island Development Agency (IDA) with more powers and resulted-oriented composition. Union Home Minister Rajnath Singh is the Chairman of the agency while the executive head is Admiral DK Joshi (retd.), former Indian Navy chief and currently also the Lieutenant Governor of Andaman-Nicobar Islands. The Agency the Cabinet Secretary, Secretaries of Home, Defence, Environment and Forest, Civil Aviation, Shipping, Finance and CEO of NITI Aayog. Since its formation, the agency has drawn up a focused, result-oriented plan to develop the island chains for dual—military and civil—purposes. Accordingly, Lt. Governor now oversees conceptualisation, planning and execution of several big, strategic and development projects across the islands.

Four islands of ANI, namely, Smith, Ross, Long and Avis and five islands of Lakshadweep group in the Arabian Sea, namely, Minicoy, Bangaram, Thinnakara, Cheriyam and Suheli have been selected for preparation of sustainable development plans. An additional 12 islands/ locations in ANI and 5 in Lakshadweep are under consideration. Issues like relaxation of restrictive area permits and e-visa/visa on arrival are under consideration. This is a good sign, at last, of some awakening taking place at the highest level in the Government of India. It has been reported in the press that two out of three projects have been cleared by the expert appraisal committee of the Ministry of Environment at Lalaji Bay in the Long Island and Smith Island in the Andamans, with riders. The Lalaji Bay project involves 220 rooms while the Smith Island project involves 70 rooms.[23] However, these are ad hoc decisions but no policy decision with regard to these islands has been announced.

Economic and Strategic Benefits of Direct Air Connectivity with Four Airports of Andaman and Nicobar with ASEAN Countries

It has been proved at many places that mass tourism can degrade the environment if appropriate policies are not followed. On the other hand, limited high-end tourism can improve the environment. How does one achieve limited high-end tourism? This can be achieved if appropriate policies are put in place and implemented. This calls for a change in philosophy for Andaman and Nicobar Islands. In a recent order of the Supreme Court banning tourism in core areas of tiger reserves, it said that it was not averse to permitting regulated tourism activities, subject to revised guidelines, to protect the depleting wild cat. It granted four weeks to the centre to evolve fresh guidelines after consultation with states, all stakeholders, hotel associations affected by the ban, guides and tour operators. They also stated, "There is always a watch when tourism is allowed. If there is no tourism there will be no human to watch the tigers. Poachers will immediately be caught by tourists and guides. Poachers actually work under cover. If no tourists are allowed, it will be a field day for poachers." However, so far, no guidelines have been issued.

Issues of Connectivity to Andaman and Nicobar Islands

Aviation and tourism, have a very close relationship. If tourism is to be encouraged, direct flights from South East Asia and other places need to be encouraged. Granting of liberal bilateral rights or even declaring open skies for the Andamans may be a solution as Port Blair has already been declared an international airport, but there are no scheduled flights from any foreign country interested in coming in, due to poor tourism infrastructure. Use of aviation as a catalyst and an enabler should be employed. This involves permitting and encouraging direct flights from South East Asian countries like Singapore, Thailand, Malaysia or Indonesia. All these countries have developed excellent tourist spots and we need to leverage them to attract tourists directly from there without coming into the Indian mainland. Further, with four airstrips in Andaman and Nicobar Islands, namely, Port Blair and Diglipur in the Andamans and Car Nicobar and Campbell Bay in the Nicobars should be put to use for limited and controlled tourism also. Besides this, use of small amphibious aircraft to take tourists to remote locations in various islands should be encouraged. This will be restricted to high-end travellers due to higher ticket prices. Port Blair in the Andaman Islands is about 1,200 km from the Indian mainland. The other airport at Campbell Bay is only 3,000 ft long but with the announcement of the establishment of the forward base, called Baaz, for the Naval Air Force, it is being extended to 9,000 ft. Night landing facilities will also be provided in due course. The Diglipur airfield is about 3,000 ft but its extension to a full length is a work in progress. Presently, an odd private plane from abroad lands in Port Blair on an average of one per month. *Otherwise, foreign travellers have to travel to mainland India and then take a domestic flight to Port Blair. Indian domestic flights are costly and a trip from mainland India during the season can be very expensive as prices of domestic tickets tend to fluctuate. Tickets from the mainland to Port Blair during season are often prohibitive. Direct international flights will correct this imbalance.*

Direct International Connectivity to Andaman and Nicobar Islands

Why is direct international connectivity necessary for Indian policy of leveraging the strategic potential? It is significant for various reasons. These islands are closer to Straits of Malacca than mainland India. This aspect needs to be brought out in the international tourist circles and through them conveyed that India's soft power jurisdiction extends right up to Straits of Malacca. However, the route to the Andamans can be circuitous for foreign tourists as there is no direct international flight to these islands.

Andaman and Nicobar Islands

While domestic connectivity has improved with about 10 or more commercial landings a day, there is still no international connectivity. In order to expose these islands to high-end foreign tourists India needs to have direct connectivity from South East Asia. Otherwise, for a foreign tourist, it takes very long to connect to a flight from mainland India. Direct connectivity with Phuket, Bangkok or Singapore may be the answer. This is so because the distance from Port Blair to Phuket is shorter than distances between Port Blair and the mainland. However, efforts by Andaman Trade Association which signed an MoU with their counterpart in Thailand failed to get a direct flight to Port Blair because of the reluctance of Civil and Defence authorities to giving clearance.

Why is direct international connectivity necessary for Indian policy of leveraging the strategic potential? It is very significant for various reasons. It is, in fact, a must to implement the Act East Policy. These islands are closer to Straits of Malacca than mainland India. The public perception in South East Asia and the world is that India means peninsular and not the Bay of Bengal. This aspect needs to be brought out in the international tourist circles and through them conveyed that India's soft-power jurisdiction extends right up to Straits of Malacca. The present route to the Andamans and Nicobars can be circuitous for foreign tourists who are coming from east of India. They have to travel to mainland India and then take a domestic flight to Port Blair as there are no direct flights from abroad. Further, Indian domestic flights are costly and a trip from mainland India during the season can be very expensive as prices of domestic tickets tend to fluctuate. The tickets from mainland to Port Blair during season are often prohibitive. Direct international flights will correct this imbalance. Flights to and fro Andaman and Nicobar

Map 5: Air Distances between Port Blair and Yangon, Bangkok and Phuket

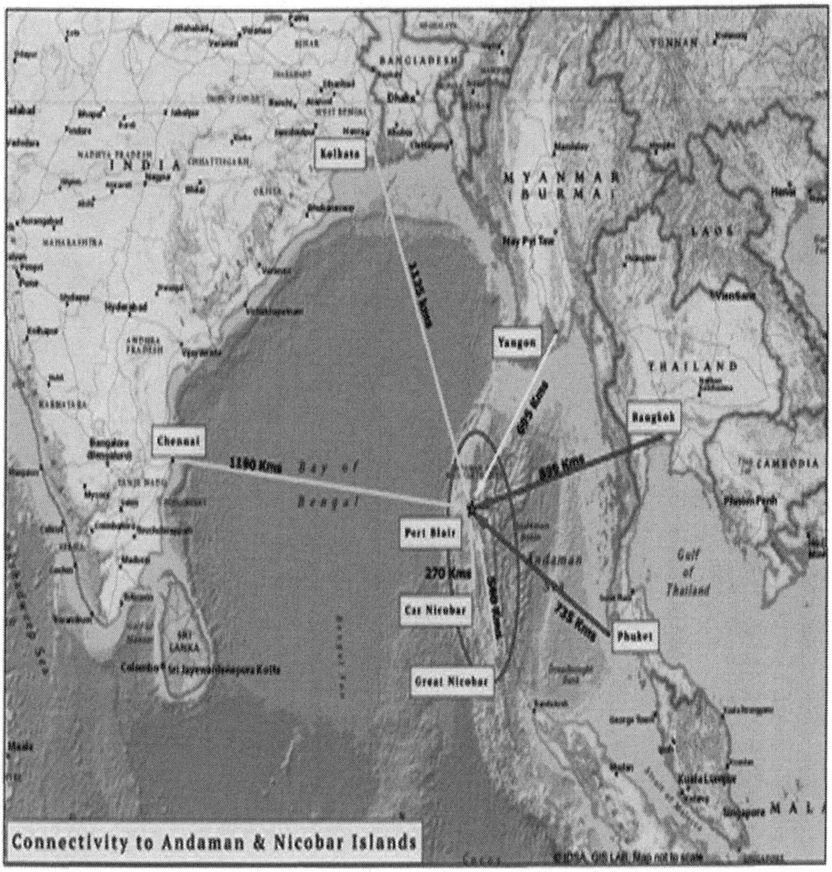

can start under the International Connectivity Scheme or ICS. A good tourist season is from October to March. Monsoons are also pleasant, but rough seas could discourage water-based activities.

A new terminal complex at Port Blair is coming up and should be ready by mid-2021.[24] It will have two aerobridges and a separation between domestic and international flights. Customs and immigration facilities will be provided as international traffic increases. At the same time a proposal for a new greenfield airport is also under preparation for Port Blair on the assumption the existing airport will not suffice as it is unidirectional with many limitations. Similar new terminal facilities could be considered for other airfields at Car Nicobar, Diglipur and Campbell Bay.

MoU With Phuket: Sister Cities—Proof of the Unwritten Policy of Masterly Inactivity and Benign Neglect

The business community of Andaman Islands as well as the tribals on Nicobar Islands are keen on greater economic prosperity for the islands. The Andaman Chamber of Commerce and Industry has been making efforts to increase tourism and other trade. On November 30, 2003 an MoU was signed between Phuket Chamber of Commerce and Andaman Chamber of Commerce with the Governor of Phuket and First Secretary of the Embassy of India as witnesses. The MoU's objective, as stated in its preamble, is to further the development of bilateral economic relationship by a forum of businessmen to discuss and explore business opportunities in trade, investment, transfer of technology, services and other industrial sectors. Again, on June 29, 2005 an agreement was signed at Phuket between the Lt. Governor of Andaman and Nicobar Islands and Governor of Phuket Province to promote and undertake regular exchanges and interaction in the following areas:

1. *Tourism.* Exchange of tourist missions for fairs, expositions, tourists' fairs, promotion of tourist destinations for each sister city, and finally promotion of international tourism between one another.
2. *Education and Culture.* Cultural Exchanges—Phuket days in the city of Port Blair and City of Port Blair's days in Phuket Province. Cultural exchanges between students, artists and professionals.
3. *Urban Development.* Exchange of expertise in innovative water harvesting techniques; upgradation of water treatment plants; study of old water supply network and rationalisation of water distribution network; desilting-relining of old sewer lines.
4. *Solid Waste Management.* Study of modern and sustainable methods of solid waste management particularly in the areas of Andaman and Nicobar Islands, of roads and public places, safe disposal through

transportation, development of proper Andaman and Nicobar Islands landfill sites, segregation of biodegradable solid wastes and recycling.

5. *Commerce.* Exchange of Commerce Missions and participation in expositions, fairs and other promotions with increased flow of goods and services between parties.
6. *Investment.* Exchange of business missions, information sharing of investment possibilities and business opportunities.

None of the activities mentioned in the MoU have been carried out and both the MoUs are lying defunct.

A major factor which comes in the way of implementing the two MoUs is the indifference shown by the governments and lack of direct connectivity between the two. Both of these have proved that the present set-up is not conducive to a new proactive policy.

While Port Blair has been declared a major port and the airport international, it has made little difference to the present position. No direct scheduled or even charter flights come into Port Blair nor do any international ships. Who should be held responsible for it? While the Andaman Chamber of Commerce was keen and they even went to Thailand to meet their counterparts, they found a different atmosphere in the Ministry of Civil Aviation/Director General of Civil Aviation.

Another issue which is related to the development of the islands is good telecom. It is surprising and shocking that these islands are still not connected properly. While cellphone connectivity is available in some inhabited islands, the quality and reach are not good enough to reach all the inhabited islands. It is for the Andaman and Nicobar Islands Administration to ensure that there is good connectivity in all the inhabited islands. Even under the UN Millennium Development Goals (MDGs), bridging the digital divide applies to these islands also. The Telecom Ministry has a Universal Service Obligation Fund (USOF) which can be used to provide cell and internet service to all the inhabited islands. It is necessary to lay out a good telecom infrastructure with good quality internet. This is also a requirement of the defence forces and it needs to be taken up on a more serious and urgent basis. A project to lay under sea fibre-optic cable for Rs. 1224 crores measuring 2,313 kms was been inaugurated on 10th August, 2020. Internet connectivity with broadband is a must for promoting these islands.[25]

A New Administrative Set-up and a New Policy Framework for ANI: A Proposal

There is a need to change the narrative from a philosophy of "Masterly Inactivity and Benign Neglect" to a policy of "Leveraging the Potential".

Creation of North East Frontier Agency (NEFA): What happened in Assam in the 1950s. While NEFA territory was a part of Assam, it remained a buffer region between Tibet and India and there was practically no administration in this huge hill tract going South of the McMahon Line. It was in the 1950s that India decided to set up a full-fledged administrative set-up right upto McMahon Line, in a hostile and difficult hilly terrain with about 50 tribal groups living isolated with no friendly links with Assam. It was also decided that these tribals need to be befriended and not fought and killed, as it happened in the US and other frontier countries. Therefore, a policy and philosophy for NEFA was developed. NEFA was carved out of Assam as a special Agency and put under the Governor of Assam and made a direct charge of Ministry of External Affairs for 10 years, and not under the Government of Assam. A cadre of ex-military officers, called Indian Frontier Administrative Service, was created to serve in this inhospitable terrain. Thus developed a philosophy and a strategy for NEFA in the 1950s and 1960s; as a forward strategy, NEFA was carved out of the northern hill districts of Assam in 1954 with the aim of extending the administration up to the Indo-Tibetan Border based on the McMahon Line of 1914 and integrating the various tribes of NEFA without destroying their tribal traditions and culture. Dr. Verrier Elwin, a famous anthologist, was made the advisor to the Governor of Assam for this purpose. Tribal Welfare and Protection was the cornerstone of this philosophy. During its early years NEFA was given very special treatment and massive air support by the air force; some private companies were provided to open up the region which was otherwise inaccessible. Today, after so many years, NEFA has got the new name of Arunachal Pradesh and is a full-fledged State, much more accessible as a large number of roads have been constructed and dependence on air support is negligible. This special action is proof of India's actual administration over this territory and has stood well internationally in spite of Chinese claims over the entire erstwhile NEFA, now Arunachal Pradesh. Further, it is proof that India can do it provided there is a will.

On similar lines a Philosophy and Strategy for Andaman and Nicobar Islands now needs to be developed so as to implement the Act East Policy. The time has come to evolve a new policy and philosophy for the Andaman and Nicobar Islands as well an administrative setup.

The fact is that these islands are closer to countries of ASEAN where tourism is already booming. Direct air and sea connection with these countries is essential to leverage the advantage of their goodwill built up all over the world and also to bring ASEAN closer to India. This will give a fresh impetus to India's Look East Policy. In order to do so India needs to develop a Special Tourism Plan for Andaman and Nicobar Islands with this philosophy in mind, rather than the present tourism policy which is aimed more at integrating India's mainland domestic tourism with Andaman and Nicobar Islands with no regard to the quality of tourism or strategic implications. A strategic master plan needs to be redrawn for this purpose after taking into account the various environmental concerns integrating the civil and military requirements and merging it with India's AEP of 2014.

Policy Suggestions for Leveraging the Political Advantage

Can the present set-up at Andaman and Nicobar Islands deliver a policy change and deliver the needs of the Act East Policy as proposed in this book? As already discussed, it is unlikely that the present set-up, geared towards preservation of the status quo, will be able to deliver. The Ministry of Home Affairs (MHA), which is the administrative Ministry for the Islands, has too many problems in hand to look into its development, security and environmental issues which if mixed together in the right proportions can bring about a lasting change in India's security scenario without sacrificing the environmental aspect. There is, perhaps, a need for a new administrative set-up for these islands. The role of MHA over the years has been to keep these islands secure and without trouble. However, if India adopts a progressive policy towards these islands, there is a need to seriously review the administrative structure and take it out of the MHA. Like North East Frontier Agency (NEFA)—which was created out of Assam and made into an agency under the Foreign Ministry for a decade—a similar policy should be followed by putting it under a new structure similar to what has been done for North-East India. The most appropriate and proven method would be to put it under the Ministry of External Affairs so that they are able to implement the Act East Policy.

However, before these islands are opened to tourism a well-thought-out tourism policy should be put in place. Within ecotourism, scuba diving and fishing should be given their due in view of paucity of revenue land. Strict rules with an implementation mechanism should be evolved. Pollution of the crystal-clear water of these islands has to be stopped. With a few precautions like these, a good tourism policy can be evolved for the next stage of growth of these islands. The Environment and Forest Department should be more involved in the management of this policy. Although joint patrol is conducted with the army, navy, coast guard, marine police and forest department in remote islands and sometimes a camp is set up for a day or so, surveillance in these islands with countless creeks is a gigantic job. It is, therefore, felt that tourism in these islands should be dealt with as a strategic tool and should complement the defence services. Only such a step can bring about the necessary changes in policy and its implementation towards Act East Policy. This will enable the transformation of the security scenario, the public perception that India's limits go right up to the Malacca Straits and give the requisite fillip to our Look East Policy.

Tribal Policy and Tourism: Opening of Nicobar Islands for Tourism. Andaman and Nicobar Islands Protection of Aboriginal Tribes

Regulation, 1956 and the Rules framed thereunder provide the framework of the Tribal Policy. There are four tribes in Andaman Group and two in Nicobar. Only Nicobarese Tribals have now started joining the mainstream and they should be integrated into normal life slowly. The islands can be slowly opened to tourism also.

Island Development Authority (IDA)

The IDA was formed in 1986 by a government order after the visit of Prime Minister Rajiv Gandhi to Andaman and Nicobar Islands, in which the Prime Minister was the Chairman with about a dozen Cabinet Ministers including ministers of home and defence as members. It remained dormant all these years. In June 2017, the government scrapped the Island Development Authority and constituted the Island Development Agency (IDA) with more powers and resulted-oriented composition. Union Home Minister is the Chairman of the agency while the executive head is Admiral DK Joshi (retd.), former Indian Navy chief and currently also the Lieutenant Governor of Andaman-Nicobar Islands. The Agency includes among its members the Cabinet Secretary, Secretaries of Home, Defence, Environment and Forest, Civil Aviation, Shipping, Finance and CEO of NITI Aayog. The Agency has drawn up a focused, result-oriented plan to develop the island chains for dual—military and civil—purposes.[26]

Many of the items in the Supreme Court orders have not been implemented. The Hon'ble Supreme Court in its order, while keeping these islands green has allowed "low volume-high value" ecotourism to come up. This has not been implemented either in letter or spirit.

Further, the security scenario has undergone a change with terrorists having their own ships, and human trafficking by boats taking place in the Bay of Bengal. It has been reported that theft of Sea Cucumber from the beaches and sands of Andaman and Nicobar Islands is taking place by organised syndicates, and there is a need to take a fresh view of these islands from a security and strategic point of view. There is a need to bring out the synergy between security, ecotourism and environment protection. The real ecotourism of these islands lies in its fabulous coral wealth and the big fish which will attract scuba divers and deep-sea anglers from all over the world. Of course, the ecosystem of these islands is fragile and needs careful management. This means that limited tourism can flourish in these islands without necessarily opening the hinterland. The sport of scuba diving is a major specialised tourist attraction.

United Nations Development Programme (UNDP) Report on Development Strategy for Environmentally Sustainable Tourism in the Andamans (1996)

As mentioned earlier, on a request of the Andaman and Nicobar Administration, World Tourism Organisation (WTO), with UNDP funding, had prepared a detailed report on Sustainable Tourism in the Andamans. However, this report has never been implemented and is gathering dust in Port Blair. This now needs to be taken out to study and implement. Further, Nils Finn Munch-Petersen, who had submitted the preliminary project formulation framework for UNDP in 1992, had stated that "In Tourism Industry, down market drives out the upmarket." He gives the example of Bhutan and Galapagos as upmarket, Maldives as mid market and a planned tourism area, while Nepal was an example of unplanned tourism. He emphasised the need and importance for planned tourism development as "well planned tourism may be a vehicle for growth". In this context, he further states that "Andaman & Nicobar Islands are dangerously close to defining themselves as a down market destination in the future." It is unfortunate that the detailed UNDP report on Environmentally Sustainable Tourism Policy carried out under supervision of the WTO has been ignored by the Andaman & Nicobar Administration. This is yet another case of 'Masterly Inactivity'.

Tourism Masterplan: A Critique

It is unfortunate that the existing master plan of 2003 is a very restricted one and has considered only the following islands. The locations covered as part of the study included only:

• Port Blair • Havelock • Baratang • Rangat • Mayabunder • Diglipur
• Little Andaman • Nicobar District

The study covered hitherto uncovered destinations like Little Andaman, Car Nicobar, Katchal and Great Nicobar 7,000 sq km of land surface out of 8,249 sq km are now coming under National Parks, Sanctuaries or Reserve Forests. While it may be difficult to go in for tourism activities in national parks and sanctuaries, reserve forests do allow limited use for ecotourism. However, the Forest Department of Andaman & Nicobar Islands has as yet no plans for development of tourism inside reserve forests which is a practice worldwide. Once this issue is sorted out there is possibility of limited high-end eco-friendly tourism in remote locations. Worldwide reser forests have been developed for ecotourism under certain rules and guidelines which are strictly followed. Wildlife sanctuaries like Kruger National Park also have enclaves for tourists where they can stay under strict rules of not making noise or throwing garbage, etc.

Further, a tribal reserve area like Nicobar can certainly have controlled tourism which will be discussed later. And lastly, there should be no bar on developing eco resorts in reserve forests as is being done worldwide as long as it conforms to some guidelines which are properly enforced. Internationally forests and games reserves like the Kruger National Park of South Africa has tourist enclaves where tourist stay and follow a strict discipline of the Park. Even the Supreme Court has endorsed this view after accepting the Shekhar Singh report mentioned earlier.

Andaman & Nicobar Islands is also a great attraction for bird watchers as well as for its rich, unique and endemic biodiversity. As many as 270 species and sub-species are reported by ornithologists. These islands are part of the 218 Endemic Bird Areas (EBA) of the world. Its mangrove vegetation protects these islands from soil erosion. Its wildlife consists of wild pigs, dugongs, elephants, turtles, snakes. Coral reefs, sea cucumbers, and shells of various types form part of marine wild life. It has 96 wildlife sanctuaries, nine national parks and one biosphere reserve. This can be a great attraction for nature loving tourists only if facilities for stay are provided and tours under control conditions are made mandatory.

From the above chart it may be seen that Andaman & Nicobar Islands has the highest percentage of forests at 90 per cent of land surface and lowest percentage of agriculture. This figure should be seen as an advantage as ecotourism with dense forests and beaches is a preferred option with ecotourists. In fact, the high level of forest reserves gives Andaman & Nicobar Islands a special place for nature related activities and reduces the pull of social resort tourism. Forest area has a number of restrictions which have to be honoured and generally allow only upmarket tourism because of these restrictions. Worldwide forest tourism in reserves is becoming popular. However, Andaman and Nicobar Islands have hardly any forest related tourism especially when the forests of Andaman and Nicobar Islands are extremely dense rain forests, rarely found in the world today. Andaman and Nicobar Islands do not have any major animals in the forest which are likely to be hunted. There are iguanas, other reptiles and birds. The protected species have already been listed by the Forest and Environment Department. Unlike forest departments in countries like the US, Australia and New Zealand and even some forest departments of Indian States, there has been very little work done by the Forest Department to promote ecotourism in the forest areas. There is a need to plan out the high quality of the limited number of tourist resorts inside these forests. There is a growing breed of nature lovers who travel to all corners of the world to such locations. It will not only be a revenue earner but also bring awareness of the environmental degradation. The Tourism Policy document issued by the Andaman and Nicobar Islands clearly states in its strategy to go in for Strategic Partnerships. It states, "Formulate strategic tourism partnerships with neighbouring international destinations like Phuket for leveraging increased visits to these islands." So far no such partnership has been signed or even negotiated. The only document is the MoU signed between the Lt. Governor of Andaman and Nicobar Islands and Governor of Phuket signed in 2005 but which remains unimplemented. This is unfortunate as this agreement talked of tourism promotion, solid waste management and cultural exchanges amongst other things (see Appendix 1). In order to compare tourism policies of other countries, given below is a comparison with Bhutan, South Pacific Islands based on a UN Report, the Maldives Model and Report of Ecotourism Association of Australia (EAA).

A Policy Prescription for Positive Discouragement of Mass Tourism. It may be seen from above examples that Andaman and Nicobar Islands also need to come out with more detailed policy guidelines and regulations for their tourism policy. Its policies have to be compliant to the Supreme Court's order which is very clear on high value-low volume tourism. While it has identified activities for tourists such as scuba diving, cruise tourism, canopy walkway, mass tourism will be a spoiler. As already pointed out in the case of Bhutan, Maldives, South Pacific Islands and Australian tourism, mass tourism can lead to the destruction of the environment, especially if implementation of the policy is weak. India has already seen degradation of the environment in tourism areas in the Himalayas due to mass tourism and lack of enforcement. The recent 2012 incident reported in all national newspapers that local tour operators in Port Blair in connivance with police have been taking groups of tourists to Jarawa tribal reserve areas and forcing Jarawas to dance before them. This is a case in point of how a laid-out policy was violated not only by travel agents but also local administration and police who connived in this activity. Such activities are proof of "poor surveillance", and show a need for a tourism and environmental regulator for these islands. It would be in the fitness of things to decide upfront how to control decline in the quality of enforcement because of forests, which are likely to be damaged by illegal immigrants.

Leveraging Soft Power

Good air connection, fast travel to islands, clean environment, availability of clean water, clean beaches, low crime rate all form a part of tourism essentials. Expenditure on these items needs to come mainly from the government but wherever possible, private sector participation should be welcome. One of the problems of Andaman and Nicobar Islands is shortage of water for about three months in the year when it is dry there. While there is adequate rainfall, the months from January to March are dry and there is shortage of drinking water in most areas. These are also the best tourist months. For promotion of tourism and supply of water during the dry months, there is need for extensive rainwater harvesting technology to be implemented in all islands where people live and tourism is to be promoted. This is a solvable problem as there is adequate rainfall the rest of the year.

Responsible Tourism. Responsible Tourism is the current mantra of tour operators. However, it is not enough to allow the slogan but penalties should be put in the legislation and fines imposed on hotels/guest houses that do not follow it in letter and spirit. Opening of these islands will give a better appreciation to the whole concept of use of tourism for security purposes. Will tourism development improve, or further degrade the environment? This is a complex question. Mass tourism has shown in many places that it can degrade the environment if correct policies are not followed. However, limited high-end tourism can improve the environment. How does one achieve limited high-end tourism? This can be achieved if appropriate policies are put in place and implemented. This calls for a philosophy for Andaman and Nicobar Islands. In the recent order of the Supreme Court banning tourism in core areas of tiger reserves, it said that it was not averse to permitting regulated tourism activities, subject to revised guidelines to protect the depleting wild cat. It granted four weeks to the centre to evolve fresh guidelines after consultation with states, all stakeholders, hotel associations affected by the ban, guides and tour operators. The Supreme Court also stated, "There is always a watch when tourism is allowed. If there is no tourism there will be no human to watch the tigers. Poachers will immediately be caught by tourists and guides. Poachers actually work under cover. If no tourists are allowed, it will be a field day for poachers."

Tribal Policy and Tourism

There are four tribes in Andaman Group and two in Nicobar. Tribes of Andaman are Jarawas, Adamanese, Sentinelese and Onges, each residing in a separate region. The Sentinelese reside in Sentinal Island which is isolated and they are hostile to other human beings. They are still in hunting and gathering stage and do not want to be disturbed. There is, therefore, no problem with them as long as they are left alone. The Andamanese were the residents of Port Blair region about half a century back but are now relocated in Strait Island, shifted by the British Government. They are about to get extinct with less than 20 members left. The Onges are in Little Andamans living under the Tribal Department's Welfare Scheme and there is no issue with them. The only conflict of the people is with the Jarawas Tribals who are primitive and where a road called Andaman Trunk Road (ATR) has cut through their territory and is causing a lot of problems for them. This has become a case of litigation in the court by environmentalists/ anthropologists. The Supreme Court had ordered closure of a certain part of the road going through the Jarawas reserve which has not been done as yet. These four tribes are still primitive and the existing policy to leave them by themselves without allowing tourists enter their areas is fully accepted and appreciated. There is no need for tourists to have any interaction with them.

The Nicobars, however, is another story. The Nicobar Group of Islands has Nicobarese tribals in practically all islands of Nicobar. These are progressive tribals who have joined the mainstream. Nicobarese boys have been winners of All India Subroto Mukerjee Trophy in Football many times. The Nicobarese children are all literate and are attending schools. They are also working in various government departments including defence forces and are doing well. In fact, according to a senior Nicobarese officer, Nicobarese are now facing issues of educated unemployment as the children passing out of schools and colleges are not getting absorbed in Nicobars and have to seek a living outside their homes. Another very small group of tribals called Shompens is found in Great Nicobar Islands. They are still hunters and gatherers and can be called primitive. These tribals are shy and live in the forest areas. Yet they are friendly and come into settled areas to exchange their products like honey. They should be allowed to live their own life. They have some contact with the tribal department in the Great Nicobar Islands but they feel shy to mix with other settlers. There is no problem with them. Although, the Tribal Policy of Andaman and Nicobar Islands has insulated the primitive tribes (except for some breaches in implementation), time has come to review it especially in respect of Nicobarese.

The Nicobarese have now reached the stage of development and integration that they need to be more actively involved with the rest of the country. Further, their main activity in the Nicobar Islands is around coconut trade, which has suffered due to the tsunami of 2004 and reached a saturation point. They need a new economic venue to absorb the youth, especially the educated youth and a policy of controlled tourism after taking into confidence their Tribal Council. Leading Nicobarese have stated that their coconut trade has reached a saturation point and they need to start a new economic activity. The obvious choice would be to allow growth of tourism in Nicobars. As part of India's enlightenment policy adopted towards the Nicobarese there is a need to enter into a dialogue with them regarding regulated tourism in these islands. It is necessary that all decisions are taken after due consultation with their Tribal Council, which they respect. As the younger generation looks for jobs and is getting educated, there is a need to allow tourism in these islands but managed by them and not outside companies. They are well organised and capable of managing business themselves. While the Nicobar Islands are still very remote and isolated, their interaction with foreign fishermen and traders has always been there prior to 1947. The government policy since World War II of prohibiting foreign boats from entering these islands has made them more insular and isolated. However, reopening these islands to foreign tourists/cruise ships will not be such a major change.

The island of Car Nicobar is the most progressive of them with a full-length airfield and is ready to welcome a limited number of tourists. For the rest of the islands cruise ships stopping for a few hours, like in the Greek Islands, would be a win-win for both the tribals and display of soft power. The scope of leveraging India's soft power by tourism promotion and allied activities is immense keeping in mind full environmental protection. Not only that, while hard power is a costly drain on the exchequer, soft power through tourism and its allied activities, is revenue generating for the local economy, the region as well as for the country. Tourism is now the biggest industry in the world and the share of Andaman and Nicobar Islands is insignificant. However, the need for promoting tourism in these islands should not be for generating revenue but for supplementing the incomes of the tribals and complementing military power with soft power to increase the strategic vision in the national context. Opening of Nicobar Islands for Tourism may require modification of Andaman and Nicobar Islands Protection of Aboriginal Tribes Regulation, 1956 and the Rules.

In conclusion, the Andaman and Nicobar Islands have a major role to play in the Act East Policy. They need to be leveraged for their soft and hard advantages. The islands need to be opened up for 'High End Tourism' keeping in mind the environment. Security, Tourism and Environment have to synergise and take advantage of its geographic location.

Is direct international air connectivity a necessary requirement for Indian policy of leveraging the strategic potential? Yes, indeed. It is very significant for various reasons. These islands are closer to Straits of Malacca than mainland India. This aspect needs to be brought out in the international tourist circles and through them conveyed that India's soft power jurisdiction extends right up to Straits of Malacca. The route to Andamans can be circuitous for foreign tourists who are coming from main land India. They have to travel to mainland India and then take a domestic flight to Port Blair. Further, Indian domestic flights are costly and a trip from mainland India during the season can be very expensive, as prices of domestic tickets tend to fluctuate. The Port Blair tickets during season are often prohibitive. Direct international flights will correct this imbalance and save time of foreign tourists.

The strategic location of the Great Nicobar Island on the mouth of Straits of Malacca gives it great potential for bunkering of ships with huge tonnage passing by. With the opening of Naval Air Station (NAS) Baaz at Campbell Bay at Great Nicobar Islands, opportunities to fully exploit the geographic location of Great Nicobar Islands in commercial terms in coordination with defence requirements should be carried out without any delay. This will complement the soft power that India needs to display at the western entrance of Straits of Malacca. About one-third of the world's seaborne trade passes by Great Nicobar Island. This activity will not disturb the forest and biosphere reserves but will enhance India's status in the Malacca region. The Nancowry-Kamorta harbour in the Nicobars is yet another fantastic feature of the Nicobar. This harbour is excellent for keeping ships and submarines and is quite close to Great Nicobar Island.

These islands offer India a great opportunity to exert its hard and soft policy in the Bay of Bengal and can show the world that west of Malacca Straits is a region of peace and harmony. Opening of these islands for high-value tourism with environmental safeguards is therefore most important. The change in narrative is required, similar to the creation of NEFA.

Notes

1. Sanat Kaul, *Andaman and Nicobar Islands: India's Untapped Strategic Assets*, published by the Institute for Defence Studies and Analyses/Pentagon Press.
2. Robert Kaplan, *Monsoon: The Indian Ocean and the fury of American Power* (Random House, 2011).
3. John G. Botcher and Reelson, *Sovereignty and the Sea: How Indonesia Became an Archipelagic State* (National University of Singapore, 2017), p. 179.
4. See Sanat Kaul, *Andaman and Nicobar Islands: India's Untapped Strategic Assets*, published by Institute for Defence Studies and Analyses/Pentagon Press.
5. Bert Lintner, *The Costliest Pearl: China's Struggle for Indian Ocean* (Madison, MS, USA: Context, 2019), p. 72.
6. Joseph Nye, Rhodes Scholar at Oxford University and Professor Emeritus at Harvard, who introduced the concept. "Soft Power. The Means to Succeed in World Politics", Harvard University.
7. Indonesian Coordinating Minister for Maritime Affairs, Luhut Binsar Pandjsitan, in *Times of India*, May 30, 2018.
8. Bert Lintner, *The Costliest Pearl: China's Struggle for India's Ocean* (Madison, MS, USA: Context, 2019), p. 78.
9. Liu Jianzhong, at www.researchgate.net
10. Ma Ying, "An analysis of India's Maritime Strategy", *Pacific Journal*, 18 (6), 2010.
11. Ren Huaifeng, "On the Intervention of Extra Regional Power in the Changing Security Dynamics of South Sea Region", Forum of World Economics and Politics, 5, 2009, p. 55.

12. Liu Quing, "The String of Pearls' Strategy: Indian Assessment and Response", *South Asian Studies Quarterly*, 2, 2010, pp. 26-27.
13. Sanat Kaul, "The Andamans Hold the Key to India's Strategic Role in the Asia-Pacific", in *Global Dialogue Review*, April/May/June 2015, pp. 92-97.
14. Sanat Kaul, "An Alternative to Hong Kong Possible in the Great Nicobar Island", *The Sunday Guardian*, July 26-August 1, 2020.
15. *The Hindu*, October 16, 2019.
16. Guo Yingzhe, Wen Simin and Zhou Wenmin, "Hong Kong's Plan for 30 per cent Stamp Duty Hike Sinks Stocks", in *Caixin Global*, February 24, 2021.
17. Sanat Kaul.
18. Sanat Kaul, "An alternative to Hong Kong possible in Great Nicobar Island", in *The Sunday Guardian*, July 25, 2020.
19. "India Plans Rs. 10,000 cr transshipment port at the Great Nicobar Island: PM Modi", PTI, August 10, 2020.
20. "Green Terror", *India Today*, October 15, 2012, p. 19.
21. Nils Munch-Peterson was a short-term consultant sent to the Andaman and Nicobar Islands by UNDP in 1992-1993.
22. UNDP-WTO Project IND/93/032: August 1996.
23. *Hindustan Times*, February 19, 2019.
24. "Port Blair airport to have a new terminal building by 2021—AAI", *Mint*, September 16, 2020.
25. PM inaugurates undersea cable linking Chennai, Andaman & Nicobar:thehindubusinessline.com 10th August 2020: https://www.thehindubusinessline.com/news/national/pm-modi-inaugurates-first-ever-optical-fibre-project-for-andaman-and-nicobar/article32314905.ece
26. Nitin A. Gokhale, "Andamans as Springboard for India's Act East Policy", *Strategic News International*, New Delhi, October 22, 2018.

6
Aligning Civil Aviation Policy with Foreign Policy: The Proposed International Connectivity Scheme (ICS)

Viability of integrating Civil Aviation Policy with Foreign Policy

Is there is a need to reorient India's Civil Aviation Policy to meet the requirements of our foreign policy? We have shown earlier in Chapter 1 how India's very large and growing economy should reach out with direct air connectivity to its immediate neighbours based on our foreign policy requirements. Our increasingly close relationship with SAARC and ASEAN countries, and our policies in the west with Iran and it's Chabahar Port providing us a land link to Afghanistan, the Ashgabat and INSAT Agreement countries must also get direct air connectivity with Indian cities. At the same time, aberration in our aviation policies with regard to 5/20 as well as grant of too many bilateral air services rights at the cost of our own airlines and too many points of landings to be corrected. Both the Economic Survey of the Ministry of Finance and the Report of Comptroller and Auditor General of India have pointed out these mistakes in our policies. We, therefore, need to reconcile and correct the past mistakes.

While the Ministry of Civil Aviation has introduced a Regional Connectivity Scheme (RCS/UDAN) for domestic service it has also put up a draft proposal on their website for International Air Connectivity

(IAC) Scheme for State Governments to promote international air services from their States. The states may have there own needs like connecting with their diaspora in specific countries or encourage inbound tourism to boost their domestic economy. In this chapter an attempt will be to further promote a modified IAC to meet our foreign policy requirements which has been termed International Connectivity Scheme (ICS).

We have also seen in Chapter 5 how China is able to divert its huge outbound traffic by use of its Approved Destination Status (ADS) for its foreign policy requirements. However, this may not be possible for us but we could incentivise our outbound traffic to go to countries which meet our Foreign Policy requirements through certain steps detailed earlier. The details of these incentives will form a part of ICS. We have also shown how the states/provinces of China are subsidising its airlines going abroad from their towns.

In order for Indian Civil Aviation to serve Foreign Policy under ICS, the strategy is twofold: encourage our airlines to go to destinations which are not directly accessible and to encourage Indian outbound travellers to go to these destinations and invite citizens of that country to visit India. If it is in our foreign policy interest to connect directly to all ASEAN countries from as many Indian cities as possible and not to have our outbound travellers hub at airports of Singapore, Thailand and Kuala Lumpur in the east to connect, then we need a mechanism for having direct flights even if they are not viable at present. For example, our political interests require to have a direct flight to Cambodia for Angkor Wat, the world famous UNESCO heritage temples, Indonesia, the Philippines, etc. In the west of India we need to connect to Chabahar Port in Iran and to many other cities of Central Europe/West Asia like Iran, Uzbekistan, Kazakhstan, Azerbaijan which are on the routes of the Ashgabat or INSAT Agreements.

We have mentioned at page 24 the concept of International Connectivity Scheme (ICS) under which such a scheme can be floated. This Scheme can be similar to the IAC but instead of State Governments who would sponsor the flight, it would be Ministry of External Affairs.

As far as bidding methodology and concessions by Airports Authority are concerned, the Ministry of External Affairs could negotiate the same in collaborative arrangement with the Ministry of Civil Aviation. The final decision to launch a flight between an Indian city and a city abroad should be left with the Ministry of External Affairs.

Direct Connectivity and Passenger Preference Issues

One important ingredient in trade and tourism is direct connectivity as both business people and tourists do not want to waste time in changing planes in hubs, and any delay in arrival for connecting flight can be tiresome, time-consuming and could upset the entire plan. Delays can become expensive also. While earlier, Indians did not mind changing planes at convenient airport hubs, such as Singapore or Dubai due to the attraction of duty free shopping, this is no longer the case. With the advent of better quality, smaller (single aisle) with long-range aircraft, this is also no longer necessary. Direct flights between city pairs is now possible within the areas of our concern. The need to go to the nearby metro city to catch a flight will not be necessary in future. In India, Delhi, Mumbai, Kolkata and Chennai were the four declared international airports in the 1970s. All Indians had to go to one of these hubs to take an international flight and that too to another hub like Singapore, Dubai or London to connect. This should be no more necessary. With about 30 international airports declared by India, international flights can take off from any of these airports for airlines of India while foreign airlines need a specific mention in their Air Service Agreement with India. The single aisle aircraft with long endurance are already available.

Airline Requirements

However, there is a rider. The airlines always look to profitability. While they are always looking for new markets to enhance their connectivity and turnover, they are also looking to profits and cannot sustain loss-making routes for long. Therefore, airlines by nature are cautious in opening new routes. Here the role of state and its foreign policy comes into play. If the state has an ambition to reach out to some country or region, it must provide incentives to airlines to open and sustain a route. If this is given for a period of, say, 3 years, the airline will build up the market to make the route sustainable/profitable. It is said that when Bali in Indonesia was not connected directly with Singapore, Singapore Airlines was given a three-year right to go to Bali to the exclusion of other airlines. This helped Singapore Airlines to build up this direct route to Bali and it was successful in helping make Bali a tourist destination. Birmingham is a popular destination with Indians but there was no direct flight from India. Travellers had to go to London and then go by land route. Now that there is a flight, it's a booming route from India. Further, in the contract there could be provision that if the occupancy reaches a certain percentage then the subsidy could be stopped or the subsidy could be based on a minimum occupancy. There can be many more refinements to it.

Analysing our past failures reveals that our attempts for seeking better connectivity to ASEAN and SAARC countries failed essentially because we did not offer incentives to airlines to cover various cities of India with various cities of SAARC and ASEAN. This has, however, never been analysed properly. It is, therefore, necessary at this stage to look at past mistakes and see how corrective action can be taken. Private airlines do attempt a new route but when they are not able to sustain it, they close it down. For example, Air Asia started a daily flight between Bhubaneshwar and Kuala Lumpur but closed it down because occupancy was poor. Under these circumstances an airline will have to think twice on stopping a flight or reducing its frequency. Jet Airways had a flight from Mumbai to Ho Chi Minh City (Saigon) via Bangkok. They kept it going for one and a half year but had to close down between Bangkok and Ho Chi Minh City due to poor response. Similarly, a flight from Guwahati to Bangkok had to be abandoned due to poor load factors.

It is interesting to note private airlines of India too have expressed their desire to have an extended UDAN type scheme for external destinations. It was reported that "SpiceJet Lobbies for International Route Subsidies: Mr Ajay Singh, Chairman of Spice Jet, a Budget airline of India stated at the Hyderabad Air Show held in April 2018, that he would like to see the Regional Connectivity Scheme (RCS) extended to international destinations."[1]

"We are looking at a (new) version of UDAN," said Singh, referring in particular to the untapped potential of eight hilly states of the Northeast Region (NER), many sharing a common border with China and Southeast Asia.

While SpiceJet has not taken any subsidy in the first two rounds of auction of UDAN scheme, a subsidy for the third round of auctions will be required for the smaller towns. SpiceJet has already connected 10 Tier II cities with 70 flights a week to Dubai. Singh said cities such as Guwahati in the state of Assam could serve as a regional hub from India to neighbouring countries. Major airports in Bangladesh, Cambodia, Laos, Myanmar, and Vietnam all lie within a short flying distance of around 45 minutes to an hour from Guwahati. Already Guwahati ranks as India's eighth busiest airport, thanks to traffic from the North East Region. It handles 800 flights a week, compared with just three a week three decades ago. SpiceJet is also going to participate in the proposed International Connectivity Scheme (IAC) starting with connecting Guwahati with Bangkok and Dhaka. On the west, Mumbai or some towns of Saurashtra in Gujarat can be connected to Chabahar port or other cities in Iran and in CIS countries.

Commercial Airline and Profitability

Once air connectivity is firmly established, investors and tourist start coming. So, just as we have an Act East Policy, as enumerated in the Press note of December 23, 2015, favourable conditions for direct air connectivity have to be established. This means that in order to implement the policy there must be a plan for direct services to multiple destinations from multiple points in India. This can be done only if a plan for Air Connectivity is made and monitored by the government to connect various points from India to various points in foreign countries that India is seeking to get involved with and not leave it to forces of the market and profitability of airline operators.

Once the policy decision is taken, implementation will need detailed planning, including incentives to be provided, wherever necessary. Therefore, instead of general proclamations of good intent, a follow-up with a detailed plan needs to be made and implemented. Institutions like Indian Council for Cultural Relations (ICCR) and India Tourism Development Organisation (ITDC) could be involved also. A special fund to meet the subsidy charges could be created in ICCR. In hindsight, the follow-up on Prime Minister Vajpayee's unilateral offer in 2003 to SAARC and ASEAN was never followed up and it was left to the airlines to take to it. Airlines are business ventures and they always look to a Business Plan. Business Plans are based on profitability of a route. Airlines do make a pre-feasibility study to look into the viability and profitability of a route. Often, they take a risk and start a route and watch it for some time. If it does not show profits or shows persistent losses, they tend to close down the route. This option, though based on the principle of profitability, is not the best option when looked at from a foreign policy and strategic angle. Consistency of service is important from a strategic angle.

In view of the proposal by Government of Assam to make Guwahati as a regional hub for North-East India for air travel to countries in SAARC/ASEAN region, the Ministry of Civil Aviation has made Guidelines called International Air Connectivity (IAC) Scheme or IAC Scheme and put it up on their website to invite suggestions. This is the first indication that MOCA is serious about having an UDAN like Scheme for international travel.

There is, therefore, an appreciation by the Ministry of Civil Aviation that time is ripe for having a Subsidised Scheme for International Connectivity on lines of UDAN/RCS. This is similar to the methodology adopted by China for international connectivity from their States/ Provinces on a subsidised basis as described earlier in this book.

International Air Connectivity (IAC) Scheme: August 2018

Starting with the request of Government of Assam to make Guwahati an international hub for the North-East for which they are prepared to provide funds up to Rs. 100 crores per year for three years, the Ministry of Civil Aviation has formulated this draft Scheme so that other state Governments desirous of the same can follow and would not attract audit objections if properly followed. While Regional Connectivity Scheme has already started with over 300 routes already allotted through reverse auctions in the second round of auction,[2] this IAC as a draft has come at the right time to complete the Domestic with International Connectivity.

This Scheme is demand driven and originates from State Governments and has no links with the needs of our foreign policy. Under this Scheme, the concerned State Government shall provide financial support to Selected Airline(s) in the form of subsidy for operations of IAC Route(s). For avoidance of doubt, the Subsidy Support under the Scheme shall be available only to the selected Airline for the IAC Route.

Concessions offered by the Central Government under the Scheme shall be as follows: Selected Airlines will have the freedom to enter into code-sharing arrangements with domestic as well as international airlines pursuant to applicable regulations and prevailing air service agreements.

Concessions offered by the Airports Authority of India shall be as follows:

> In the event that the IAC Airport connected by an IAC Flight under the Scheme is operated from an airport of the Airports Authority of India, the AAI may consider to provide additional discounts, at its own discretion, on the applicable Landing, Parking and Housing charges for operations of such IAC Flight under the Scheme. For a start, in order to promote international flights to Andaman and Nicobar Islands, the Ministry of Defence has exempted international flights from landing charges (as Port Blair airport belongs to the Indian Navy) and the Andaman and Nicobar Administration has relaxed the VAT on ATF from 10 per cent to 0 per cent.[3]

The Subsidy Support by the State Governments and Airports Authority of India as decided will be provided for IAC Flight(s) under the

Scheme for a period of three (3) years from the date of commencement of IAC Flight operations on any IAC Route under a Selected Airline Agreement (the "Tenure of Subsidy Support").

Subsequent to the completion of such period of three (3) years, the Subsidy Support under the Scheme to the Selected and any other benefit as envisaged under the Scheme shall cease, unless unforeseen or exceptional circumstances—such as a court order or other factors beyond the control of the MoCA, the State Government(s) or the Airports Authority of India, constrain the ability of the MoCA, the concerned State Government and/or the Implementing Agency to continue with the Scheme. In the previously mentioned circumstances, the Implementing Agency shall endeavour to honour agreements already entered into with Selected Airline Operators for the remaining term of such agreements.

The IAC subsidy-based scheme document states:

"Enhancing international air connectivity:

1.1.1 The Ministry of Civil Aviation (MoCA), Government of India released the National Civil Aviation Policy 2016 (NCAP 2016). It envisions increasing the international ticketing to 20 crore by 2027.

1.1.2 NCAP 2016 also seeks to sustain and nurture a competitive market environment in the civil aviation sector. It is believed that it would be best for growth in the sector and establishment of international air connectivity to materialise through open market mechanisms in terms of airlines assessing demand on various routes, developing networks through deployment of appropriate capacities & technologies, etc.

1.1.3 However, certain State Governments of India also felt that facilitating/stimulating international air connectivity would be desirable from a public policy perspective and may need financial support, at least in the initial period, to trigger participation of airlines. Such State Governments desire to have direct scheduled flights between their respective states and select international destinations to promote socio-economic growth. It is in this context that the subsidy scheme (the Scheme) was envisaged for promoting international air connectivity between select destinations in the state and international destinations, as decided by the State Governments ("International Air Connectivity Scheme"), hereinafter called "IAC Scheme or the Scheme".

Thus the Scheme will not make the airline route unprofitable even from day one.[4] The extracts are as follows:

1.1.4 The operation of the Scheme is proposed through a State Government led mechanism. According to which, the State Governments will identify the list of routes to be connected, airline operators will assess demand on the identified routes, submit proposals for operating/providing connectivity on such routes; seek subsidy, if any, while committing to certain minimum operating conditions.

1.1.5 While, it is the intent and focus of the Scheme that the proposed mechanism facilitates discovery of the optimum subsidy requirements within specified subsidy caps, Ministry of Civil Aviation (MoCA) recognises that a market based discovery of optimum subsidy requirements may not happen due to lack of competition/uncertainty in market conditions and varied nature of operations on international sectors. The specified subsidy caps may end up seeming to be higher than the actual subsidy requirement in future on account of factors like higher airfares or yields, higher load factors, etc. Given that the focus of the Scheme is to provide international air connectivity where it does not exist and the nature of operations on international routes, the quantum or probability of such eventualities/outcomes in future cannot be ascertained by MoCA or the State Governments and potentially even the market ex-ante on account of the multiplicity of unascertainable factors. Further, the Scheme is premised on and encourages an open market mechanism where operators will be assessing demand on routes, developing networks through deployment of appropriate capacities & technologies, and take risks on account of factors like marketing of capacities, realisable demand, effect of ATF prices on costs /fares, etc. Accordingly, in consultation with stakeholders, MoCA recognised that the risks retained with the operators and agreed to provide a subsidy based system.

Therefore, we need concrete steps to channelise our outbound tourism from India with an incentive scheme for airlines and passengers. This will be a Scheme like the Regional Connectivity Scheme (RCS), but for International Connectivity based on foreign policy requirements. The proposed name is International Connectivity Scheme or ICS. Here are some suggestions for the incentives which could be given.

International Connectivity Scheme (ICS) as a Supplementary Scheme to IAC Scheme

International Connectivity and Foreign Policy Requirements

While the IAC Scheme proposed by the Ministry of Civil Aviation is good from an aviation perspective, it does not meet the needs of our foreign policy. Therefore, there is a need to tweak it further.

The Research and Information System for Developing Countries (RIS), a research institution set up under the Ministry of External Affairs has produced a report on ASEAN-India Air Connectivity.[5] In its recommendation it has suggested that:

"Promote Air Services to Tier II and Tier III Cities between ASEAN and India: Air services could facilitate larger numbers of tourists between India and ASEAN countries. This is very important at a time when India has offered e-Visa to most of the ASEAN countries. On Buddhist circuit, there is considerable interest from the ASEAN countries to visit Northeast and other parts of India. To promote tourism particularly in Tier II or Tier III cities, we shall facilitate operation of more flights. Given the BASAs (Basic Air Service Agreements) we have and in view of proposed 5th freedom rights of traffic, new air services may be explored on the following routes:

(i) Guwahati → Dhaka → Yangon → Guwahati;
(ii) Guwahati → Bangkok → Guwahati;
(iii) Imphal → Dhaka → Bangkok → Imphal;

(iv) Bagdogra → Dhaka → Bagdogra; Bagdogra → Bangkok → Bagdogra;
(v) Kolkata → Yangon → Bangkok → Kolkata;
(vi) Kolkata → Port Blair → Phuket → Port Blair → Kolkata;
(vii) Vizag → Kuala Lumpur → Vizag;
(viii) Kolkata → Port Blair → Bangkok → Port Blair → Kolkata; and
(ix) Gaya → Yangon → Gaya.

Preparing such a wish list is easy but persuading Airlines to go on these routes is another thing. Airlines are not only commercial in nature but they have a volatile profitability cycle. As such they are not able to take risk for long.

While the IAC Scheme, provides a mechanism with which the state governments can meet their needs for certain external flights, the ICS scheme routes will be decided by Ministry of External Affairs also on a similar mechanism with some modifications. This is to ensure that government procedures are followed with similar rules and procedures for RCS/IAC/ICS schemes and unnecessary audit objections are avoided. In case of ICS an MOU between MOCA and MEA or its agency like ICCR could be signed. Since ICCR is a subsidy giving institution for cultural affairs, it can be entrusted with this additional job also. The recommendations in the RIS report can then be considered for ASEAN nations. ...

For making ICS more attractive to our citizens the following addition incentives are suggested:

(a) Government and Private Sector offers a "Leave Travel Concession (LTC)" to its employees. In this scheme an employee with wife and family can travel to any part of India once in four years. Companies are allowed to claim this facility as tax deductible for income tax purposes. This is hugely popular as it involves around over 10 million persons. Government of India including Income Tax authorities, State Governments, Banking sector, Municipalities could include certain destinations abroad in the east like Cambodia, Laos, Vietnam, or in the west like central Asian countries duly selected by

Ministry of External Affairs. Further, this concession should be made applicable on only airlines of India. This itself would bring some assured passenger traffic to a route under the Scheme. Presently, main attraction for private sector companies is that the LTC is tax exempt. This will need some modification done in the Income Tax Act also to allow this deduction for restricted destinations abroad. Therefore, if LTC policies are modified a bit to allow claim of LTC to certain foreign locations like Angkor Wat or Hanoi/Ho Chi Minh City on the east or towns of Chabahar, Kabul, Tashkent etc. in the west by an Indian carrier then it will go a long way in encouraging an air operator to take up these specific routes.

(b) In addition, if Indian Film industry could be encouraged to shoot films in such destinations then it will further induce the outbound traffic to these locations. For this various concessions to film industry could be thought of, including tax concessions. The host countries could also be asked to provide some concessions to the film making company coming from India as is done by some western countries and in particular Switzerland.

(c) Another issue which can attract passengers over restricted overseas destination is the concession given by airlines to Senior Citizens. While Air India is offering 50 per cent off on normal fare for domestic routes and SpiceJet and Indigo about 8 per cent, there is a need to make a substantial discount for senior citizens on restricted ICS routes. Senior Citizens are increasing in numbers in India. Many have saved up well and are ready to spend on travel. If this concession is extended to limited number of overseas flights like Siem Reap in Cambodia for Angkor Wat, Bali in Indonesia, or Uzbekistan then it could work well and become viable. Like the Prime Ministers' pilgrimage scheme, this could be funded by ICCR of Ministry of External Affairs central of MEA.

The decision to select the countries under this Scheme should be with the Ministry of External Affairs who, in turn, should also consult travel trade and in particular the Outbound Tour Operators Association on India (OTOAI).[6] This will encourage Indian tourists eligible under

LTC rules to go abroad to these selected countries on Indian carriers. For example, Angkor Wat complex are world famous Hindu and Buddhist temples. They have been declared by UNESCO as a World Heritage monument. It is also a part of India's extended heritage. If Siem Reap, the airport serving Angkor Wat in Cambodia is declared as eligible under LTC rules, IT Rules and under ICS rules then we will be able to divert a part of our LTC traffic there.

In a similar way we can designate other airports like that of Yangon or Mandalay in Myanmar, Phnom Penh in Cambodia or Hanoi or Ho Chi Minh City (Saigon) or Bali in Indonesia etc., then it will give boost to our foreign policy objectives. It has been ascertained that in past also Ministry of External Affairs did take up the matter to include five Asian countries namely, Kazakhstan, Turkmenistan, Uzbekistan, Kyrgyzstan and Tajikistan in LTC. Prior to this a proposal for similar action for SAARC countries was mooted. However, this was never agreed upon. There is a need to put greater emphasis once again on our foreign policy requirements to get the proposal approved.

The author having discussed with many airlines and travel business persons regarding the ICS scheme, it was felt that it is very much doable. This Scheme will have the twin advantage of correcting the existing anomaly in our civil aviation policy of giving away too many seats and points of landing to foreign airlines in India, which has also been highlighted by CAG and the Economic Survey and on the other providing direct connectivity to countries of diplomatic interest but not part of the Indian outbound tourist demand. This will also help encourage tourism from these countries/cities.

Another feature of the ICS scheme is that since Indian tourists are considered fairly high spending, such a visit may be substantially economically beneficial to some of the receiving countries.

For ICS—the outbound service there will have to be some differences. We could keep the exclusive rights for three years for the Indian carrier selected and designated for this purpose so that no other Indian carrier will fly this route. We cannot, however, stop carriers from the opposition side come to India as long the bilateral Air Servive

Agreement provides for it. But we can offer more incentives in other forms to Indian carriers like:

- Offer relaxation of 0/5 rule, i.e., to those airlines that are prepared to join ICS routes abroad.
- With the help of ICCR and ITDC, incentivise Bollywood film makers to make films in some of these locations, i.e., Angkor Wat or Vietnam or Afghanistan, etc.
- Use social media to promote some destinations by getting articles written on them in mainstream media by known travel writers. Travel Blogs are another important source to attract outbound tourists.
- Cash subsidy to Airlines of India can also be considered. The $ 1 billion line of credit at the Kuala Lumpur summit of November 2015, offered by India for both digital and physical connectivity in ASEAN countries has really not taken off. As a result India has decided to give a grant of $ 40 million for a pilot project in Cambodia, Laos, Myanmar and Vietnam (CLMV) countries to help kick start the credit line. This fund can also be used to provide subsidy/line of soft credit to Airlines of India to certain preselected destinations under our Foreign Policy.
- Concessional rates for senior citizens for some identified tourist destinations could also be considered.
- The ICS scheme should be a dynamic scheme. Depending upon the budget available new locations abroad from different Indian cities could be introduced. There are some "don'ts" for the government to follow to build up a good connectivity. This is mainly not to open up any more our smaller towns to foreign carriers and let them concentrate in existing towns. Also not give more seat rights to the existing smaller towns. This applies more in the case of countries who do not have many airports in their country to offer.

As already pointed out earlier that even after the Prime Minister offering a $ 1 billion line of credit at the Kuala Lumpur summit of November 2015, for both digital and physical connectivity in ASEAN countries, it has really not taken off. As a result, India has decided to give a grant of $ 40 million for a pilot project in Cambodia, Laos, Myanmar and Vietnam (CLMV) countries to help kick start the credit line.[7] If another small grant is given from this for starting direct air connectivity between Indian towns and unconnected towns of CLMV countries under ICS, it would go a long way in meeting the vacuum and correcting a past wrong. Further, Ministry of External Affairs has saved about Rs. 700 crores per annum since 2018 from Haj subsidy as it was stopped as a result of a Supreme Court order. This saving could also be justified for diversion to ICS scheme.

Another issue that has been raised is whether spending money in a third country on a project like road or port or hospital gets better goodwill than people-to-people contact. While no quantitative analysis could be done for such an issue, these are two separate manners of achieving the same objective. People-to-people contacts bring in goodwill and have great potential of improved trade through this especially at Small and Medium Enterprises level.

Notes

1. Neelam Mathews, www.ainonline.com, March 29, 2018.
2. Airports Authority of India to partially fund Regional Connectivity Scheme flight, PTI, January 25, 2018, at Financialexpress.com
3. United News of India (UNI), February 21, 2021, at www.uniindia.com
4. Draft Scheme Document of International Air Connectivity Scheme UDAN (International) was placed in the website of Ministry of Civil Aviation and Airports Authority of India for wider consultation of the stakeholders. This Scheme intends to enhance air connectivity between Indian States and selected international destinations. Ministry of Civil Aviation: 21-08-2018 https://www.civilaviation.gov.in/sites/default/files/Draft%20UDAN%20Scheme%20document.pdf
5. ASEAN-INDIA Air Connectivity Report: RIS (Research and Information System for Developing Countries) May 2016.
6. http://www.otoai.org/
7. *The Indian Express*, April 4, 2018.

7
The Way Ahead

We have seen how the Regional Connectivity Scheme (RCS), popularly called UDAN, has been proposed in the NCAP 2016 and implemented. The response to this has been encouraging. Four reverse auctions for subsidy have been conducted till 2021 and operations from unserved airports and under-served helipads have stared on routes that have been allotted with lowest subsidy bidder (or with no subsidy in some cases). All these routes have been given to selected operators on a three years exclusive right, so that no other airline will be able to ply this route and the selected operator will be able to build up this route. Some additional concessions have been offered like subsidy, low landing charges/lower sales tax on aviation fuel, etc. However, such an allotment carries obligations too. It is obligatory for the operator to run a minimum of three services per week for three years. Further, ticket prices for half the aircraft capacity have to be on controlled prices while the other half can have free pricing. There are penalties for violation of the terms. From accounts available, the Scheme has been a great success. About 90 per cent to 95 per cent occupancy has been reported in many sectors. SpiceJet has announced that they will not be needing any subsidy under UDAN as the incentives provided including exclusive rights are sufficient. However, it now appears that funds collected under UDAN Regional Connectivity Fund may not be sufficient for the subsidy, and therefore some funds will need to be diverted from Airports Authority of India funds to the Regional Air Connectivity Fund.[1] The NCAP 2016 is silent on extending UDAN/ RCS beyond India.

Is There a Need for Connectivity Abroad for Foreign Policy Requirements?

We have seen that both late Prime Minister Vajpayee in 2003 and Foreign Minister late Sushma Swaraj had aspired for greater connectivity to our neighbouring countries but without a well-thought-out scheme. Civil Aviation Minister Jayant Sinha had offered to extend the domestic subsidised scheme of UDAN to the neighbouring countries. We have also seen how Haj pilgrimage was being subsidised to Saudi Arabia till 2018 by the Ministry of External Affairs to the tune of nearly Rs. 700 crores in the end. Another grant of $ 1 billion, about Rs. 8,000 crores, which was given to CLMV countries has also been only 25 per cent utilised and the scheme has been given up due to lack of demand.

Air India as a public sector, in the past, did oblige the Ministry of External Affairs with connectivity to a foreign destination even if the flight was not viable. It was able to meet the loss on such routes by cross-subsidising from profitable routes. Air India was then India's flag carrier with a monopoly of foreign flights. Although it never got budgetary support for this kind of unremunerated flights, it continued to support government requests till the Air Corporation Act of 1953 was repealed in 1994 when its monopoly was taken away. After this it was not able to support government policies as it was facing competition from within the country.

The second attempt at use of aviation in foreign policy was tried by Prime Minister Atal Bihari Vajpayee when he announced certain concessions to invite ASEAN and SAARC country airlines to multiple destinations in India. The announcement of invitation in 2003 was to SAARC and ASEAN countries' airlines to up to 18 destinations in India, namely, Patna, Lucknow, Guwahati, Gaya, Varanasi, Bhubaneshwar, Khajuraho, Aurangabad, Goa, Jaipur, Port Blair and Cochin, Thiruvananthapuram, Calicut, Amritsar, Visakhapatnam, Ahmedabad and Trichy, was subject to reciprocal rights. This did not achieve the desired result as only strong airlines of a few countries took advantage of it and improved their hub by connecting to more points in India.

The recent mention of improving direct overseas connectivity by Minister of State for Civil Aviation, Jayant Sinha, was stated during a curtain raiser to mark the 20th anniversary of BIMSTEC in June 2017. As has already been quoted earlier, "that it is worth considering whether we can work with countries that are in the BIMSTEC to see whether we can create a policy package that will enable us to connect smaller towns across the entire BIMSTEC region."

The proposed scheme was to be an extension of India's RCS/ UDAN scheme with different features. This proposal was never formally offered to BIMSTEC members nor was any enthusiasm shown. It was a mere idea.

Further, as already mentioned, Mr. Ajay Singh, Chairman of SpiceJet, an LCC of India, stated at the Hyderabad Air Show held in April 2018, that he would like to see the Regional Connectivity Scheme (RCS) extended to international destinations. Finally, the Chief Minister of Assam has announced a subsidy fund of Rs. 100 crores per annum for three years to start subsidised flights from Guwahati to SAARC and ASEAN countries and make Guwahati a hub for North-East India, both for domestic and international flights, during a conference on 'Advantage Assam' on December 5, 2017.

We have described in chapter 5 how China is pushing its airlines to go abroad. State governments in China are also offering subsidy to airlines to go to new destinations abroad. China is also using its huge outbound traffic of its nationals to help or punish states by restricting the movements of their outbound tourists to desired locations.

There does appear to be the requisite political will as well as the business keenness to go for a subsidised International Connectivity Scheme on the lines of RCS for foreign policy purposes, even if the flights are not viable initially. The potential of diverting a part of the projected 50 million outbound traffic from India to desired directions needs to be channelised by methods already enumerated earlier, such as LTC modification; use of Bollywood films and social media; put ICCR and ITDC to work on these ideas, requirements for these routes; create a subsidy fund under the Foreign Ministry.

As a result of all the demands of the State Governments the Ministry of Civil Aviation has in August 2018 put up on their website a Draft 'International Air Connectivity' (IAC) Scheme.

Draft International Air Connectivity (IAC) Scheme: August 2018
Starting with the request of Government of Assam to make Guwahati an international hub for the north-east for which they are prepared to provide funds up to Rs. 100 crore per year for three years, the Ministry of Civil Aviation has formulated this draft Scheme so that other state Governments desirous of the same can follow. While Regional Connectivity Scheme has already started and in the 13 months since, 25 new airports and airstrips, belonging to states and privately-held, have been added to the aerial network, with airlines, both new and established ones, signing up for over 300 routes in the first two rounds of bidding under UDAN.[2] A third auction has also taken place. There were 15 airlines that bid for 111 initial proposals, which were then placed for counter-bidding. Among these 15 airlines, six airlines participated in counter-bidding and these six airlines put in a total of 17 counter-proposals.[3]

This draft IAC Scheme, however, is a demand driven scheme meant for State Governments and has no links with the needs of our foreign policy. Under this Scheme, the concerned State Government shall provide financial support to selected Indian airline(s) in the form of subsidy for operations of IAC Route(s) for three years only. There will also be exclusive right for that airline for three years. This exclusivity will be for Indian airlines and not airlines of the other country. The international routes in this case will be determined by the State Government for 'socio-economic growth' and the subsidy will also be provided by them. The State of Assam is likely to be the first to avail of this Scheme, probably followed by the state of Gujarat.

In this book a new scheme called International Connectivity Scheme (ICS) has been proposed for International Connectivity under our Foreign Policy requirements as our outbound travellers are not inclined to go to these places. This Scheme would be based on International Air

Connectivity (IAC) Scheme with modifications. Further, this Scheme has looked into the Chinese system of outbound promotion but, being impractical for India, has proposed a new methodology for diverting our outbound traffic by use of Bollywood, promotion by ICCR/ITDC, the two government promotion bodies, and subsidy and some suggestions where required.

The Missing Link of Act East Policy: The Soft Power of Andaman and Nicobar Islands

Finally, this book comes up with the missing part of Act East Policy: Leveraging the Potential of Andaman and Nicobar Islands due to its location has been covered. This book has discussed the issue of Malacca Straits which China has referred to as their Malacca Dilemma. It has recommended that a similar approach be adopted, as to what happened in the North-East India in the 1950s when North East Frontier Agency (NEFA) was carved out of Assam and put under charge of Ministry of External Affairs for 10 years to implement then foreign policy of extending the Indian Administration right up to the McMahon Line, with massive air support. This omission in the implementation of Act East policy by not leveraging the strategic importance of these two archipelagos in the Bay of Bengal with the Great Nicobar Island near the western entrance of Malacca Straits is a strategic blunder and needs to be corrected.

The issue of importance of Air Cargo has been dealt in chapter 2. As air cargo now constitutes 35 per cent of total cargo in value terms, its importance is immense. Further, air carries perishable items like fresh fruit and vegetables besides fresh fish. It is also the preferred means to carry electronic goods and Gems and Jewellery.

A New Beginning at Air Cargo: India-Afghanistan Subsidised Air Cargo Corridor Established in 2018

The decision to establish an Air Freight Corridor between Afghanistan and India was taken in the meeting between Prime Minister Shri Narendra Modi and President Ghani in September 2016 during the President's visit to India.[4] The *Economic Survey 2017-2018* also mentions it as a proposal.[5]

Finally, in September 2018 budget carrier SpiceJet announced the launch of its Delhi-Kabul freighter service, named under brand SpiceXpress, from October 15, 2018 after signing of an agreement with the Afghanistan Chamber of Commerce and Industries (ACCI) for transporting fresh fruit, dry fruits, carpets and other commodities from Kabul to India.[6]

SpiceJet has further informed that it would be transporting these commodities from Kabul using its freighter aircraft to Indian metro cities and through its pan-India passenger flight network to 47 cities in India. It has also been reported that SpiceJet would transport this Cargo to other foreign destinations also. However, SpiceJets cargo services to Afghanistan had to stop after sometime for other reasons.

In a recent case on cargo issue was when Bangladesh approached India to help them clear their export air cargo for their export orders, mainly garments, but also perishables like vegetables, fruit and fish, dry fish and crabs. As direct cargo flights between Bangladesh and London got disrupted, India helped out through Delhi airport.[7] If India can establish for itself a regional international cargo hub it will help SAARC/BIMSTEC countries and will boost our image in these countries.

Bilateral Air Rights

We have also pointed out the harm that we have done to our industry by giving away excessive bilateral rights and too many points in India to countries which have barely a single airport, such as Singapore or Dubai. We have also not encouraged our own airlines to go abroad directly to our neighbouring countries and build up a hub in India itself.

We have also shown that India outbound has a very healthy growth and Indians were expected to reach 50 million mark for outbound travel by 2020 delayed due to COVID-19. This is a significant number which, if channelised to countries of our political requirement, can be a great advantage to our foreign policy objectives. Preparing such a wish list is easy but persuading airlines to go on these routes is another thing. Airlines are not only commercial in nature but they have a volatile profitability cycle. As such they are not able to take risks for long.

We have considered in this book our Civil Aviation Policy 2016 (NCAP 2016), our Foreign Policy on Act East and Look West and we have discussed how the Chinese are channelising tourists from mainland China to desired destinations through the mechanism of Approved Destination Status (ADS) and leveraging its foreign policy through them. We have also discussed the missing link in our Act East Policy: our untapped asset of Andaman and Nicobar Islands with the Malacca Advantage. We have also discussed in detail how China is using its outbound traffic as a lever of its foreign policy. We have, further, discussed how our attempts at using Aviation in our drive to connectivity to countries of our foreign policy interest failed. Finally, we have proposed a Scheme called International Connectivity Scheme (ICS) as a possible answer to Integration of Civil Aviation to our Foreign Policy.

Opening ANI for High-Value International Tourism: The Missing Link

Another proposal is the opening of Andaman and Nicobar Islands as part of the missing link of the Act East Policy, described as an enigma in our Act East Policy, by connecting it internationally by air under the ICS Scheme. Here the emphasis on air connectivity is reversed. The purpose is to invite inbound tourists from ASEAN and other countries directly to these islands as a part of 'Soft State' projection. The purpose is to show to the world and to South-East Asia in particular, that Andaman and Nicobar group of islands in the Bay of Bengal is a part of India, and thereby Indian territory extends right up to Malacca Straits. A new Administrative set-up has been proposed for these islands for about 10 years under the Ministry of External Affairs, as was done earlier in the case of North-East with setting up of North East Frontier Agency (NEFA) in the 1950s for opening these tribal areas to a formal administration.

Notes

1. See Interview of Chairman AAI, Dr. Guruprasad Mohapatra, in *Cruising Heights* magazine, May 2018, p. 24.
2. *Financial Express,* May 21, 2018.
3. *Business Line,* January 7, 2019.
4. The Ministry of External Affairs, Media Centre, June 19, 2017.
5. *Economic Survey 2017-2018,* p. 140.
6. *The Economic Times,* September 13, 2018, at EconomicTimes.indiatimes.com//economictimes.indiatimes.com/articleshow/65798939.cms?utm_source=contentofinterest&utm_medium=text&utm_campaign=cppst
7. *Cruising Heights* magazine, May 2018, vol. XII, "Delhi rushes to help Bangladesh exporters", pp. 59-60.

Appendix 1

Memorandum of Understanding between Phuket Chamber of Commerce and Andaman Chamber of Commerce and Industry, November 2003

Objective

The fundamental objective of the MOU is to further the development of bilateral economic relations by providing a forum for businessmen of both the countries to meet, discuss and explore business opportunities in trade, investments, transfer of technology, services and other industrial sectors.

Cooperation

The Phuket Chamber of Commerce and The Andaman Chamber of Commerce and Industry formally undertake to initiate and develop bilateral actions of cooperation within the principle of mutual assistance and support, in line with the following priorities:

- To develop strong institutional relations in order to establish a sustainable mechanism of dialogue and forums of discussions;
- To provide their members with information on the general economic situation, taxation, investments opportunities, trade policies and legislative changes therein;
- To promote the establishment of legal and administrative conditions favourable to the creation of a business climate enhancing the development of trade and economic relations between The Andaman & Nicobar Islands and Phuket.
- To encourage businessmen of both countries to participate in exhibitions and fairs held in The Andaman & Nicobar Islands and Phuket.
- To develop tools for co-operation between The Phuket Chamber of Commerce and The Andaman Chamber of Commerce and Industry which would allow an attractive role of both parties in the implementation of The Andaman & Nicobar islands/Phuket trade and co-operation agreements.

1. The Phuket Chamber of Commerce and The Andaman Chamber of Commerce and Industry undertake to promote within their respective regions and institutions all aspects related to economic development and trade relations between Andaman & Nicobar Islands and Phuket.
2. The present agreement shall enter into force upon its signature.
3. Modifications and amendments to this agreement must be approved by the competent bodies of each organisation.
4. This agreement may be terminated by either party by written notice to the other party with a sixty days notice.
5. All agreements on commerce will be ratified by each Chamber of Commerce.

The present agreement has been established in two copies, equally authentic, each party recognising having received its copy.

Signed:

Pamuke Achariyachai
Chairman, Phuket Chamber of
Commerce and Industry

Mohammed H. Jadwet
President: Andaman
Chamber of Commerce

Witness:

Udomsak Usawarangkura
Phuket Governor

J. R. Sharma
First Secretary Commercial
Embassy of India—Bangkok

Date: 30 November 2003

Appendix 2

Agreement of Friendship/Cooperation between City of Port Blair and Phuket Province, June 2005

The City of Port Blair, Capital of Andaman & Nicobar Islands, Republic of India, and Phuket Province of the Kingdom of Thailand (hereinafter referred to as "Parties");

Desiring to establish and develop relations of friendship between the parties for the good of their citizens; wishing to contribute to the strengthening of relations between the Republic of India and the Kingdom of Thailand as a whole;

Have agreed as follows:

Article 1

The Parties agree to promote international understanding and strengthen the relationship through tourism, education, culture, urban development, commerce and investments.

Article 2

The Parties shall undertake regular exchanges and interactions in the areas which include, *inter alia*:

- Tourism: Exchange of tourist missions for fairs, expositions, tourist festivals, promotion of tourist destinations for each sister city, and finally, promotion of international tourism between one another.
- Education and Culture: Cultural exchanges—Phuket days in City of Port Blair and City of Port Blair days in Phuket Province. Cultural exchanges of students, artists and professionals.
- Urban development: Exchange of expertise in innovative water harvesting techniques; upgradation of water treatment plants; study of old water supply network and rationalisation of water distribution network; desilting—relining of old sewerage lines.
- Solid Waste Management: Study of modern and sustainable methods of solid waste management particularly in the areas of Andaman & Nicobar Islands of roads and public places, safe disposal through transportation, development of proper

fill sites, segregation of biodegradable and non-biodegradable solid wastes and recycling.

- Commerce: Exchange of commerce missions and participation in expositions, fairs, business forums and other promotions with the increased flow of goods and services between the parties.
- Investments: Exchange of business missions, information sharing of investment possibilities and business opportunities.

Article 3

The parties shall make every effort to contribute to the fostering of relationship and cooperation particularly in the areas of tourism, education and culture, urban development, solid waste management, commerce and investments.

Article 4

The Parties shall utilise any or all of the following methods to carry out this cooperation:

- Organisation Andaman & Nicobar Islandisation of seminars, conferences, meetings, symposiums, workshops etc.
- Exchanges of experts and students in the areas of activity.
- Exchanges of information.
- Exchanges of visits by cultural troupes.
- Technical consulting.

The parties can agree on other means of cooperation other than these referred to in this Article.

Article 5

The Department of Local Self Government (LSG), Government of Andaman & Nicobar Islands, and the Department of Local Self Government of the Kingdom of Thailand, are responsible for implementing the objectives and programmes envisaged under this agreement.

Article 6

The exchange of civil servants and technicians shall be made according to international practice, under which the Party that sends councillors, civil servants and/or technicians takes charge of the international transportation costs and the host Party takes charge of the local transportation, meals, and accommodation costs of the councillors, civil servants and/or technicians.

Article 7

The agreement may be modified by mutual consent of the parties. The said modifications shall come into effect from the date of their approval and notification by the parties. *Andaman and Nicobar Islands.*

Article 8

This agreement shall enter into force on the date of its signature and shall remain in force for a period of five years, renewable automatically for equivalent period, unless one party notifies the other in writing, at least six months before the end of its period, of its desire to terminate the agreement.

Article 9

The termination of this agreement shall not affect the validity of those on-going cooperative programmes and projects made under it.

Done in duplicate at Phuket, Thailand, on June 29, 2005 in the English language.

(Ram Kapse)	(Udomsak Uswarangkura)
Lt. Governor of Andaman & Nicobar Island	Governor of Phuket Province
Republic of India	Kingdom of Thailand

Glossary

Airports Authority of India: A statutory Authority constituted by the Parliament by Airports Authority of India Act of 1994. It manages 126 Airports including 26 Civil Enclaves in Military Airports.

Airports Council International: An Association of International Airports which represents its case to governments and International Agencies/ Organisations.

Andaman and Nicobar Islands: Two archipelagoes consisting of 572 islands and islets running from Myanmar to Malacca Straits in the Bay of Bengal and belonging to India.

Air Service Agreement: A bilateral Agreement between two countries which controls commercial air services between them.

ASEAN: Association of South East Asian Nations consists of 10 nations across South China Sea and Bay of Bengal.

BIMSTEC: Bay of Bengal Initiative for Multi-Sectoral Technical and Economic Cooperation consists of 7 countries, namely, Bangladesh, India, Myanmar, Sri Lanka, Thailand, Nepal and Bhutan with 14 identified sectors of cooperation.

CPEC: China-Pakistan Economic Corridor runs from Xinjiang in China to Gwadar in Pakistan and is a part of Belt and Road and Initiative of China.

DGCA: Director General of Civil Aviation: The most powerful and regulatory office in the Civil Aviation sector. Besides licensing it is also the safety regulator.

EEZ: Exclusive Economic Zone is a concept adopted by the Third United Nations Conference of Law of the Seas (1982) whereby a coastal state assumes jurisdiction over exploration and exploitation of marine resources. EEZ limit extends upto 200 nautical miles. But there is no sovereignty over it.

GNI: Great Nicobar Island: The last island of the Nicobar archipelago near Indonesia's Sumatra and also on the tip of western entrance of the Malacca Strait.

ICAO: International Civil Aviation Organisation was constituted by the Chicago Convention of 1944 and it legislates of Air Laws. While it is older than the United Nations, it is now a Specialised Agency of the UN.

ICCR: Indian Council for Cultural Relations: An attached institution of Ministry of External Affairs, its mandate is to promote Indian culture abroad.

International Connectivity Scheme: A scheme proposed in this book to have flights from India to foreign destinations based on foreign policy requirements.

INSTC: International North-South Transport Corridor: A 7,200-km long multi-modal network of ships, rail, road route between India, Iran, Afghanistan, Armenia, Azerbaijan, Russia, Central Asia and Europe.

North East Frontier Agency: In 1951 North East Frontier Agency was formed and placed under charge of Ministry of External Affairs and in 1965 it was transferred to Ministry of Home Affairs. Presently it is a full-fledged State of India called Arunachal Pradesh.

Route Dispersal Guidelines: On March 1, 1994 Ministry of Civil Aviation issued Route Dispersal Guidelines under which all scheduled operators were required to deploy at least 10 per cent of their capacity on trunk routes to North Eastern Region, Jammu and Kashmir and Island Territories of India. These guidelines are still in vogue and are being followed.

ADS: Approved Destination Status: Started in 1990s by Chinese government, ADS is controlled outbound tourism by Chinese nationals in organised groups by certified travel agents. ADS status is based on an ADS Tourism Agreement with Chinese government by another country. China does not allow its tourists to go on their own.

Bibliography

Abeyratne, Ruwantissa. *Aero politics*. New York: Nova Science Publishers, 2009.

Abeyratne, Ruwantissa. *Air Navigation Law*. Springer, 2012.

Abeyratne, Ruwantissa. *Strategic Issues in Air Transportation: Legal, Economic and Technical Aspects*. Springer, 2012.

Air Transport Action Group. "Aviation/Benefits beyond Borders".

ANI Administration Study Group Report. "Comprehensive and Sustainable Development of Andaman and Nicobar Islands". A&N Administration, 2016.

Arvis, Jean-François and Ben Shepherd. *Air Connectivity Index*, 2011. *The air connectivity index: measuring integration in the global air transport network (English)*. Policy Research working paper no. WPS 5722. Washington, D.C.: World Bank. http://documents.worldbank.org/curated/en/859151468161649899/The-air-connectivity-index-measuring-integration-in-the-global-air-transport-network

ASEAN-India Air Connectivity Report, RIS 2016.

Canadian Tourist Commission, GTW India 2013.

Deloitte Touché Tohmatsu India Pvt. Ltd. 2013. "Promotion of Regional and Remote Area Air Connectivity in India: Final Report".

http://www.oag.com/Insight/Free-Reports/end-boom-and-bust-indian-aviation

IFFAAD. "Improving Connectivity: Role of Aviation in Socio-Economic Development of Remote Locations: Case Study of Andaman & Nicobar Islands". Area Research Project Funded by ICSSR.

India Ministry of Tourism. Indian Outbound Travel—SILO of Research Documents. https//silotips. *Literature Survey*.

Jakhu, R. S., T. Sgobba and P. S. Dempsey, editors. *The need to Integrate Regulatory Regime for Aviation and Space: ICAO for Space?* Springer, 2011.

Jakhu, Ram, Sanat Kaul and Kuan-Wei Chen, editors. *Emerging Trends in Aviation and Space Applications* McGill University, Institute of Air & Space Law, 2014. …

Kaul, Sanat. *Development and Growth through Regional Air Connectivity in India.* Monograph Series II. McGill University, Institute of Air & Space Law.

Kesharwani, Tulsi. *Privatisation of Aviation Infrastructure.* Asian Institute of Transport Development, 2002.

Martono, Prof. K., Faculty of Law, University of Tarumanagara. *Aviation Laws and Regulations Applicable in Indonesia.*

Mukerjee, Shakko and Suyash Sinha. *Marriages in the Sky: Airline Cartel.*; Monograph Series II. McGill University, Institute of Air & Space Law.

National Council of Applied Economic Research. "Emirates in India: Assessment of Economic Impact and Regional Benefits".

OTTI Indian Market Profit le 2013 and Singapore Tourist Board.

Singapore Tourist Board. *Leisure Segmentation Study* 2013.

Singapore Tourist Board. www.visitsingapore.com

Singh, Prof. (Dr.) Ranbir, Prof. Srikrishna Deva Rao and Dr. Sanat Kaul, editors. *Current Developments in Air and Space Law.* National Law University Press, 2012.

Source: Tourism Australia Consumer Demand Project 2014.

Source: Tourism Australia Market Profile 2015.

Source: Tourism Australia. *Knowing the customer.* www.tourismaustralia.com

Source: VisitBritain. https://www.visitbritain.org/markets/india

Sources: Singapore Tourism, VisitBritain.

The Convention on International Civil Aviation, also known as the Chicago Convention, established the International Civil Aviation Organization (ICAO), a specialised agency of the UN charged with coordinating and regulating international air travel. The Convention establishes rules of airspace, aircraft registration and safety, and details the rights of the signatories in relation to air travel. The Convention also exempts air fuels in transit from (double) taxation.

Visitor Economy Bulletin 5.

Wickramasinghe, Anusha and Lasantha Hettiarachchi. *An overview of South Asian Perspective on Liberalisation of Air Transport.*

World Bank document. "Ease of Doing Business".